Eugène Arnaud Casalis

My Life in Basuto Land

Eugène Arnaud Casalis

My Life in Basuto Land

ISBN/EAN: 9783743349353

Manufactured in Europe, USA, Canada, Australia, Japa

Cover: Foto ©ninafisch / pixelio.de

Manufactured and distributed by brebook publishing software (www.brebook.com)

Eugène Arnaud Casalis

My Life in Basuto Land

WORKS BY THE SAME AUTHOR.

HISTORICAL STUDIES. One vol. 12mo. 1850.

BIOGRAPHICAL STUDIES. One vol. 12mo. 1860.

NATHANAEL GREENE: an Examination of some Passages in the IXth Volume of Mr. Bancroft's "History of the United States." 8vo. 1866.

THE LIFE OF NATHANAEL GREENE, Major-General in the Army of the Revolution. Three vols. 8vo. 1871.

HISTORICAL VIEW

OF THE

AMERICAN REVOLUTION.

GEORGE W

LATE NON-RESIDENT PROFESSOR OF AMERICAN HISTORY IN CORNELL UNIVERSITY,
AUTHOR OF "THE LIFE OF MAJOR-GENERAL NATHANAEL GREENE,"
"THE GERMAN ELEMENT IN THE WAR OF AMERICAN
INDEPENDENCE," ETC., ETC.

"As to those, however, who shall desire to have a clear view of past events, and indeed of *future* ones (such and similar events being, according to the natural course of human affairs, again to occur); for *those* to esteem them useful will be sufficient to answer every purpose."

THUCYDIDES, Book I., c. cxxii.

FOURTH EDITION.

NEW YORK:
PUBLISHED BY HURD AND HOUGHTON.
Cambridge: The Riverside Press.
1876.

TO CHARLES BUTLER,

OF NEW YORK.

MY DEAR MR. BUTLER:— You know the history of this volume. You know, also, of my other studies in the field of our Revolutionary History, and my hope to contribute something more to the just appreciation of the great men it produced. You will not, therefore, deny me the gratification of connecting your name with my labors by this public expression of the respect and affection with which
    I am, most truly,
      Your friend,
        GEO. W. GREENE.

GREENESDALE, February 2, 1865.

PREFACE TO THE FOURTH EDITION.

THE following pages were written in the darkest hour of the War for the Union. Unable to take an active part in the contest, and unwilling not to put my convictions upon record, I gave them expression in these pages. They have met, I am told, a general want, and I gladly offer them anew in this Centennial Edition.

To make them more acceptable in a class-room, if they should find their way there, I have added to them an Analytical Table of Contents.

G. W. G.

WIND MILL COTTAGE,
    EAST GREENWICH, R. I.
        April 1, 1876.

PREFACE.

THE following Lectures were written for the Lowell Institute of Boston in 1862, and read before it in the January and February of 1863. A part of them was also read before the Cooper Institute of New York in March and April of the same year. Relating to a past of great present value, they have already, I am told, done some good; and I publish them in the hope that, in a more accessible form, they may do still more. No nation can neglect the study of its own history without exposing itself to the danger and disgrace of repeating past errors. No statesman can confine his attention to the present, without losing sight of the principles from which the present grew, and thus becoming a groper in the dark, instead of a trustworthy guide.

It is impossible to read our history without seeing that we, like all other historical nations, have been controlled by general laws. It is a universal law that every principle works out its own development; and hence, as an inevitable corollary, if you accept the principle, you must sooner or later accept its consequences. Our Puritan forefathers claimed freedom of judgment for themselves, and founded their Colonies that they might have a home of their own to exercise it in. But they failed to see that what was true for one was true for all; and the dark pages of their history are the pages which record their fruitless struggle with the fundamental principle of their own institutions.

It is a principle of English law, that the King cannot take the subject's money without the subject's consent. Denying this principle, England attempted to tax the Colonies through the Imperial Parliament instead of the Colonial Assemblies, and lost them. Appealing to this principle, the Colonists claimed the right to dispose freely of the fruits of their own labors, and established their claim by the War of Independence. But they failed to see that, if the principle was true, it was true as a law of universal humanity, and therefore must sooner or later demand and obtain universal application. And this failure to accept all the consequences of the accepted principle left the bitter and bloody war — *bella plus quam civilia* — through which we are now passing as a part of their legacy to their children. Will not history say that wise statesmanship should have foreseen this as a logical sequence, and consistent Christianity should recognize it as the act of that divine justice which could not have imposed the obligation of personal responsibility without according the right of personal freedom?

The conduct too of the War of Independence is full of lessons. More than half its waste of blood, treasure, and time was caused by the want of an efficient general government. What a comment is the history of the civil government of the Revolution upon the doctrine of State rights! When Washington, in his proclamation of the 25th of January, 1777, called upon those who had accepted British protections to give them up and take an oath of allegiance to the United States, a delegate from New Jersey, Mr. Abraham Clark, condemned his proclamation as "exceptionable in many things and very improper"; adding, with an air of infinite condescension, "I believe the General is honest, but I think him fallible." Has not the present war given rise to many accusations which history will record with the same wonder and disgust with which she records this?

Another cause of the profuse expenditure and protracted sufferings of the War of Independence, was the neglect to raise an army for the war when popular enthusiasm was so high that the ranks might have been filled with hardly any effort but that of making out the rolls. If I were to copy from Washington's and Greene's letters all the paragraphs against short enlistments and temporary levies, I should fill a volume. Have we not seen the lesson blindly and fatally neglected?

A copy of Washington's letters in every school and district library of the country, to serve as a text-book in clubs and debating societies, and a manual for public men in every department of civil and military administration, would do more for the formation of our national character, would stand us in better stead in difficult emergencies, and furnish us more appropriate examples of that wisdom which we need at all times, than any other source to which we could go for guidance and counsel. A careful study of them by our statesmen at the beginning of the present war would have saved us thousands of lives and millions of treasure.

> "Why have the fathers suffered, but to make
> The children wisely safe?"

I have not attempted to give my authorities for the statements and opinions contained in these Lectures, for the form of Lectures does not admit of it; and if my purpose in publishing them is reached, they will carry the reader directly to the original sources. But I cannot permit them to go forth into the world without acknowledging my obligations to the able and trustworthy volumes of Mr. Hildreth, to the judicious and accurate Annals of Holmes, and to that admirable series of publications by which Mr. Sparks has connected his name indissolubly with the history of our Revolution. Force's Archives unfortunately cover only the first two years of the war; but for those years they leave nothing to be desired. What a disgrace to the administration of 1853, and its immediate successor, that such a work should have been suspended, and the exhaustive researches and wonderful critical sagacity of such a man lost to historical literature, by the arbitrary violation of a solemn contract.

In using Gordon, I have often felt the want of the critical edition which was promised us some years ago in the name of Mr. George Henry Moore of the New York Historical Society. In using the Journals of Congress, I have constantly had occasion to regret the awkward separation of the secret journals from the main collection, and the want of a new edition based upon an accurate collation of the original manuscript, and completed by the insertion in their proper places of the fragments of debates and speeches that are scattered through the works of Adams, and Jefferson, and Gouverneur Morris, and other members of that body.

Among the other sources from which I have drawn, I would particularly mention the documents in DeWitt's valuable work upon Jefferson, and the elaborate Life of Steuben by Mr. Kapp. Since these Lectures were written, this profound and careful writer has published in German two other works which bear upon my subject, — "The Life of DeKalb," and "The Trade of German Princes in Soldiers for America." I will not say with Vertot, *mon siége est fait;* but I have felt in reading them that, if they had reached me before my own work was written, I might have enriched it by new and important details. I trust that these valuable contributions to our history will soon be made more generally accessible to American readers. Mr. Kapp has proved by his Steuben that he writes English well enough to be his own translator.

GEORGE WASHINGTON GREENE.

GREENESDALE, NEWPORT,
    February 2, 1865.

CONTENTS.

LECTURE		PAGE
I.	THE CAUSES OF THE REVOLUTION	1
II.	THE PHASES OF THE REVOLUTION	33
III.	THE CONGRESS OF THE REVOLUTION	67
IV.	CONGRESS AND THE STATE GOVERNMENTS OF THE REVOLUTION	104
V.	FINANCES OF THE REVOLUTION	137
VI.	THE DIPLOMACY OF THE REVOLUTION	173
VII.	THE ARMY OF THE REVOLUTION	210
VIII.	CAMPAIGNS OF THE REVOLUTION	245
IX.	THE FOREIGN ELEMENT OF THE REVOLUTION	282
X.	THE MARTYRS OF THE REVOLUTION	320
XI.	LITERATURE OF THE REVOLUTION. (PROSE.)	357
XII.	LITERATURE OF THE REVOLUTION. (POETRY.)	389

APPENDIX.

CHRONOLOGICAL OUTLINE	445
STATISTICAL TABLES	449
ADDRESS TO GENERAL GREENE	458

ANALYSIS

OF THE

HISTORICAL VIEW OF THE AMERICAN REVOLUTION.

LECTURE FIRST.

CAUSES OF THE REVOLUTION.

	PAGE
The Revolution a decisive epoch of civilization	1
No good true Republic in existence, when the American Republic was formed	1
The Republics of Europe. Holland; Venice	1
Genoa; Lucca; San Marino	2
The Monarchies contrasted with them; Prussia; Russia; Austria	2
England; Spain; France	3
The feudal system in antagonism with modern ideas	4
The dependence of the American colonies on England a natural one	5
The colonists thoroughly English in their sympathies	6
All these changed in a few years	6
The Revolution eclipsed for a time by the events which followed it	7
Impartiality of History	7
The Revolution viewed in this light both a cause and effect	7
What was the cause?	8
Two classes of causes	8
First, in the colonial system	9
Reverence for law a national characteristic	9
The spirit of English liberty an animating principle of the colonists	9
The spirit of English liberty defined and traced to its origin	10
Its form when transported to America	10

The Navigation Act, the first interference of Parliament
  with colonial rights 11
The feelings which it awakened 12
After this the relation between England and her colonies
  a business relation in her eyes 12
The feelings caused by this relation among Americans . 13
Anecdote of Attorney General Seymour illustrating the
  English feeling 13
English ignorance of America a second cause . . 14
Alienation caused by a lack of appreciation . . . 14
English conceptions of the colonies 15
Their thoughts of investment and gain, not brotherhood . 15
Their unfavorable opinions of America and Americans 16
Their treatment of the American traveller . . . 17
Alienation a result of these prejudices 17
The nature of municipal institutions a third cause . . 18
The European colonial system a false one . . . 18
Freedom of the English system an advantage over other
  systems 18
Importance of municipal institutions in the history of civ-
  ilization 19
The colonists' form of municipal institutions English . 20
A separation in time inevitable from these three causes 20
Two more causes 20
England in her dealings with the colonies at war with her
  own political system 21
England oppressed by debt 21
England's misfortune, adopting an erroneous system and
  adhering to it 22
Possibility of a reconciliation before 1763 22
Part of George III. in the contest 23
The course of the English tax-payers during the war . 24
The dispute a question of constitutional rights . . 24
Effects of this 25
Many steps before actual war 26
American feeling of dependence vague and undefined . 27
All questions discussed in the colonies 27
Alienation a slow process 28
The American struggle in connection with the state of
  European politics 29
The Treaty of Paris and its results 30
The course of French and English statesmen contrasted 30

THE SECOND CLASS OF CAUSES.

A great question sure to be agitated 31
The colonial question a great one 31
A new principle of government 32

ANALYSIS.

All nations agitated by the contest	32
The interests at stake	32
The American Revolution a war between natural and hereditary rights	32

LECTURE II.

THE PHASES OF THE REVOLUTION.

Recapitulation of Lecture I.	33
The first colony and the first league	33
The growth of the colonies and their relations to the mother country	34
Their relations to each other	35
The first interference of the home government	36
Position of England toward the colonies during the commonwealth	36
English estimation of the Act of Navigation	37
The thirteenth clause	37
The object and spirit of the Act	38
The enumerated commodities	40
The King's claim on Maine woods	41
Its results	41
The feelings of the colonists in regard to this claim	42
The contest between Maine lumbermen and royal surveyors and its consequences	43
A law in violation of public opinion a fatal error in Legislation	44
An effect of the Act of Navigation on the colonists	45
The effect of the reservation in the new Massachusetts charter	45
The ways by which England drives the colonies to seek independence	46
A new phase, the French and Indian war	47
The action of the colonists. The Congress at Albany	47
England's great opportunity	48
Her misuse of it and the result	49
A critical moment	49
A separation inevitable and foreseen by men of intelligence	50
The wisest course for England	51
Another phase, aggression and resistance Grenville's policy	52
The Stamp Act	52
Its Repeal. A reconciliation still possible	53
The "Declaratory Act." Townshend's Resolutions and their spirit	53

The relative position of the two countries . . . 53
Resistance a necessity 54
Patrick Henry's Resolutions and the "Declaration of
 Rights" by Congress 54
Their influence on Americans 54
The formal declarations of both countries in regard to
 taxation 55
The American opinion confirmed by Henry's Resolutions
 and the Declaration of Rights 56
Aggression on the part of England met by Retaliation on
 the part of America 56
A British garrison in Boston and the effect . . . 57
The Tax on tea and the Boston "tea-party" . . 57
The Committees of Correspondence 58
Their results. The last phase of the Revolution . 58
Regret of many Americans at the separation. Prepara-
 tions for war 59
Lexington 59
Ticonderoga 60
The Revolution accomplished 60
Mistakes on both sides at the beginning of the war . 60
First period of the war. Washington's rise in public es-
 teem 61
British plan for 1877. A crisis 62
How the plan is frustrated 62
The calumnies against Washington 63
His refutation of the calumnies and supremacy . . 63
The results of his supremacy and successes . . . 64
The American position viewed from the present and a
 contemporary stand-point 64
Second period; the campaign in the Carolinas . . 65
The campaign in Virginia 65
Appointment of Robert Morris as financier . . . 65
The remainder of the war 66

LECTURE III.

THE CONGRESS OF THE REVOLUTION.

Brief recapitulation of Lecture II 67
The Revolution defined 68
The first Congress, its formation and object . . . 68
The Albany Congress of 1754 69
Importance of the union 70
The men who composed this Congress and the character
 of Franklin 70
Franklin's opinions, at that time, concerning independence . 71

ANALYSIS. xvii

His plan of Union	71
The plan condemned by Provincials and Britons	71
Results of the Congress of Albany	72
The New York Congress of 1765. The manner of issuing the call for it and the answer to the call	72
Its authority and object	73
Its importance shown by the condition of the country	74
Some of the members composing it	75
The tone of the petitions sent to England	75
The contents of the petition sent to the King	76
Petitions sent to the two houses of Parliament	77
The declaration of Rights and Grievances	77
The Congress dissolved	78
— The Congress of 1774. Its object and the call for it	78
Our ignorance of its debates	79
Its meeting, the variety in the manner of appointment of its members	80
The organization, president and secretary	80
The first trouble in regard to the manner of voting	81
Patrick Henry gives up his opinion, the question settled temporarily	81
Congress opened by prayer	82
Committees appointed to draft a Bill of Rights and to report on the statues of commerce	83
The delegates from Massachusetts on their journey and in the Congress	83
Opinions of various members about their rights	84
The great end of the Congress attained	85
Joseph Galloway's plan defeated	85
The work accomplished	86
The character of the Bill of Rights given by Chatham	86
The agreement of non-importation, non-exportation, and non-consumption, and opinions regarding it	87
Congress dissolved having accomplished its object	88
Attempts to bribe the members	88
Opinions on the situation	88
A new Congress convened amid stirring events	89
The place of meeting	89
The labor to be done and the difficulties to be encountered	90
All their deliberations bring them nearer independence	91
Their opinions in regard to resistance divided	91
Hopes of a reconciliation cause fluctuations in their councils	92
Division of opinion concerning the opening of the ports	93
Disputes about this question	93
The proposal to arrest dangerous persons equally embarrassing	94

b

Rhode Island's proposition to build a navy adopted after
  much delay 95
Measures for the encouragement of manufactures, agricul-
  ture, the arts and sciences passed 96
Congress petitions the King for the last time . . . 76
It assumes full powers and denies the royal proclamation
  that its members are rebels 96
Resolutions of non-assistance to British officers passed . 97
England's course drives them to independence . . . 97
Extract from the letters of John Adams. . . . 98
A resolution for the institution of State Governments in-
  troduced 98
The Preamble added giving the grounds of the resolve . 99
Another extract from a letter of John Adams . . 99
The Colonies authorize their delegates to vote for inde-
  pendence 100
Discussions of the Resolutions of independency and the ap-
  pointment of a committee to prepare the declaration 100
A Committee apointed to prepare a form of Confederation
  and one to plan treaties with foreign powers . . 101
The discussion of the 1st of July 101
The Resolution of independence passed July 2d . . 101
The Declaration of Independence signed July 4th . 101
Its reception by the people of the colonies and of the
  world 102
Our estimation of it 102

LECTURE IV.

CONGRESS AND THE STATE GOVERNMENTS OF THE REVOLUTION.

Recapitulation of Lecture III. 104
Appearance of unanimity in the councils of Congress 105
Internal dissensions and jealousies 105
Greatness and weaknesses often joined in the same mind 106
Committees apointed 107
The difficulty of obtaining a true estimate of the Confed-
  eration 107
Various alliances and confederations 108
The difference of the relations of citizen and state in an-
  cient and modern times 109
The theory of the source of authority and the idea of of-
  fice as shown by the Italian Republics . . . 109
Importance of this principle and the errors of the Con-
  federation from disregarding it 110
The course of Congress from the Declaration to the acceptance of the Confederation by the states . . 111

Congress criticised by the people and not entirely acquitted by History	111
Washington occupies the place in popular affection formerly held by Congress	113
Congress driven from place to place	114
It loses some of its best members	114
The place it is entitled to in our esteem	115
The King the source of authority in all the various forms of provincial government	115
Another principle checking the King. The rights of Englishmen	116
These rights characterized and specified	117
The result of these rights — a free government	117
Division of powers long familiar to the colonists	118
Outlines of the English Constitution preserved in all the colonies	119
The results of these facts after the separation	119
The passage from the old to the new a critical moment	120
Perplexities regarding the Massachusetts charter	121
Instruction of Congress to New Hampshire about her form of government	121
New constitutions adopted in several states	122
Defects in the constitutions remedied	122
The authority of the constitutions derived from the people	123
Nearly all preserve two houses of the legislature	123
Jealousy of the chief magistrate a common feature	124
Religious clauses in the constitutions common	124
Educational provisions few	125
Property restrictions of suffrage	126
The transmission of real estate. Entails abolished	126
The only material change—the substitution of the people for the King	127
Suspicion of the central power natural	127
Evil results of this jealousy	128
Difficulty between General Greene and the South Carolina legislature	129
General Greene compelled to advise the legislature again	129
Contents of his letter	130
Its unfavorable reception by the Governor and Assembly	131
The Governor offers an insult to Congress through its General	131
General Greene's course in the affair	132
His report to the Secretary of War	133
The proofs of jealousy about Congress many	134
The men who indulged in it	134
A strong central power required by the law of society	135

The history of the Civil government of the Revolution the history of a struggle against this principle . . 135

LECTURE V.

FINANCES OF THE REVOLUTION.

Introduction 137
Difficulty of attaining the proper standard of historical judgments 138
The undeveloped state of political science at the time of the Revolution 139
Our more enlightened state 140
Our fathers prevented by present perplexities from seeing future difficulties 141
Early history of traffic in America. Buying wives with tobacco 141
A pernicious principle, the power of the government to regulate prices 142
The issue of bills of credit by Massachusetts, and its evil effects 143
The fact established that government paper can for a time take the place of money 144
Continental money issued by Congress . . . 145
Probable course of the debate which preceded this step . 145
Difficulty of their position, the accusation of rashness refuted 146
Discussion as to the responsibility of the bills . . 148
The form and denominations decided upon . . . 149
A committee appointed to attend to the engraving and printing of the bills 150
The scarcity of paper and engravers 150
Paul Revere one of the engravers 150
The execution and signing of the bills . . . 151
The demand for the money urgent 152
The money soon gone — fresh issues 152
The war protracted — twenty millions gone before the Declaration of Independence 153
Depreciation begins — a loan resolved upon . . . 154
The loan insufficient — a lottery voted . . . 154
The immorality of lotteries not recognized at this time . 155
The lottery unsuccessful 155
A fresh issue directed 156
The depreciation continues — the public alarmed — a tax voted 156
The difficulty of collecting the tax 157
The tax inadequate — more paper money . . . 158

ANALYSIS.   xxi

Expedients to revive national credit tried in vain	159
Speculation and luxury prevalent	160
John Jay appointed to make an appeal to the states.	160
The figures which he exhibited to them	161
He states the resolve of Congress not to exceed in issues two hundred million dollars	161
He gives the three causes of depreciation	161
His argument proving the inclination of Congress to redeem its issues	162
His closing appeal	162
The trouble complicated by State debts and paper money	163
A new expedient — redemption and reissue	164
Public spirit sinking — an unhealthy state of society	164
Failure of crops — riots and mutinies	165
Agriculture and commerce crippled — speculation active	165
1781 arrives bringing French and Spanish gold	166
The Confederation accepted. Robert Morris appointed financier and Congress votes to return to a specie basis	167
Another blow at paper money in Pennsylvania.	168
Robert Morris' fitness for his position — he establishes a bank	169
The history of American finances after this less interesting though as important	170
Measures of Morris he is blamed; but unjustly	170
A parting glance	171
Errors of Congress and of the people, and their consequences	171
Could they have been avoided?	172

LECTURE VI.

THE DIPLOMACY OF THE REVOLUTION.

Washington and Franklin the great names of the Revolution	173
Importance of the French alliance	173
Franklin, his character, studies, and ambitions	174
His philanthropy and philosophy	176
France deeply wounded by the Treaty of Paris and longing to revenge herself	177
French emissaries in the Colonies — their vigilance and their reports to Versailles	178
De Kalb one of the emissaries — his activity and farsightedness	179
Choiseul's projects and the suggestions of his agents	180
He is overthrown by intrigue	181

The probable course of events had he remained in power	181
Vergennes does not try to interfere in American affairs, but is compelled to act	182
The new power in France — public opinion favorable to the colonists from desire of revenge on England and love of humanity	183
The formation of this public opinion an important part of European civilization	184
Another French agent sent to America. England suspicious	185
The Committee of Secret Correspondence and its members	185
Franklin's diplomatic experience — his questions to De Bonvouloir	186
His correspondence with Dumas	187
Two parties in Congress on diplomatic policy — the one in favor of seeking treaties prevails	187
Agents appointed by the Committee of Secret Correspondence	188
Difficulty of obtaining a recognition of independence — Franklin the only one competent to do it	188
His arrival and reception	189
His life, occupations, vigilance, and dangers	190
His associates Deane and Lee; Lee's disparagement of Franklin aided by Ralph Izard	192
State of affairs upon Franklin's arrival. The opening of negotiations	193
Franklin perceives the policy of France. His objects	193
Franklin enabled to honor the drafts of Congress upon himself and his colleagues	195
Summer of 1777. Franklin's confidence. The news of Germantown and Burgoyne's surrender. Its result — the first treaty	196
The hall in which the treaty was made	196
The significance of the scene	196
Franklin's confidence justified by the liberal terms of the treaty	198
A rage for treaties prevailing in Congress	199
Jay's character and trying situation in Spain	199
Spain's policy	199
Important European events	200
Diplomatic relations with Holland. A treaty obtained	200
Covert intrigues defeated by Franklin's integrity	201
Diplomatic relations with Germany and Russia. John Adams' independence	202
England standing alone. The principle at stake on her part	203
The internal state of France. She desires peace as much as her rival	204

Overtures for peace. America's claims	205
Franklin's colleagues and their course	205
Preliminary articles signed after many delays	207
Franklin's delicate position	207
The treaty finally signed	207
Pecuniary aid rendered to America by France	208
Franklin risks his own fortune. His economy	208
O for one hour of Franklin!	208

LECTURE VII.

THE ARMY OF THE REVOLUTION.

The remembrances which this title awakens. The veterans of the Revolution	210
The English misled by a false belief that the Americans were cowards	211
The materials for an army in the colonies. Prominent military men	212
A grave difficulty. Can a necessary degree of subordination be obtained?	213
The people prepare for the war. A characteristic illustration	213
Massachusetts militia. Timothy Pickering, clergyman, in the ranks	214
Massachusetts takes steps toward the raising of an army	215
The army gathering	215
An instance in Rhode Island	216
The need of a warning	216
The fundamental error. Short enlistments	217
Need of a commander-in-chief	217
Congress induced to accept the army	218
Candidates for commander-in-chief. Washington appointed	218
Plan of the army	219
Heart-burnings and jealousies	219
Washington takes command. His head-quarters	220
The strength and state of the army	221
The scene around Boston	222
The feelings of the Americans. A war-hymn	222
Winter approaching. The soldiers longing for home. Their privations	223
Washington's measures. Reorganization of the army	224
Various opinions about the army. Errors of Congress	225
The army disbanding. Washington's dangerous position	227
Enlistment of a new army. The arms of the discharged soldiers retained	227

The change accomplished 228
Record of the army of '75 228
Deeds of the army of '76 229
Necessity of disciplined troops, — disadvantages of short
 enlistments and inefficiency of militia . . . 229
Congress endeavors to repair its error in vain . . 231
Lack of discipline and proper equipments in the army 232
Baron Steuben reforms the tactics of the army . . 233
The whole number in the army 235
The great privations of the soldiers, their labors and
 prospects 235
Condition of the officers 236
Mutinies few and easily quelled 237
Congress unjustly jealous of the army 238
After much delay it votes the officers half-pay for life 239
The question again revived 240
The "Newburg Letters" and Washington's treatment
 of them 241
The half-pay commuted to five years' full pay . . 241
The disbanding of the army 241
Its ungrateful treatment by the country . . . 242
Difficulty of getting justice done the survivors by Congress 244

LECTURE VIII.

THE CAMPAIGNS OF THE REVOLUTION.

Dependence of success in war upon the general . . 245
The history of a war an individual history. Examples 245
This true of the Revolutionary war. Washington, Gates,
 and Greene 246
The military genius of Washington 246
The Revolution lacking in physical grandeur, — but full
 of moral grandeur 247
The great principles of warfare shown in the Revolutionary war 247
Washington's claim to greatness proved . . . 248
The campaign of 1775. Washington's labors . . 249
The problem before him 249
A blockade begun. Lack of munitions and engineers 250
Fortifications erected 250
Washington's vigilance. Skirmishes. The decisive blow.
 The city evacuated 251
The campaign of 1776. The defence of New York.
 Washington compelled to give up the city . . 252
The retreat after the battle of Long Island . . . 253

ANALYSIS.

Untrustworthiness of the army	253
Manœuvres around New York. The retreat through the Jerseys	254
Howe thinks himself secure in possession of New York and the Jerseys	255
Washington crosses the Delaware	255
Campaign of 1777. Movements around Trenton. Battle of Princeton	256
Washington's winter-quarters at Morristown	256
Howe embarks his troops. Washington's position	257
The English enter the Chesapeake. Battle of Brandywine. Manœuvres after it. The enemy occupies Philadelphia	257
Battle of Germantown. Howe endeavors in vain to force Washington to a battle	258
Valley Forge. Steuben disciplines the army	259
1778. Battle of Monmouth	260
Events of the next two years	260
1781. Washington plans an attack on New York. It is prevented by British reinforcements	261
Washington suddenly proceeds against Cornwallis. Seige of Yorktown	261
The Northern army. Episodes of the three campaigns. Arnold's march through the wilderness. Montgomery's death. Sullivan's retreat. The laurels unjustly awarded to Gates	262
England's opportunity — the campaign of '77. Burgoyne's advance. Schuyler opposes him. Burgoyne desperate. Gates takes command of the Americans. Stillwater. Bemis' Heights. Burgoyne's surrender	263
The original plan. How it was frustrated	265
Lee's treason and its results. How it was discovered	265
The Southern campaigns	266
British uniformly successful till 1780. Their position	267
The country nearly depopulated	267
State of the American army when Greene takes command	267
Gates' plans. Greene changes them. His difficulties	268
Greene moves his camp, constructs batteaux, establishes depots, etc.	269
Cornwallis reinforced. Greene detaches Morgan	270
Cornwallis perplexed. He sends Tarleton after Morgan	271
Battle of the Cowpens. Cornwallis' advance	271
Morgan's motions. Greene's retreat. Cornwallis foiled. He issues a proclamation. The Americans after him again. Greene's manœuvres. His dangerous position. His vigilance. An anecdote	272

The battle of Guilford Court House. Retreat of the
    British 275
Greene pursues but is deserted by his militia . . . 276
Greene advances into South Carolina. Cornwallis goes
    to Wilmington 277
Greene advances on Camden. Battle of Hobkirk's Hill.
    Camden evacuated. Other forts taken. Siege of
    Ninety-Six. The siege raised. The enemy with-
    draw 277
Greene on the hills of Santee. Battle of Eutaw Springs.
    The enemy driven from Dorchester. Washington's
    commendation 278
Strategic skill of Washington and Greene compared
    with that of other great generals 279
Other names: Sullivan, Knox, Lincoln, MacDougall,
    Olney, Angell, Christopher Greene, Williams, How-
    ard, William Washington, Marion, Henry Lee, Mor-
    gan, Wayne 280

LECTURE IX.

THE FOREIGN ELEMENT OF THE REVOLUTION.

The subject interesting though difficult from lack of sta-
    tistics. A conjecture of the number of foreign pri-
    vates 282
The proportion of foreign officers 283
The usefulness of these officers 283
An American's stake in the war. Difficulty of deciding
    how far foreigners should be trusted . . 284
A glance at the state of society in Europe. The suprem-
    acy of France 285
Local attachments changed to personal ones. Instances 285
The attachment to the sovereign. How it is destroyed
    in France 286
State of public feeling in France at the time of the Rev-
    olution 287
Abundance of mercenary officers and soldiers . . 287
Varieties of character among them 288
Position of these men in time of peace 289
The American war a Godsend to these mercenaries.
    Many come to America 289
Some act as spies for the European powers . . 290
American officers alarmed at the claims of these men.
    Jealousy of promotion 290
Embarrassment of Congress 291

ANALYSIS. xxvii

The want of engineers. Duportail, Launoy, Radière and Gouvion engaged. Their services	292
Thomas Conway arrives and is made brigadier-general. The plot against Washington. Conway writes to Gates. The contents of the letter reach Washington. His conduct and that of Gates and Conway	293
Troublesome pretensions of foreigners. Fleury at Stony Point. DeKalb's death at Camden. Washington's commendation of the Chevalier Armand. Pulaski	296
Kosciusko's introduction to Washington. His services in the northern army. His usefulness to General Greene. His after life, death, and burial	297
The great names of the subject, Lafayette and Steuben. Their great services	298
Points of resemblance in their characters	299
Lafayette's early life, prospects, and education	300
Steuben's early life, education, and military experience during the Seven Years' War	300
His life from the peace to the breaking out of the American war	302
He is persuaded with difficulty by the French minister to come to America	303
His arrival	304
The romantic manner in which Lafayette came to America. His noble sentiments	304
His attachment to Washington and studies in the camp	306
The hard work of an American general	307
The popularity of Lafayette in the camp	307
American dislike of France and Frenchmen	307
Position of American statesmen in regard to France	308
Lafayette's services in removing prejudices and promoting harmony of action between France and America	309
His influence in hastening the treaty	310
His services in France and Spain	310
His services in the field and his place in American history	311
The state of affairs in America upon the arrival of Steuben. His motives for coming	311
His footing with his brother officers	313
His friendship for Washington	313
Defects of the American army in evolutions, inspection, and returns	314
The task of Steuben to remedy these	314
He adapts his plan to the army	315
He drills Washington's body-guard. Its effect	315
His method and its success	316
His reforms in other departments	317
His services	318
Their reward	318

LECTURE X.

THE MARTYRS OF THE REVOLUTION.

Unknown martyrs. Imperfections of history. The aid of the sister arts needed	320
James Otis. His popularity	321
His studies, talents and character	322
His labors and sacrifices	323
His health fails. He is assaulted. His madness	325
Josiah Quincy. His studies and tastes. He becomes a champion of his country. The Boston Massacre. Difficulty of finding counsel for the soldiers	326
Quincy defends them. A test of moral courage.	327
His health fails under his labors. The necessity of sending a delegate to England	328
Quincy chosen. His reception and labors	329
His health again breaks down	330
A messenger to America needed. Quincy knowing his danger accepts the mission	331
His courage, sufferings, and death	331
Samuel Ward. His services in Congress. He dies at his post. His resting-place	332
Martyrs in domestic life. James Caldwell and his wife. His eloquence and dangers. The enemy approaching. Mrs. Caldwell remains. Her murder. His murder. Their grave	333
Cruelty of the British	336
The heroism of our civil martyrs and the benefit of keeping them in remembrance	336
The memory of Joseph Warren and his death	337
Nathan Hale. His character and sentiments	338
He enters the army. His services while there. A spy needed. Hale volunteers and cannot be dissuaded	339
He is arrested and condemned. His brutal treatment and noble death	341
A parallel between Hale and André. Its injustice	343
The guilty motives of André. The innocence of Hale	344
Isaac Hayne. He is captured as a prisoner on parole. He is compelled to acknowledge himself a British subject, and is summoned to take arms contrary to agreement	346
Greene's advance. Hayne considering himself freed from his allegiance takes command of an American regiment and is captured	347
His execution	348
The indignation it awakened. Greene's officers ask for retaliation. Their address	349

ANALYSIS.   xxix

Retaliation made unnecessary 350
The thousands of martyrs in jails and prison-ships.
   Their sufferings 350
A case taken. The capture. Sufferings in the guard-
   house. The march to the shore. The Jersey. Tor-
   tures of the first night 351
From this picture the spirit of our martyrs shown . 355

LECTURE XI.

LITERATURE OF THE REVOLUTION.

PART I.—PROSE.

Revolutions favorable to the cause of literature by awak-
   ening intellectual activity 357
Revolutions to be favorable must receive their impulse
   from the depths of men's hearts 358
The questions that take possession of the heart everlasting 358
Instances of revolutions followed by epochs in literature 358
The intellectual portion of the American Revolution
   founded on reason rather than feeling . . . 358
Not new theories but old ones carried out . . . 359
An instance. Jefferson's maxim 360
Reason, not imagination, the guide 361
The character of the Revolutionary literature derived
   from this fact 361
Benjamin Franklin. His ambition to become a good
   writer 362
An extract from his writings showing his method to at-
   tain this object 362
Two points regarding this extract 364
Franklin's style 364
His humor and satire 365
His position affords an ample field for his genius. His
   "Edict by the King of Prussia." His "Rules for
   reducing a great Empire to a small one." Extract
   from the latter 366
The piece written on his death-bed 369
John Dickinson. His education and success as a law-
   yer. His first publications. He is elected to the
   Congress of 1765 and drafts its resolutions. His ad-
   dress to the committee of correspondence in Barbadoes. Extracts from the preface and opening paragraphs 370
His next work "The Farmer's Letters." The advantages of their form and character 374

A passage from one of them	375
The reception of the "Letters" abroad	375
Their success at home	375
He is a member of the Congress of 1774 and writes many of the papers of that body	378
His error. Refutation of the charge that he refused to sign the Declaration of Independence	378
The remainder of his public life and writings. His death	380
Points of resemblance and contrast in the style of Dickinson and Adams	381
Jefferson's style	382
John Jay's style. An example. Difficulty of finding a parallel to it	383
Alexander Hamilton. His precocity and early writings. His connection with Washington's official correspondence	384
Other writers. Otis, Quincy, Thomas Paine, Hopkinson, Samuel Adams, Livingston, Richard Henry Lee	385
Our neglect of these precious legacies	386
The newspaper press	387
The debates in Congress	387
The patriot preachers	387

LECTURE XII.

LITERATURE OF THE REVOLUTION.

PART II.—POETRY.

General character of the Revolutionary poetry. The lack of fancy	389
English poetry at this time	390
Timothy Dwight. His services. The estimation in which he was held	390
His "Conquest of Canaan" and "Greenfield Hill." An extract	391
Joel Barlow as a man	393
The opinion of his contemporaries concerning him	394
His "Vision of Columbus." Its publication. Extracts from it	394
The weakness of the verses	396
His faults as a poet. His best poem	397
David Humphreys. His verses. His personal experiences and opportunities for poetical description	397
His fault as a poet. A lack of vividness	400
His "Address to the Armies of America." Contemporary reviews of it	401

Curiosity a cause of his success	402
The opening lines	402
His description of the Battle of Lexington	403
Of Bunker Hill and Washington	404
Other extracts	405
Humphreys considered especially the poet of the Revolution	406
Phillis Wheatley. Freneau	407
The humorous poets more successful. John Trumbull. His serious poems. Specimen	407
His satire compared with that of Butler	409
"The Progress of Dulness." "MacFingal." Its success	409
An outline of the plot and extracts	410
The opening. MacFingal's origin. His second-sight and eloquence	412
The town and place of meeting	412
The morning session	415
Adjournment for dinner	417
The afternoon session	417
The liberty pole. The fight. The sentence and its execution	423
The meeting of Tories by night	426
Other points of the poem	428
Its reception	428
Songs and ballads of the Revolution	427
A specimen "The Dance"	429
Other ballads. "Clinton's Invitation to the Refugees"	430
Final specimens, "The Battle of the Kegs" and the ballad of Nathan Hale	432

CONCLUSION.

History the record of man's acts and the interpreter of God's will	437
Comparison between the Revolutionary War and the War of the Rebellion	437
Every responsibility carries a corresponding right	437
Personal freedom a result of personal responsibility	438
The war of the Rebellion a logical sequence of the war of Independence	438
The two wars alike in origin, in the practical lessons they convey and in errors	438
Errors of our fathers compared with ours	439
Our peculiar error	440
An illustrative anecdote	441
As they conquered by perseverance, endurance and faith, so we must conquer by the same means	441

APPENDIX.

Chronological outline	445
American Colonial Trade	449
List of general officers at the commencement and close of the Revolutionary War	452
Statement of troops furnished by the respective states during the war	454
Force that each state furnished for the regular army	455
Expense of the Revolutionary War	455
Emissions of Continental Money	456
State Expenditures and Balances	457
Address to General Greene	458

LECTURE I.

THE CAUSES OF THE REVOLUTION.

THE subject to which I have the honor to invite your attention is one of those events which are sometimes overshadowed for a while by the magnitude of their own results; but which, when time enough has passed to give them a proper distance, and show the extent and variety of their ramifications, take their place among the decisive epochs of civilization. When the thirteen Colonies of Great Britain dissolved their connection with the mother country, and determined that they would henceforth have a government of their own, — a government of the people and for the people, — the name of republic had almost become a byword and a reproach. The United Provinces were fast yielding to the selfish pretensions of the House of Orange, and the monarchical influences by which they were surrounded. Venice — an oligarchy from her cradle — was dying, as oligarchies die, enervated and corrupt beyond the power of regeneration. Genoa and Lucca were but names on the map, asking only to be forgotten while they lived the passive and aimless lives of beings who have survived all the associations that make life a blessing. While San Marino, still preserving in her little territory of seventeen miles square the spirit which had carried her unchanged through twelve centuries of comparative independence, seemed a living confirmation of the favorite doctrine of monarchical publicists, that republics, to be durable, must be small, industrious, and unpretending.

While the incapacity of the people for self-government seemed thus to have been set in the strongest light by the failure of every people that had undertaken to unite it with material development, the power of man to govern man, both with an absolute and a limited authority, seemed to have been set in a light equally clear and equally strong. The Seven Years' War had shown what a small state can do against fearful odds, when its resources are developed and applied by a man of genius. Russia was still pursuing, under Catharine, the career of internal improvement and external expansion which she had begun under Peter. The throne of the Hapsburgs had never appeared more firmly rooted, nor their crown more dazzling; and the hand which the young Emperor, emulous of philosophic renown, held out to his people, was the hand of imperial condescension. Never, too, had England been so powerful abroad, or so prosperous at home; and never before had so much happiness been diffused over so wide a space, under any form of government, as was diffused over her vast possessions under her aristocratical monarchy.

Spain, it is true, had fallen into a deep sleep. But the brief career of Alberoni, within the memory of men still living, had shown startled Europe how much vitality was slumbering, undreamed of, in the lethargic mass; and how much a single will may do when it is an intelligent and a strong one. And if France excited any doubts in the minds of thoughtful partisans of monarchy, was there not enough in her profane philosophy, in her infidelity under the garb of formal devotion, and her insane trifling with all that was venerable and sacred in human as well as in divine things, under the specious pretext of philanthropy, to explain the degradation of a power which had more than once given laws to the continent?

But beneath this smooth exterior there was an internal fermentation, a feverish restlessness, a longing, vague in the beginning, but growing every day more definite, and even breaking out at times in energetic protests and warnings of deep significance. To those who had read history aright, it was evident that that natural harmony which makes form the spontaneous expression of substance, enabling you to interpret the inner life by the outward manifestation, and which reconciles anomalies and contradictions by voluntary concessions and ready adaptation, was lost forever. The vassal gave grudgingly, as an extortion, the labor which his father had given cheerfully as his lord's unquestioned due. The peasant hated the noble who trampled down his grain with his dogs and horses, and forbade him to fence out the hares and rabbits who ate with impunity the vegetables which he had planted and tended for the food of his children. The merchant dreaded monopolies; the manufacturer dreaded new edicts; industry in every form feared interference and repression under the name of protection and guidance. The man of letters sighed for freedom of thought; the lawyer, for an harmonious code; the rich man, for an opportunity to employ his wealth to advantage, and make himself felt in the world; the soldier, for promotion by service; society, through all its classes, for the correction of abuses, which in some form or other were felt by all. Two worlds, two irreconcilable systems, stood face to face, — the Middle Ages, with ideas drawn from the convent and the feudal castle, and the eighteenth century, with ideas drawn from the compass and the printing-press; and every day the gulf between them grew wider and deeper.

But in the thirteen Colonies of British America there was no such contradiction between the government and the people. There were no Middle Ages to efface; no feudal abuses to correct; no institutions which had outlived their usefulness, to tear up by the roots. They had been accustomed from the beginning to regulate their domestic affairs according to their own conception of their interests; and they were contented to leave their foreign affairs in the hands of the mother country in return for her protection. But they felt that that protection was no free gift; that the restrictions which they accepted for their commerce and manufactures transmuted every shilling which the English treasury expended on their behalf into pounds of profit for the English merchant and manufacturer. Dependence in this form they could submit to, for, though sometimes pushed to the verge of oppression, there was no humiliation in it. It was the dependence of the industrious child upon the thrifty parent; a habit outliving the necessity whence it sprang. And they had too much of the English love of precedent and English reverence for law about them to wish for any changes which did not seem to be the necessary consequence of acknowledged facts. They loved their mother country with the love of children, who, forsaking their homes under strong provocation, turn back to them in thought, when time has blunted the sense of injury, with a lively recollection of early associations and endearments, — a tenderness and a longing not altogether free from self-reproach. To go to England was to go home. To have been there was a claim to especial consideration. They studied English history as the beginning of their own; a first chapter which all must master thoroughly who would understand the sequel. England's literature was their literature. Her great men were their great men. And when her flag waved over them, they felt as if the spirit which had borne it in triumph over so many bloody fields had descended upon them with all its inspiration and all its glory. They gave English names to their townships and counties; and if a name had been ground enough to build a pretension upon, more than one English noble, who already numbered his acres in the Old World by thousands, might have claimed tens of thousands in the new. They loved to talk of St. Paul's and Westminster Abbey; and, with the Hudson and the Potomac before their eyes, could hardly persuade themselves that the Thames was not the first of rivers.

More especially did they rejoice to see Englishmen and converse with them. The very name was a talisman that opened every door, broke down the barriers of the most exclusive circle, and transformed the dull retailer of crude opinions and stale jests into a critic and a wit.

In nine years, — years full of incident, and which passed so rapidly that the keenest eye was unable to see what a mighty work they were doing, — all this was changed radically and forever. The thirteen Colonies became thirteen United States, with a name and a flag, and allies, and a history of their own; great men of their own to point to, great deeds of their own to commemorate, and the recollection of common sacrifices and a common glory to bind them together. And scarcely had this great change been completed when the French Revolution came; and then for a time the splendor of the American Revolution seemed to have been eclipsed by the variety and magnitude of the events which followed it. Men forgot, as is their wont, what their fathers had done, that they might magnify their own achievements. Their eyes were too much dazzled by the meteors that were flashing before them, to feel the full force of the clear and steady light that was shining on them from the past.

But History forgets not. In her vast treasure-house are garnered all the fruits and all the seeds of civilization. At her awful tribunal men await in silent expectation, face to face with their deeds. She assigns to each his place, apportions to each his reward; and when the solemn moment arrives wherein it is permitted to lift the veil from human errors and frailties, and give to man and to circumstances their due part in the production of events, the wondrous chain of causes and effects stretches out before us into the deepest recesses of the past, uniting by indissoluble links the proud aspiration of to-day with the hope that was breathed, half formed and almost indefinite, three thousand years ago.

In this light the American Revolution has, at last, taken its place in history, both as cause and as effect; receiving its impulse from the past, and transmitting it with a constantly increasing power to a future yet unrevealed.

What now was the cause of this rapid change in the opinions and affections of three millions of men,—a change so complete as almost to justify the opinion, that it was the work of design from the beginning? How was confidence transformed into suspicion, loyalty into aversion, submission and love into defiance and hatred? How could statesmen be so ignorant of the common laws of our nature, as to suppose that the industry which had been fostered by security could survive the sense of security? How could philosophers so far forget the force of general principles, as to suppose that the descendants of men who, when few in number and hard pressed by poverty, had preferred a wilderness for their home to a yoke for their consciences, should so far belie their blood as tamely to renounce their birthright when they were become a powerful people, and had made that wilderness a garden?

And here, at the threshold of our inquiry, we must pause a moment to remember that nothing is so fatal to a correct understanding of history as the blending and confounding of the two classes of causes which underlie all human events. For while every occurrence may be traced back to some immediate antecedent, it belongs also as a part to those great classes of events, which, gathering into themselves the results of whole periods, enable us to assign to nations and epochs, as well as to incidents and individuals, their appropriate place in the progress of humanity.

(1) Keeping, therefore, this distinction in view, we find the first cause of alienation in the colonial system itself. This system had grown up gradually and almost imperceptibly; beginning with a few feeble colonists scattered over a vast extent of territory, or clustering here and there in towns which, in Europe, would hardly have passed for villages. These colonists had no wish to dissolve their legal connection with England. Reverence for law and precedent, as I have already hinted, was a national characteristic; an inborn sense which they had inherited from their fathers, and could not eradicate without changing their whole nature. They still trod and loved to tread in the footsteps which they knew. The beaten track was a safe and a plain track, full of pleasant associations, familiar to their eyes and dear to their hearts. With this under their feet they walked firmly, like men who know what is behind them and what is before.

They had brought with them the common law, and, as far as the difference of circumstances permitted, followed its precepts. They had brought their municipal forms with them, and adapted them to the wants of their new home. And above all, they had brought with them the animating principle, the vital spirit of those laws and forms, the spirit of English liberty. They had forsaken one home for it, and without it no place would have looked to them like home. It was their inspiration, their guide, and their comforter, interwoven with all their habits and thoughts and feelings, and inseparable from their conception of duty to themselves, to their children, and to their Maker.

The spirit of English liberty is not an abstract conception, logically deduced from fundamental principles, and applied to the practice and purposes of life. Neither is it a sentiment, reaching the feelings through the imagination, and giving its coloring to thought because it had already been speculatively combined with action. It is an instinctive conviction, confirmed by reason, deep, ever present and ever active. You find it first in the forests of Germany, an absolute individuality, unlike anything that the Greek or Roman world had ever seen; strong-willed, self-dependent, spurning involuntary control, yet submitting cheerfully to the consequences of its own acts. Thence it crosses the seas as a conqueror, and suffering, as conquerors generally do, from the completeness of its own triumph, it relaxes somewhat of its vigor, passes through many vicissitudes, and, having survived the associations both of its origin and its transmigration, comes out, with all the freshness of its youth about it, in the meadow of Runnymede.

Here it entered upon a new phase of existence; a phase which gradually developed all its character·

istic traits, strengthening and purifying it till it became the most perfect conciliation which the world had yet seen of the rights of the individual with the rights of society. And this was the form which it had assumed when our fathers first brought it to these shores, where for forty years it was allowed to grow at will, and had already penetrated every part of the new society, before the guardians of the old bethought them of taking it under their protection.

The first fruit of this protection was the Act of Navigation, so long celebrated as the masterpiece of statesmanship, and so tenaciously clung to as the bulwark of England's commercial prosperity. The foundation, indeed, had been laid by the Long Parliament, and confirmed by the courts of Westminster. But it was not until Charles II. had entered upon his career of profligacy and corruption, that the Colonists began to feel the chains gradually tightening around their commerce, and contracting the sphere of their industry. First came a five per cent duty upon exports and imports; then the great Act itself, closing their ports to every flag but that of England, restricting the pursuit of commerce to native or naturalized subjects, and prohibiting the exportation of certain "enumerated articles, such as sugar, tobacco, cotton, wool, ginger, or dye-woods," produced in the Colonies, to any country but England. Still the Colonies grew and prospered, and still the jealous watchfulness of the mother country kept pace with their increasing prosperity. As new branches of industry were opened, new shackles were forged, and every fresh product of their enterprise was promptly added to the lists of prohibition. The Navigation Act, in its enlarged form, was passed in 1660; in 1763 it had woven its toils around American enterprise in twenty-nine separate acts, each breathing its spirit and enforcing its claims.

It is not difficult to imagine the feelings with which these acts were received. Open resistance, indeed, was impossible, and remonstrance would have been unavailing. Still the obedience that was rendered wore oftener the air of remonstrance than of cheerful acquiescence; and although the right was generally conceded, the exercise of it excited bickerings and heart-burnings that gradually prepared the way for independence. The enterprising spirit itself could not be repressed; and smuggling, its natural outlet, became almost as reputable, and far more profitable, than regular trade.

Thus the relation of England to her Colonies, which might have been a relation of mutual good offices, became, on her part, a mere business relation, founded upon the principle of capital and labor, and conducted with a single eye to her own interests. They formed for her a market of consumption and supply, consuming large quantities of her manufactures, and supplying her, at the lowest rates, with many objects that she required for her own consumption. What they sent out as raw material, she returned prepared for use. Her ship-owners grew rich as they carried the sure freight to and fro. Her manufactures gave free play to their spirit of enterprise, for their market was secured to them by a rigorous monopoly. She had the exclusive right of buying, and therefore bought upon her own terms; the exclusive right of selling, and therefore set her own prices. If with all these restrictions and obstacles the Colonies still continued to grow in wealth and strength, it was because in a new country, where land was cheap, the spirit of industry could not be crushed from a distance of three thousand miles by the spirit of monopoly.

Still the feeling engendered by this relation was not of a kind to make it lasting. That of the Americans was distrust and suspicion, strangely mixed up with filial reverence, — an instinctive sense of injury, instantly met by the instinctive suggestion, that there must be some constitutional reason for doing it, or it would not be done. That of England was summed up with somewhat more of concision than of elegance in Attorney-General Seymor's reply to Commissioner Blair. Pleading warmly for a moderate enlargement of the moderate allowance to the churches of Virginia, "Consider, sir," said the pious commissioner, "that the people of Virginia have souls to save." "Damn your souls!" was the ready answer; "make tobacco."

A second cause, equally active, and in its effects equally powerful with the first, was English ignorance of America. Nothing alienates man from man more surely than the want of mutual appreciation. Sympathy founded upon respect for our feelings, and a just estimate of our worth, is one of the earliest cravings of the human heart. It begins with our first recognition of existence, imparting an irresistible eloquence to the eye and to the lips of infancy. It grows with our youth, and, as we rise into manhood, finds new strength in reason and experience, teaching us in their daily lessons that without it there can be no sure foundation for the purest and noblest sentiments of our nature. It is the only feeling which can reconcile us to that condition of mutual dependence in which it has pleased our Maker to place us in this life; and working, as all the feelings which he has implanted in our breasts work, for the accomplishment of its appropriate end, it cherishes in the harmonious co-operation of fellow-citizens the germ of that beneficent concurrence of human wills and human desires, which, in God's chosen time, will become the brotherhood of the nations.

Few Englishmen had accurate ideas of the nature, the extent, or even the position of the Colonies. And when the Duke of Newcastle hurried to the King with the information that Cape Breton was an island, he did what perhaps half his colleagues in the ministry, and more than half his colleagues in Parliament, would have done in his place. They knew that the Colonies were of vast extent; that they lay far away beyond the sea; that they produced many things which Englishmen wanted to buy, and consumed many things which Englishmen wanted to sell; that English soldiers had met England's hereditary enemies, the French, in their forests; that English sailors had beaten French sailors on their coasts. But they did not know that the most flourishing of these Colonies had been planted by men who, prizing freedom above all other blessings, had planted them in order to secure for themselves and their children a home in which they could worship God according to their own idea of worship, and put forth the strength of their minds and of their bodies according to their own conception of what was best for them here and hereafter.

Hence, the ideas awakened by the mention of plantations were not ideas of brotherhood and sympathy, but of investment and gain. Like landlords who receive their rents through an agent, without seeing or caring to see the farm that produces, or the men who make it productive, they merely counted their money, and asked why there was not more of it. And when more came, it was welcomed as a proof that there was still more to come:

that the soil had not yet been made to pay its full tribute; that a little more care, a little more watchfulness, a little more exaction, would multiply its increase many fold; and that every attempt to turn that increase to the advantage of the laborers was a fraud upon the state.

It was known, also, that from time to time criminals had been sent to the plantations as an alternative, if not an equivalent, for the dungeon or the gallows; — and what to many minds seemed hardly less heinous, that men too poor to pay their passage across the ocean had often sold themselves into temporary servitude, in the hope of finding a home in which they might eat in security the bread which they had earned in the sweat of their brows. Philosophers, too, comparing the animals of the two worlds, had discovered that America was incapable of producing the same vigorous race which had carried civilization so far in Europe; and that, whatever might be the grandeur of her mountains, the vastness of her lakes, and the majesty of her rivers, the man that was born among them must gradually degenerate both morally and physically into an inferior being.

And thus, when the eye of his kindred beyond the ocean was first turned upon him, the American colonist already appeared as an inferior, condemned to labor in a lower sphere, and cut off by Nature herself from all those higher aspirations which ennoble the soul that cherishes them. His success awakened no pride; his filial reverence called in vain for maternal affection. The hand that had been held out in cordial welcome to the English stranger in America, found no respondent grasp when the American stranger returned to visit the home of his fathers in England. With a heart overflowing with love, with a memory stored with traditions, with an imagination warmed by tales and descriptions that began in the nursery ballad, and led by easy transitions to Shakespeare and Milton, with a mind elevated by the examples of English history and the precepts of English philosophy, he was received with the repulsive coldness of English reserve, and the haughty condescension of English pride. Had it not been that man is never so set in his opinions as when he takes them up in order to reconcile his conscience to a prejudice, the best minds of England would have seen that America had soon produced minds fully able to cope with theirs on their strongest ground. But the choicest lessons of experience were thrown away. From generation to generation the galling insult was repeated; and still the Colonist loved the land whose language he spoke, and revered the institutions from which he had drawn his own ideas of the duties of the sovereign and the rights of the subject. But already the work of alienation was begun, and every new demonstration of English prejudice was like the loosening of another of the "hooks of steel" which had once grappled the land of his forefathers to the "soul" of the American.

A third cause is found in the nature of the institutions, and more particularly of the municipal institutions, which the Colonists brought with them. For institutions have their nature, like human beings, and will as consistently and as inevitably work it out. Society is a soil whereon no seed falls in vain. Years, and even centuries, may pass before the tender germ makes its slow way to the light. But grow it must, and thrive and bear its fruit; and not merely fruit for the day, but fruit producing a new, though kindred seed, which, passing through the same changes, will lead in due time to a new and kindred growth.

The English colonial system was false from the beginning,— formed in erroneous conceptions of the laws of national prosperity, and the relations of sovereign and subject. But still it was, in part, an error common to all the countries which had planted colonies in America, all of whom had carried it into their colonial policy, and done battle for it by land and by sea. Even Montesquieu, when he discovered the long-lost title-deeds of humanity, failed to discover amongst them, in distinct specification, the title-deeds of colonial rights.

But in the application of this erroneous system, the superiority of a free over a despotic government was manifest. English colonies prospered in a cold climate, and on a meagre soil, as French and

Spanish colonies never prospered under mild skies, and with a soil that almost anticipated the labors of the husbandman. This superiority, and not the protection of her armies and fleets, was the enduring though unconscious service which England rendered to America. Her colonists were the free sons of fathers so accustomed to freedom that they held life as of little worth without it; and so trained by their municipal institutions to the forms of self-government, that even rebellion assumed the garb of order, and resistance to constituted authority moved with the precision and regularity of legal action.

And here, permit me at the risk of a digression to remind you of the important part which municipal institutions have ever borne in the history of civilization. The natural growth of every generous soil, we find them in Italy at the dawn of history, and we find them still there through all its manifold vicissitudes. They gave energy to the long struggle with Rome. They nourished the strength which bore the imperial city to the summit of glory and power. They survived the great inroad of the barbarians, appearing even in the darkest hour of the tempest like fragments of some noble ship, to which the survivors of the wreck still cling with trembling hands, in the fond hope that the winds may yet cease and the ocean rest from its heavings. Need I remind you of those republics of the Middle Ages, which, gathering up the lessons of Greece and Rome, enriched them by new lessons of their own, lessons accepted by every free people as essential elements of freedom? Need I tell you how the spirit of industry, how commercial enterprise and mechanic invention, and, better than all these, freedom of thought and vigor of creative imagination, have followed the waxing and waning of municipal freedom, still growing with its growth and withering with its decay?

These were the institutions which our fathers brought with them in their English form, — surely one of the best; for by virtue of this, while they cherished that belief in inalienable rights which made independence inevitable as an aspiration, they preserved those habits of self-government without which it would never have been attainable as a blessing.

The three causes which I have already mentioned would sooner or later have produced a violent separation of the Colonies from the mother country. For the colonial system would have led to a collision of interests; English ignorance to ill-directed attempts at coercion; the sentiment of inalienable rights fostered by English institutions, to firm and resolute resistance. But many years, perhaps another century, might have passed before these causes alone would have brought on an open contest, if their action had not been hastened by the concurrence of two other causes, one of later growth, the other almost contemporary with the first three.

CAUSES OF THE REVOLUTION. 21

4. This last was the fact that, in her war upon the freedom of colonial industry, England was at war with the spirit of her own political system. She had left nothing undone to break down the barriers with which Spain had fenced in her American Colonies. The illicit trade which she punished by a fine and imprisonment on her own colonial coast, was long pursued on the Spanish Main, almost under the shadow of St. George's cross. Her true interest required an enlargement of her commerce, new markets for her manufactures, an expansion of her navigation in every direction; and the true interests of a country will always, sooner or later, infuse somewhat of their spirit into its conduct, even where they fail to commend themselves to its rulers. By nature and by position England was the champion of free trade. But her statesmen, unable to raise themselves above the prejudices of the age, seem to have vied with each other, during every period of her colonial history, in doing all that depended upon them to transform a nation of merchants into a nation of shopkeepers.

5. The cause of later growth was the fact that England was oppressed with debt,— her landholders overburdened with taxes. The monopoly which brought golden streams to the merchant and the manufacturer, brought no evident advantage to the country gentleman. He could not see in what his condition was to be bettered by an increase in the shipping of Bristol; just as at this very time the

moneyed men of Liverpool were unable to see how the Duke of Bridgewater's canals were to be of any use to them, and allowed his note for £ 500 to be hawked about from broker to broker in quest of a purchaser. Town and country railed at each other, as they have always done, and the landholder, as he gave vent to his indignation, called loudly for some one to share with him the burden of taxation. What class so able as the rich colonists who were thriving under his protection? That protection, as he understood it, was an advantage well worth paying for; and with a foresight worthy of his motives, he hailed the Stamp Act as the harbinger of that happy day which was to send the tax-gatherer from his own door to that of his American factor.

It was England's first misfortune that she adopted an erroneous system. But this might have been pardoned her, as a common error of the age. Her second misfortune was that she persevered in it long after its erroneousness had been demonstrated, and for this her only apology is the humiliating confession that her rulers were unfit for their places. There was no period previous to 1763 wherein a real statesman might not have reconciled the just claims of both countries; giving to each all that, in the true interest of civilization, it had a right to ask; imposing upon each all that, in the true interest of civilization, it was bound to bear.

For what is statesmanship but the art of adapting the actual condition of a nation to what must inevitably be its future condition, — the art of connecting the present with the past and the future, — distinguishing the permanent from the casual causes of national prosperity, and thus knowing what to lop off as an excrescence, what to root up as a noxious growth, and what to foster with all the arts of sedulous cultivation? More than half the blood that has been shed upon this blood-stained earth of ours, has been shed because mankind have persevered in intrusting their dearest interests to the guidance of men who have no reverence for the past, no intelligent appreciation of the present, no prophetic visions of the inevitable future.

How much to attribute to individuals, and how much to general causes, is one of the most difficult problems of philosophical history. But the publication of George the Third's letters and billets to Lord North leaves no room to doubt the part which the monarch bore in the contest with America. George the Third, notwithstanding his English birth and nominally English education, had all the arbitrary instincts of a German prince. To free himself from the hereditary control of the great Whig families, and to exalt the royal prerogative above the aristocracy and the people, was the hope with which he ascended the throne, and to this end all his policy was directed as long as he was able to direct it. In the searching light of history it matters little that he was a pure man in his domestic relations, and an industrious man in his royal functions. Not even the sincerity of his convictions can cleanse him from the taint of unnecessary bloodshed; for he erred in things wherein it is not permitted to man to err and hold himself guiltless. With none of the characteristics of greatness himself, he could not bear great men around him; and while no one can blame him for seizing the earliest opportunity to throw off Grenville as a tedious formalist, no one should forget that the ear which was reluctantly opened to Chatham and Fox drank in with avidity the congenial counsels of a Bute and a Wedderburn.

And thus the English tax-payer, groaning under his burdens, joined heartily with short-sighted ministers and a narrow-minded king in the attempt to draw a revenue from the Colonies by Parliamentary taxation. While the contest lasted, he supported government with his vote and his purse, submitting, though not without an occasional murmur, to an increase of his present load, in the firm hope of future relief. And when, at length, the inevitable day of defeat came, he was the last to see that the attempt had been hopeless from the beginning.

And this brings to view a circumstance which, though not an original cause of alienation, added materially to the difficulty of effecting a cordial reconciliation when the dispute became a discussion of Parliamentary rights. It is one of the great advantages of the English constitution, that it has grown up with the growth of the English nation. Thus, as society has continued its progress, the constitution has nearly kept pace with that progress; never much in advance, never long in the rear; sometimes guiding, sometimes waiting upon its footsteps; but always the faithful exponent of the feelings and convictions of the bulk of the nation. Some of these adaptations and expansions have been made silently; the statute-book reflecting, as it were with an instinctive sympathy, the mind and the heart of the people. But by far the greater part have cost long and bitter contests, — convulsions some of them, and some of them blood. And in them all the spirit of the constitution has been preserved, although the letter has often changed, — its spirit of freedom, which was already a living spirit under the Plantagenets, though a feeble one, which tempered the arrogance of the Tudors, and never was truer to its mission than when it crushed the Stuarts.

But while this gradual development has been attended by many advantages, it has been productive also of an unusual degree of that uncertainty and contradiction which always attend the interpretation of a constitution, whether compressed within a few pages like our own, or scattered through hundreds of folios like that of England. An absolute government — France or Spain — would have brought the claims of the Colonists to the decision of the sword from the beginning; for the French and Spanish colonist, in resisting the pretensions of the mother country, would have had no legal or constitutional ground to stand upon. What one arbitrary sovereign had given, another arbitrary sovereign might take away; and the colony that was too feeble to resist had no choice but to submit.

But with English colonists the question of Parliamentary supremacy was a constitutional question, a discussion of legal rights, leading, as men's blood grew warm, to the sword, but necessarily beginning with the pen. In this discussion, individual opinions and party opinions were soon enlisted, awakening fiery zeal, and gradually preparing both sides for a solution from which they would both have shrunk at the outset. The Parliament that "languidly" voted the Stamp Act, would have debated long and divided often before it voted an armed invasion. The men who resisted it would have repelled with indignation the charge of disloyalty. It was by steps which to them who were taking them seemed very slow, that the final step of an open war was reached. Both sides had much to study and much to say. Englishmen, though fully agreed upon the question of Parliamentary supremacy as a constitutional principle, were far from agreeing upon the interpretation of that supremacy. Did it imply the right of taxation? If it did, what became of that other fundamental principle, — taxation goes with representation? Were the Americans represented in Parliament? If not, what would be the final effect of this taxing without representation upon England herself? The field of discussion was immense, almost boundless, — embracing, as some of Dean Tucker's tracts show, a prophetic glimpse of the true laws of trade; and, as Chatham's speeches show, a foreshadowing of Parliamentary reform.

On the part of the Americans, the feeling of dependence was very vague, very indefinite. In some form and degree they all acknowledged it; but the form was nowhere clearly defined, the degree nowhere distinctly marked out. The most important Colonies had been founded at a moment when all the best minds of the mother country were actively engaged in discussing the claims of the royal prerogative, — the very best, in trying to set bounds to it. With this feeling towards royalty, the Colonists laid the foundations of the new state, and laid them more in harmony with the rights which they came here to secure, than with the claims which they came here to avoid. As the state grew, those foundations became more firmly fixed. The great problem of social organization — how far the rights of the individual can be carried without interfering with the rights of society, or impeding its legitimate action — was met as a practical question, susceptible of a practical solution. All the forms of their society compelled them to think and to discuss. They discussed in their town meetings. They discussed at their elections. They discussed in their General Courts and General Assemblies. Every question was brought to the final test of individual opinion; and when this became merged in the general opinion, every individual felt that he could still recognize therein something of his own. They were all parts of the state, and, as parts, had an equal interest in it, an equal claim to its protection, an equal right to control its action.

To counteract this, there was their love of England, their Anglo-Saxon love of precedent, their instinctive sense of legal subordination; — feelings so strong and so deep rooted, that it was not until the Act of Navigation had, by the slow growth of a hundred and four years, reached its logical conclusion in the Stamp Act, that "the strong man arose from his slumber, and, shaking his invincible locks," burst forever the bands that had bound him to an ungenerous and unsympathizing parent.

Thus a false colonial policy led to false relations between England and her American Colonies; an unjust depreciation of colonial character undermined the sentiments of reverence and love which the Colonists had piously cherished for their mother country; an insane hope of alleviating his own burdens by casting part of them upon his American brethren led the English tax-payer to invade in the Colonies a right which he would have cheerfully died for at home; and a narrow personal ambition combined with gross ignorance of the science of statesmanship prevented the adoption of any effective measures for adapting the relations of the two countries to the changes which a century of marvellous prosperity had produced in their respective positions. And thus alienation and opposition grew, advancing step by step — twenty-nine in all — from the Act of Navigation to the Boston tea-party and the battle of Lexington.

Thus far I have spoken only of the relations arising from the connection between England and her Colonies. But both England and her Colonies formed part of a larger system, — the great European system, not merely as a system of policy, but as a form of civilization. And during the whole period of Colonial history, this system was under constant discussion, — discussion with the pen and with the sword. While the Pilgrims were making for themselves a home at Plymouth, and preparing the way for Roger Williams and the doctrine of soul liberty, Richelieu was undermining the aristocracy of France, and preparing the way for Louis XIV. and absolutism. While the claims of hereditary monarchy as the most peaceful method of transmitting sovereign power were receiving a bloody confutation in the wars of the Spanish and the Austrian succession, England was taking firm possession of Newfoundland and Nova Scotia, making sure the fur trade of Hudson's Bay, the fisheries of the Great Banks, planting new Colonies in the Carolinas, and preparing herself for the great, and, as she fondly thought, the final struggle, in the valley of the Ohio, and on the banks of the St. Lawrence. American clauses gradually crept into European treaties. Diplomatists, with the map of Europe before them, began to cast longing eyes on the vast territories beyond the Atlantic. At last came the treaty of Paris, in 1763, — the proudest treaty which England had ever signed, wherein a needy partisan, grasping at the succession of a great statesman, set his name to the act which stripped France of the Canadas, and shut her out forever from the valley of the Ohio.

And now, thought the King and his counsellors, we have our Colonies to ourselves, and can henceforth make war or peace in Europe as we choose, without taking them into account. But not so thought the French Minister at Versailles, and the French Ambassador at London; and while George Grenville, the man who, according to Dr. Johnson, could have counted the Manilla ransom if he could have enforced the payment of it, was eagerly counting in advance the profits of his Stamp Act, French emissaries were passing through the thirteen Colonies in their length and breadth, and Durand, Francès, and Du Châtelet were sending to the Duke of Choiseul long and minute reports of the character, resources, and spirit of the Colonists. When the ministry of Louis XVI. were called upon to decide between England and America, the archives of the Foreign Office at Paris afforded materials for the formation of a sound opinion, hardly less abundant, and far more reliable, than those of the Foreign Office at London. Cool observers now, if not absolutely impartial, French statesmen saw clearly in 1766 what statesmen on the other side of the Channel were too much blinded by pride and false conceptions of their interest to see in 1776. "They are too rich to persevere in obedience," wrote Durand, just nine years and eleven months before the Declaration of Independence. "They are too rich not to share our taxes," reasoned Grenville, and half England marvelled at his wisdom.

And this brings us to that second class of causes which I have already alluded to as gathering into themselves the results of whole periods. Lord Bacon tells us that "a great question will not fail of being agitated some time or other." What question so great for our thirteen Colonies as free labor in its broadest sense, and with its train of mighty consequences? For free labor implies freedom of will, — the right to think as well as the right to act. And all Europe was agitated by thoughts which, translated into action, led to an entirely new principle of government, — the greatest good of the greatest number. The doctrine of inherited rights was gradually calling in its detachments, and forming the line of battle for the decisive struggle with the doctrine of natural rights.

All through its ranks gleamed the burnished arms of its devoted allies, — waved the proud banners which had waved over it in triumph for more than half a thousand years. And in front, as far as eye could reach, stretched the firm phalanx of the enemy; calm, deliberate, resolute, fearless, confident of victory. For it was no longer a war of king against king, a war to decide whether an Austrian or a Frenchman should sit on the throne of Spain, — whether a few millions more or less of Italians, or of Flemings, should be thrown, as make-weights, into the scale, when their owners were tired of fighting, and satiated with military glory; but the great war of the ages, which was to crush forever the hopes of civilization, or open wide the gates of progress as they had never been opened before. And therefore it was meet that the signal of battle should come from men who saw distinctly for what they were contending, and were prepared to stake their all upon the issue. As a chapter of English and American history, the American Revolution is but the attempt of one people to prescribe bounds to the industry of another, and appropriate its profits. As a chapter and one, too, of the brightest and best in the history of humanity, it is the protest of inalienable rights against hereditary prerogative; the demonstration of a people's power to think justly, decide wisely, and act firmly for themselves.

LECTURE II.

THE PHASES OF THE REVOLUTION.

IN my first Lecture I endeavored to show the historical position of the American Revolution, and point out the causes which produced it. We saw, that, as a purely English and American question, it was the necessary consequence of the colonial system, — a struggle for monopoly on one side, and free labor on the other. We saw that, as a chapter in the history of European civilization, it was a struggle between hereditary prerogative and inalienable rights. Both of these views will be confirmed by the historical sketch which I propose to give you this evening of the phases through which it passed in the progress of its development.

The first permanent English Colony in America was planted in 1607, and by 1643 the foundations of New England had been so securely laid, that Massachusetts, Plymouth, Connecticut, and New Haven formed a league for mutual protection against the French and Indians, under the significant title of the United Colonies of New England.

History has nowhere recorded greater perseverance, or a more marvellous growth. On what, as we look at the map, seems a narrow strip of land betwixt the wilderness and the ocean, with a wily enemy ever at their doors, they had built seaports and inland towns, and extended with wonderful celerity their conquests over man and over nature. There were jealousies and dissensions among them. There were frequent misunderstandings with England about undefined rights. The Church, too, from which they had fled that they might worship God in their own way, had already cast longing eyes upon their new abode, as a field ripe for her chosen reapers. But their strong municipal organization controlled jealousies and dissensions, even where it failed to suppress them. However vague English ideas of their rights might be, there were certain points whereon their own were perfectly defined. And when the Church from longing prepared to pass to open invasion, they prepared for open resistance. They had hardly emerged from infancy when they began to wear the aspect and speak the language of vigorous manhood. For they had been planted at happy moments, — when James was starting questions which compelled men to think, and Charles doing things which compelled men to act. Those among them which had charters watched them jealously and interpreted them liberally. Those that had not yet obtained them spared no exertions to obtain them; falling back, meanwhile, upon their municipal institutions as a resource that met all their present wants. A few more years like the past, and the whole seaboard would be peopled.

As yet, however, one element of strength was lacking, — a spirit of union; for the New England Union was rather the expression of an immediate want, than a natural aggregation of sympathetic parts. Plymouth was soon merged in Massachusetts, and New Haven in Connecticut. And both Massachusetts and Connecticut, which had never admitted little Rhode Island to their confederacy, would gladly have divided her between them. New York was still Dutch, and remained Dutch in feelings and habits long after it had become English in name. New Jersey was not yet settled. A few Swedes were trying to build up colonies in what some years later became Pennsylvania and Delaware. Catholics, with an uncongenial code of religious toleration, held Maryland, — while Virginia, the oldest and wealthiest Colony of all, had grown up under the shadow of the Church, and with a reverence for the King which seemed to place an insuperable barrier betwixt her and her unbishop-loving and more than half republican sisters of the East. Thus each Colony still stood alone; each still looked to England as to a mother to whom they were all bound by natural and not unwelcome ties.

Yet something which might have awakened suspicion had already occurred. The Pilgrims had not yet gathered in the first harvest which they wrung with weary hands from the ungrateful soil of Plymouth, when an English Order in Council was issued, forbidding the exportation to foreign countries of any colonial product which had not previously paid duty in England. The only Colony to which this order could as yet apply was Virginia; but what would not a mother be likely to ask of her children in the day of prosperity, who already asked so much in the day of trial?

Twenty-two years passed, and a warning voice came from New England; "where," says the chronicler, "the supplies from England failing much, men began to look about them, and fell to a manufacture of cotton." Prophetic glances, these, into a distant future; but, like so much of human foresight, thwarted and made useless by human passion.

It was in no unkind spirit towards New England that Parliament passed the Navigation Act of 1651, but partly to curb the aggressions of Holland, and partly to arouse the slumbering energy of English nautical enterprise. New England might have asked much of the rulers of the Commonwealth which she wisely refrained from asking. There was little that Virginia could have asked which would not have been granted grudgingly, if granted at all. The Commonwealth passed away, and the Restoration found the Colonies stronger in population, in wealth, and in that spirit which makes population and wealth availing.

The period of indefinite relations was passed; the first phase of revolution, the period of definite subjection, was begun. For now — 1660 — that Act of Navigation of which that of 1651 was but the outline, and which Lords and Commons, historians and orators, united in extolling as the palladium of English commerce, a *charta maritima* second only to Magna Charta itself, first took its place on the statute-book. "It will enable your Majesty to give the law to foreign princes abroad, as your royal predecessors have done before you," said the Speaker of the House of Commons to Charles, as he presented the bill for approval. "By this act," says an historian of commerce, "we have absolutely excluded all other nations from any direct trade or correspondence with our American plantations." By this act, a philosopher might have said, you have opened a breach betwixt yourselves and your Colonies, which every year will widen, till the sword completes what the pen began, and severs you from them forever.

It might have been supposed that there was little in those Colonies, as yet, to excite the avaricious longings of commercial monopoly. But monopoly has a keen eye, if not a prophetic one; and seldom does an immediate interest escape its eager search. "No sugar, tobacco, cotton-wool, indigo, ginger, fustic or other dyeing woods, of the growth or manufacture of our Asian, African, or American colonies, shall be shipped from the said colonies to any place but England, Ireland, or to some other of his Majesty's said plantations, there to be landed, under forfeiture as before. And to make effectual this last-named clause, for the sole benefit of our own navigation and people, the owners of the ships shall give bonds at their setting out for the due performance thereof." Thus reads the thirteenth clause. A few years later, Ireland, which, as you will observe, is here put upon the same footing with England, was excluded by name. You will observe, too, that the American Colonies stand last upon the list; so much had England yet to learn, both about their importance and their character. The articles mentioned in this clause obtained the name of "enumerated commodities," henceforth an irritating and odious name in our colonial history.

Thus England took her position towards the Colonies deliberately and definitely. Henceforth they were to work for her; to grow strong, that they might add to her strength; to grow rich, that they might aid her in heaping up riches; but not to grow either in strength or in wealth, except by the means, and in the direction, that she prescribed. It behooves us to ponder well this thirteenth clause; to weigh it word by word, that we may understand the spirit in which it was conceived, and the spirit which it awakened. Its object was the general increase of shipping and navigation,—"wherein," says the preamble, "under the good providence and protection of God, the wealth, strength, and safety of this kingdom are so much concerned." Words well chosen, and whose truth none can gainsay; for it is only by the portion of truth which is mixed up with them that radical errors ever succeed in commending themselves to the human mind. And here the proportion of truth was not only large,—for national prosperity is closely allied with commercial prosperity,—but the error was singularly in harmony with the opinions and feelings of the age. "So long as your Majesty is master at sea," said the Speaker, "your merchants will be welcome wherever they come." Change the form of expression, and what does this mean, but that superior strength is to dictate the laws of commerce, as it dictates the terms of a treaty? And what is this but the alliance of commerce, whose power is founded upon interest,—I use the word in its true sense,—with the sword, whose power is founded upon fear? Follow it a little further; push it to its logical consequences, and you have that simple formula, so repugnant to truth, to morality, and to religion, My gain is your loss; your loss is my gain.*

---

* A great empire has been established for the sole purpose of raising up a nation of customers, who should be obliged to buy from the shops of our different producers all the goods with which those could supply them."—SMITH, Wealth, &c., B. IV. Ch. VIII. Vol. II. p. 517.

LECTURE II.

But could we expect men to foresee the disastrous consequences of this narrow and selfish policy, who undertook, as this Parliament did, in the same session in which they passed the Navigation Act, to encourage the "fish trade" by prohibiting the eating of flesh on Wednesday?

It was a necessary consequence of this system, that England should henceforth watch American industry in order to check it whenever it entered upon a track which she deemed inconsistent with her own interest, rather than with a view of encouraging it whenever it opened a branch useful to the Colonies. The enumerated list was ever at hand, a happy embodiment of the great principle, and susceptible of indefinite extension. Not many years passed before rice and molasses came more largely into demand; and the spirit of enterprise was presently rewarded by their prompt insertion upon the catalogue. Then the hardy trader, who, at the hazard of his life, had penetrated to the banks of the Ohio, and established trading-posts in the wilderness, was cheered in his industry by seeing his furs and peltries honorably classed with the other privileged articles which were reserved exclusively for the English market. Copper ore stands close by their side, — an enumeration of the same year, the eighth of George I., and showing how well prepared the House of Hanover came to tread in the footsteps of the House of Stuart. A still wider sweep was taken by George II., when pitch, tar, turpentine, masts, yards, and bowsprits were condemned by the ready *Yeas* of the House of Commons to make a voyage to England — and eleven weeks in those days was nearly the average length of the voyage — before they could be offered at any other market.

The same spirit extended to royal charters. Already, in the charter of Pennsylvania, the right of taxation had been expressly reserved to Parliament. And when the charter of Massachusetts was renewed by William and Mary, or rather a new charter granted after the arbitrary sequestration of the first by Charles, all the pine forests of Maine, not already granted to individuals, were treated as the property of the King, and every tree in them of more than twenty-four inches diameter at above a foot from the ground reserved to furnish masts for the royal navy. A hundred pounds sterling was the penalty for cutting one of those trees without a special license, with the addition of twenty lashes on the bare back if it was done in disguise.

The position was taken. All that remained to do was to enforce the law. This required officers, and they were easily found. There were already officers of the customs, with their registers of entry and clearance. And now, to protect the interests of the royal navy, a new officer was appointed, — a "Surveyor-General of the King's Woods"; and, as he could not them all in person, he was furnished with a goodly band of deputies and underlings, who, from the chief with his ample salary and large perquisites to the subaltern with his fees for specific services, were bound, each in his degree, to uphold the King's claims to the pines that had been growing there for centuries, so straight and tall, without the King's aid or permission. It was a goodly net-work, spreading far over the land, and gathering, what such nets in such hands always gather, a full draught of litigation and discontent.

For the Colonists could not bring themselves all at once to look upon the doings of Parliament as kind and wise. They had worked hard to make for themselves comfortable homes, and felt that the labor they had bestowed upon those homes gave them a right to enjoy them in their own way. When the Pilgrims first came, their chief care was provision and shelter; how they could most readily make the earth give them food; how they could most readily construct for themselves, out of the trees of the forest, dwellings which should be a protection both from the inclemency of the weather and a sudden attack of the savages. They planted and reaped with arms at hand for immediate use. They went to meeting with their guns loaded for instant service. All around them was wilderness, — a leafy canopy of boundless forest. In a few years, fifteen thousand acres of this wilderness were under cultivation. Everywhere, as you went, your eye was greeted by cornfields and orchards and cottages that told of peace within doors and without. And now, as a new generation — a generation born upon the soil — was beginning to reap the fruit of their fathers' sacrifices, they were told that they must not use their strength so freely; that, before they employed the means which they had created, they must ask permission of that mother three thousand miles off, who had looked on so coldly, if she had looked at all, while they were creating them. With all the love they bore that mother, — and we have already seen that they loved her, — there was an instinctive rising of the Colonial spirit against claims which the tamest among them could not but regard as an unjust restraint upon their industry. Even if the farmer could submit, could the merchant fail to see whither these restrictions were tending?

The merchant did see, and became the ally of smugglers. The farmer did not submit without murmurs that prepared the way for questionings; and these questionings, growing bolder year by year, and more searching, led, at last, to open resistance. Among the pine forests of Maine there was a hardy race of lumberers, men who could not understand the King's claim to the trees which they had been so freely cutting down as their own. From the first appearance of the "Surveyor-General" among them, they began to make his office uncomfortable for him. A feud sprang up between them, which no mediation, no authority could allay;

for it had its origin in that instinct of right which often leads man to resist aggression, even where he fails to perceive its remoter consequences. The contest between the Maine lumbermen and the royal surveyors was the prelude of the greater contest which was to set American industry free from every restraint but such as American legislators should see fit to impose upon it for the good of Americans. As the old French war prepared Washington for the peculiar trials of the Revolutionary war, this petty warfare between obscure men prepared the popular mind of Massachusetts — of which Maine was as yet a part — for the discussion of that broader application of the same comprehensive principle which led step by step to the Declaration of Independence.

Of all the errors of legislation, there is none so fatal as the making of laws against which the public mind instinctively rebels. For it is only when law is in harmony with the society for which it is formed, that men will give it that cheerful obedience which makes it strong for the protection of good men and the punishment of evil-doers. A law which violates the public conscience excites first hatred, and presently contempt for those who undertake to enforce it; and from them the feeling soon extends with increased vigor to the source from which the law emanated, confounding the sense of right and wrong, and undermining the very foundations of society.

Thus one of the natural effects of the Act of Navigation was to raise up a generation of law-breakers; of merchants, who went regularly to meeting, doing the greater part of their business, the while, in a way that might have sent them to jail; of lawyers, who dressed their wives and daughters in stuffs that the law would have confiscated; of mechanics and farmers, who daily put upon their tables what they could not have put there if they had been compelled to obtain it through the regular channels of commerce; and sometimes, I fear, of clergymen, who quieted their consciences by drawing subtle distinctions between direct and indirect participation, — between the statutes of man and the statutes of God.

The first and only effect of the reservation in William and Mary's charter was to set in action a class of men who never act without making other men think; and thus, by action and thought combined, and directed to one object, bringing out principles and awakening convictions that broke through reservations, and made charters useless.

For thoughtful men, earnest men, cannot break laws often without calling in question the authority as well as the wisdom of the lawgiver. Where habit is not formed by principle, principle falls naturally under the control of habit. American merchants engaged in smuggling because they wanted a market and money. In time they came to look upon it as something that everybody participated in, though nobody cared to talk about it. Next came the unavoidable question, how men who were upright and honorable in everything else could be dishonest and dishonorable in this. And this brought them to the true question, When had they intrusted a legislature, so far removed from them by habit, by association, and by interest, with authority to control their industry and set bounds to their enterprise?

But it was not till after many trials, and a full experience of the true character of such legislation, that this question was asked. The Colonist longed for freedom without aspiring to independence. It was not till the spirit of monopoly had spread from their foreign to their domestic commerce, — it was not till each Colony had been put by statute in the position of a foreign nation towards its sister Colony, — that they saw what a vile spirit they were dealing with, and to what an unnatural condition it was leading them. When a hatter was forbidden to take more than two apprentices at a time, or any apprentice for less than seven years, — when he was encouraged to buy slaves, and forbidden to use them in the only way wherein he could make his purchase profitable, — he felt aggrieved, deeply aggrieved. But when he was forbidden to send his hats to an adjacent Colony that was ready to pay him a fair price for them, and to which he could send them without inconvenience or risk, and get something in return that he wanted very much, he felt that the legislator who made these laws for him had made them in wanton defiance of his interest and his rights. Woollen manufacturers were subjected to the same restraints. Iron might be taken from the mine. America produced, and England wanted it; but every process which could add to the value of the unwrought ore was reserved for English hands. It could neither be slit nor rolled; nor could any plating forge be built to work with a tilt-hammer, or any furnace for the making of steel. It was just ninety years from the passing of the Navigation Act when this last link was added to the chain. Such laws defied nature, and they for whom they were made, obeying nature, learnt to defy the law.

But now a new phase begins. There are rumors of war on the frontiers; not the war of the white man with the red man, but the long-cherished hatred of England for France, and of France for England, transplanted to America; English colonists and English soldiers against French colonists and French soldiers, with Indian wiles and cruelty to aid them in the work of destruction. Already, in the last war, the Colonies had displayed their strength as efficient and active allies, by taking the strong post of Louisburg without help from England. It was resolved in this to bring out their strength with more system and regularity, and a Congress was convened at Albany to consult upon the best way of doing it. Franklin availed himself of the opportunity to bring forward a plan of Union, which, by giving them a common rallying-point, would have been a first step towards emancipation. The English ministry condemned it, and substituted another plan, which, by putting the control of the united strength of the Colonies into the hands of royal agents, would have confirmed them in their subjection. Both failed. But two great words had been uttered, — <u>Congress and Union</u>; and henceforth men began to think about them and talk about them in a way which soon gave them that place in the public mind which no ideas can hold long without gaining a place in the public heart.

Yet England had never before had such an opportunity of confirming the Colonists in their love for their haughty mother. The war was in one sense as much their war as hers. Success would rid them forever of a dangerous enemy. Failure would fix an enterprising rival upon half the long line of their frontiers. Military glory had attractions for their young men. The prospect of a secure frontier and enlarged territory had attractions for their statesmen. And the old English feeling of hatred for France, the old leaven of national hostility, had lost little of its strength by being transplanted from the Old World to the New. Then was the time for taking as brothers the hands which the Colonists held out to them as children. Then was the time for soothing dissensions, rooting

PHASES OF THE REVOLUTION. 49

out jealousies, uniting judiciously by feeling what might still have been long united by interest.

You all know how England profited by the opportunity. You know how English regulars looked down upon Provincial volunteers, on the parade-ground and in camp; and how they were compelled to look up to them in the woods, and with the war-whoop ringing in their ears. You know how Provincial colonels were outranked by Royal captains; how the distinctions which are the elements of military discipline were made to depend upon the caprice of an official who came to-day to go to-morrow, instead of the sure ground of tried merit and approved service. You all know that a Washington asked in vain for a King's commission, while the honor of the King's soldiers and the safety of the King's subjects were intrusted to a Braddock. And knowing this, can you wonder that Americans thought somewhat less reverently of English wisdom, and spoke with somewhat less confidence of English invincibility? that, while they rejoiced in England's laurels, they should remember their own wounds, and be prepared to look more closely and more sceptically upon their mutual relations?

These relations had now reached their most critical moment. Canada was conquered; the North was free from the danger of foreign invasion; England was triumphant everywhere, though loaded with debt; the Colonies jubilant over their own successes, and prepared to spring forward with increased elasticity in the career of industrial development.

There were few intelligent men, on either side of the Atlantic, who did not foresee that sooner or later the Colonies must become independent. It was evident that what had already been done to develop their natural resources was but a feeble beginning, if compared with the immense results which must follow the opening of the valleys of the Ohio and the Mississippi to that race of sturdy farmers and resolute woodsmen who had so promptly carried cultivation from the shores of the Atlantic to the foot of the Alleghanies. Their population was fast approaching three millions. The Earth gave them iron, lead, copper, all the metals required for calling forth all her strength. They were hardy sailors as well as robust farmers, as familiar with the compass as with the plough, and as skilled in finding their way on the pathless ocean as in the illimitable forest. On every side the thousand voices of streams and water-courses seemed to be calling for the busy wheels that were to enable them to join their mightier sisters in the great work of civilization. And when all these forces were combined, what was to prevent these Colonies from dissolving their connection with England, and establishing a government of their own? Such strength could not long be held in bondage by a small island three thousand miles off. Such enterprise could not always submit to the laws imposed by interested jealousy. Such energy could not always be the minister of another's will, the agent of another's power. The historian Robertson, fresh from the study of Charles the Fifth's vain attempt at universal dominion, saw clearly that the same natural laws which had concurred in frustrating the designs of the mighty Emperor, would some day set bounds to the aspirations of England, and make America the seat of independent empire. The philosopher Smith, while tracing the laws which govern the growth of nations in wealth, found a law among them which marked out the limits of colonial subjection; and, following it in its development, believed that the day would come when England would voluntarily transfer the sceptre from an island to a continent, and English kings build their palaces on the banks of the Hudson or the Potomac.

Had the rulers of England been statesmen, they would have assumed ultimate independence as inevitable, and set themselves in all earnestness to prepare the way for it. There was yet much that England could do for the Colonies, and still more that the Colonies could do for England. Mutual good offices, cherishing mutual affection, might still prolong a connection useful to both. And when the day of separation came, when, by the sure action of an inherent principle, both were brought to see that it was now better for both that they should henceforth live apart, they might pass by an easy and natural transition, that would leave no heart-burnings behind it, from the relation of sovereign and subject to the relation of friend and ally. But the rulers of England were not statesmen.

We enter upon a new phase, — a phase of systematic aggression and prompt resistance. George Grenville, looking out from the little watch-tower that he had built for himself on a crumbling wall of the constitution, saw that the Colonies were forbidden to trade with the colonies of France and Spain, and presently resolved to enforce the laws against smuggling. Naval officers were made officers of the customs, and exerted their authority in a manner far more fatal to legitimate trade than to contraband. The regular officers of the customs, not to be outdone in zeal, applied for writs of assistance to authorize them to extend their searches to private dwellings. And thus was brought on that celebrated trial, so eventful in Massachusetts annals; and then, too, was first heard from the mouth of James Otis the watch-word of the Revolution, — "Taxation without representation is tyranny." The ministry persevered in its stringent enforcement of the laws of trade. The Colonies remonstrated against the restraints upon legitimate commerce; pointed in vain to the steady flow of the wealth it brought them towards the manufactories and counting-houses of England, and thus, eventually, into the exchequer itself. The line of sight from Grenville's watch-tower did not reach as far as this. He only saw that the exchequer was low, and — exact logician — to fill it, devised the Stamp Act.

How resolutely that act was met, and how promptly it was repealed, you all know. Had the spirit of that repeal been adhered to, the day of separation might yet have been put off almost indefinitely, in spite of the fermentation of the public mind, and the pregnant questions that had been started. For if any already thought of independence, it was rather as a contingency to be feared than as a blessing to be asked for. Even what George the Third called " the waste-paper of the Declaratory Act" would have failed to gall the Colonists to resistance, if it had not been closely followed up by the resolutions of Charles Townshend, imposing a real tax under the name of impost duties on glass, paper, painters' colors, and tea. But there was a contemptuous spirit in those resolutions, far more galling than the resolutions themselves; for they seemed to say, with a civil sneer, if you do not choose to let us bind your hands, we will bind your feet, and much good may your hands do you! Other irritating acts were passed, renewing the agitation of the public mind, and foreshadowing still more arbitrary legislation if this were tamely submitted to. England took her ground, arrogant and menacing, with a threat on her lips, and her sword half drawn. America took hers, indignant and resolute, prepared to meet threats with defiance, and the sword with the sword.

Resistance was organized; — no longer an ebullition of popular feeling, easily aroused by the presence of an object, easily allayed by its removal; no longer dependent upon a few leading minds or a few warm hearts; — but a system, thoughtfully devised and thoughtfully accepted; a necessity from which there was no escape but unconditional submission; a resource which, promptly and wisely used, would establish freedom on foundations that could not be shaken. Patrick Henry's Virginia Resolutions, and the Declaration of Rights by the Congress of 1765, told the American story in language so clear, so firm, and so earnest, that no man not passion-blinded could read them and doubt the sincerity of conviction in which they were conceived. And to us, at this distance from the blinding passions of the hour, it seems marvellous that an English statesman could have read them without recognizing in them the principles and the spirit which had raised England to such prosperity. But unfortunately for England, her statesmen did not recognize in them either those principles or that spirit, and the few who read them understandingly had no influence with the King, no controlling voice in Parliament.

But Americans read them and felt their ideas grow clearer, their hearts wax firmer, as they read. There is a period in the growth of the public mind, just as there is in the growth of the individual mind, when ideas and feelings are so mixed up, that men can hardly think clearly or act firmly without something to arrange their ideas and define their feelings for them. There was a general persuasion among the Colonists that their rights had been invaded, and that there was a design of invading them still further. There was a deep-rooted conviction that resistance was lawful; a feeling, second only to their religious feelings, that it was a duty. The doctrine that an English Parliament had no right to tax them was not a new doctrine. New York had announced it by a solemn act of legislation as early as 1691; Massachusetts, in an enumeration of her rights and privileges, in 1692. Both of these acts, it is true, were formally disallowed by the English government; but they remained none the less a part of American history.

Nor was the doctrine that England had a right to tax America new in England. For in 1696 it was deliberately advocated in an elaborate pamphlet, and no less deliberately refuted in two pamphlets, upon the ground which Americans always put it upon, — that taxation went with representation. There had been various other indications, too, at various times, of the continued existence of both doctrines; — of what some Englishmen wanted, and of what every American who had ever thought upon the subject was determined not to submit to. Walpole's advisers were not alone in their longing for American places and pensions, when they advised him to tax America. But Walpole was almost alone in his wisdom when he answered that America was already paying her full tax in the manner most agreeable to the constitution of England and her own.

Patrick Henry's Resolutions, and the Declaration of Rights of the Congress of 1765, brought these ideas and convictions, which had been floating to and fro in the popular mind, to a definite shape; gave them a form which every one could take in at a glance; expressed them with a distinctness which left no room for misinterpretation, and a solemn earnestness which left no doubt of the depth and intensity of the convictions from which they sprang. Henceforward American statesmen had a chart to guide them in the stormy sea upon which they were entering; a chart whereon many of the shoals, many of the rocks they were to meet, were not set down, but which contained, nevertheless, in bold and accurate lines, the course they were to steer, and the haven in which they might hope for rest.

Resistance first took the form of retaliation. England attempted to reach the American purse by taxation. America returned the blow by agreements of non-importation. England sent out shiploads of tea subject to the new duty. America refused to receive it. England knew that America needed her woollens. America stopped eating lamb, and ate very little mutton, that she might raise more wool and make woollens of her own. Had England's bitterest enemy dictated her policy at this critical juncture, he could not have prescribed a course better adapted to train the Colonists to resistance, and familiarize them betimes with the sacrifices which successful resistance required.

Events followed rapidly. It soon became evident that force must be employed; and Boston being the chief sinner, a British garrison was sent to overawe Boston. But all that ministers gained by their garrison was to bring on a collision between the citizens and the soldiers, which embittered the public mind, and prepared it for further resistance. The act of indirect taxation — Charles Townshend's act — was modified on commercial principles; the duties on glass, paper, and painters' colors were repealed; a small duty on tea alone being left, like the declaratory clause in the repeal of the Stamp Act, to establish the right. Ministers could not see that what they were treating as a question of money, America treated as a question of principle. The tea ships came. Some were sent back with their cargoes. Some were allowed to unload, and the tea stored in cellars and other places, where it presently became worthless from damp. Boston went a step further, and threw it into the bay. Never had King George been so insulted before; and, glowing all over with royal indignation, came the Boston Port Bill, and the bill for altering the charter of Massachusetts.

But already the minds and hearts of the Colonists had been brought into close communication by the establishment of Committees of Correspondence; "the foulest, subtlest, and most venomous serpents that ever issued from the egg of sedition," says a royalist; "the great invention for organizing the Revolution," says an historian of the United States; first organized in Massachusetts in 1764, but not felt in all their strength till their reorganization there in 1772, as a Provincial measure,* and in Virginia in 1773, as a Colonial measure. The chain was now complete in all its links. Every pulse-beat of Massachusetts throbbed through the Colonies; every fiery word of the great orator of Virginia was felt from New Hampshire to Georgia; and every bold resolve, every wise counsel, every budding aspiration, was transmitted from Colony to Colony for examination and approval. The foundations of the Union were laid. The Revolution entered upon its last phase; and it was henceforth but a question of a year more or a year less, how soon a new Congress

---

* "These last [Committees of Correspondence] were engines which operated with more energy and consistency than any others which were put in motion in the commencement of our opposition: they may be called the corner-stone of our revolution or new empire." — Mr. Dana to Mr. Gerry, Austin's Life of Gerry, Vol I. pp. 299, 390.

should gather up the rich inheritance of the Congress of 1765, and declare the independence of the Colonies.

We, with the whole of this past before us, with all its scattered elements wrought into an harmonious series, can see this necessity plainly enough But it was by no means so easy to see it then Many Americans, who loved their own country devotedly, still clung with lingering affection to the country of their forefathers; watching with saddened eyes each cherished tie as it snapped asunder, and hoping in hope's despite that some one among them might yet prove strong enough to hold parent and child together. Of those who thus hoped to the last was Washington himself. It may well be doubted whether reconciliation was any longer possible. But the great Congress of 1774 did not doubt it, and gave their hopes utterance in a new memorial and new addresses, which led to no other result than to show how completely they had overrated the heart of the King and the intelligence of his ministers. Meanwhile, the country was arming. Old soldiers, the veterans of the old French war, furbished up their arms. Young men met to learn the drill and go through their evolutions together. On the 19th of April, 1775, the collision between British soldiers and American citizens, which had already occurred in the streets of New York and Boston, was renewed in the fields of Lexington. Too much blood was shed on that holy day to be forgotten, either by those who shed it or those who gave it so freely. On the 10th of May the second Congress met; and at the dawn of that same day, before they were yet organized, Ethan Allen took possession, in their name, of Ticonderoga, the key of the Canadas.

Thirteen anxious months, twenty-four feverish days, were yet to pass before the irrevocable step was taken. But independence had already been foreseen as a necessity before it was accepted as a boon; and when the solemn declaration was sent forth on its errand of justice and mercy, the last lingering hope of reconciliation had long been extinguished in the heart of Washington. The Revolution was accomplished; the War of Independence began.

A war which, at first, neither party was prepared for; of which neither party had comprehended the magnitude, nor foreseen the duration. England had rated the courage of the Colonists too low to call out her strength for a serious contest. America had rated her patriotism too high to take advantage, as she might and ought to have done, of the first fervor of popular zeal. Lexington and Bunker Hill taught the English to respect irregular troops. But they respected them too much. They taught the Americans to rely upon undisciplined ardor; but they carried their reliance too far. In a few months, the men who had forsaken their fields and firesides for the camp before

Boston forsook the camp as their terms of service expired, and they began to think how profitless their fields and how lonely their firesides must be without them. New men came in very slowly to take their places, and the work of instruction and discipline was to be begun anew at the beginning of each campaign.

The first period of the war covers a series of reverses and humiliations, imperfectly redeemed by occasional success. Washington was firmly taking his place as the controlling mind; but there were still some who thought themselves his equals, and a few who fancied themselves his superiors. The surprise of Trenton, the brilliant winter march into the Jerseys, tore away the scales from most eyes. Yet more than one still wilfully turned away from the light; men who, having read of Cæsar and Cromwell, forgot, or failed to see, that America was neither corrupt Rome nor aristocratic England, — that there were neither the elements of a monarchy in her institutions, nor of a usurper in her pure-minded leader. And thus new obstacles were wantonly thrown in his way; even a rival brought forward to divide the public mind, and supplant him, if possible, in the public heart.

The spring, summer, and autumn of 1777 were critical moments. England was meditating a fearful blow; nothing less than the severing of the Eastern from the Middle States, by seizing the line of the Hudson and opening communication with

Canada by Lake George and Lake Champlain. Burgoyne was coming down, with his English and German veterans, and their Indian allies. Howe was going up, with his ships on the river, and his troops on its banks. Severed from her Southern sisters, would New England have fallen? Cut off from New England, with their principal city already in the hands of the enemy, their second city defenceless, and their long seaboard exposed to hourly invasion, could the Middle and Southern States have persevered? Thank God, we need not seek to penetrate these recesses of a once possible future. It is enough for us to know that His mercy spared us the trial, and averted the blow when it seemed to be already descending upon our heads.

We now know by what human ministry it was done. We now know that Charles Lee, then a prisoner in New York, brooding over the failure of his own schemes of selfish aggrandizement, prepared for the Howes a plan of operations in the South, which, if vigorously carried out, would have been no less fatal to our cause than the invasion that was threatening us from the North. We know that the English General, without accepting it in its full extent, accepted it so far as to renounce his plan of co-operation with Burgoyne, and turn his arms against Philadelphia. Thus Schuyler was left free to heap up obstacle upon obstacle in the path of Burgoyne, and Gates to reap the fruit of Schuyler's labors.

This, too, was the time when Washington's personal enemies were busiest and fullest of hope; when his prudence was condemned as sloth, his caution as irresolution; when his wisest measures were misrepresented, and failures, which he had not the means to prevent, boldly laid to his charge, because it was well known that he would never reveal the secret of his country's weakness to his country's enemies in order to shield himself from the calumnies of his own. And thus, through calumny and reproach, the great, good man went firmly forward in the path of duty, and cast the bold attack of Germantown into the scale which, turning wholly towards us by the capitulation of Saratoga, gave us the long-coveted alliance with France.

From that time, Washington's superiority was scarcely disputed. He became the representative of the Revolution; towering above all others in America, as Franklin towered above all others in Europe. The army looked up to him with reverence, warmed by love. Citizens acknowledged that his virtue was as exalted as his wisdom. And Congress, which — no longer the Congress of the "Declaration" — had lost much of its hold upon the public mind, was mainly indebted to the respectful deference with which he continued to treat it, for that portion of public confidence which it still retained.

The autumn of 1777 and the winter that followed it were the turning points in the war. The establishment of Washington's supremacy gave a more decided character of unity to our civil as well as to our military councils. The moral effect of the military successes of the autumn was confirmed by the introduction of a uniform system of discipline and manœuvre, under the direction of Baron Steuben. And Congress had formed the plan of a general government under the title of Confederation, which, with all its imperfections, corrected some mistakes, supplied some deficiencies, and possessed some of the elements of legislative strength.

As we look back upon these events from our present point of view, with the results as well as the causes before us, it is difficult for us to understand how anybody could still have doubted the success of the Americans. They had a skilful leader; they had a powerful ally; they had the early hope of an organized government; they had resources which industry, judiciously directed, would soon multiply many fold. But to their eyes the horizon was still dark with many clouds. Their army was half clad, imperfectly equipped, badly fed, inadequately paid; their agriculture was exposed to the inroads of the enemy, their commerce to the enemy's cruisers; their credit, already low, was daily sinking lower; their currency was chiefly a depreciated and depreciating paper; and even of that there was not enough to meet the daily demands of the civil and military service. We wonder less that some should have doubted, than that so many should have continued to hope. Month after month wore slowly away. Campaign followed campaign, with a loss here and a gain there, a small victory to-day, a small defeat to-morrow; things little changed in the North, but the South nearly lost; and thus we reach the winter of 1780-81.

Then began the brilliant period of the war: first, that brilliant campaign of a Northern general in the Carolinas,— a campaign in which skill supplied the place of strength, judgment and energy created resources, and a leader, who never won a decisive victory, never fought a battle by which he did not compel his enemy to retreat. Thus Guilford drove Cornwallis back upon Wilmington; Hobkirk's Hill compelled Lord Rawdon to evacuate Camden; the repulse before "Ninety-six" was followed by the immediate withdrawal of the British garrison; and Eutaw sent the British army, in swift retreat, upon Charleston. The year which, in Carolina, had opened so auspiciously for the British arms, left them nothing at its close but an insecure foothold on a narrow strip of coast.

Equally rapid and equally fatal to their hopes was the progress of the campaign in Virginia. First Arnold's invasion; then Cornwallis's; and opposed to them, Lafayette and Steuben,— the gay young representative of France, and the gallant German who had followed Frederic through the

Seven Years' War; and last, that miraculous march of the whole Northern army upon Yorktown; so boldly conceived, so judiciously planned, so skilfully executed, so wonderfully concealed, while concealment was necessary, and which burst at last upon the astonished enemy like a thunder-storm at midnight, when the peal and the flash are the first that men know of its approach.

And making possible this triumph of the sword, the appointment of Robert Morris as financier, who saved his country from bankruptcy, and barely escaped dying in the debtor's prison.

The infatuation of the King, the intrigues of placemen and men who wanted places, protracted the war through another year; adding a few rills to the torrents of blood that had already been shed, a few broken hearts to the hearts that had already been broken; but independence was secure, and the Peace that was formally signed in Paris in 1783 had been virtually signed in 1781, on the plains of Carolina and in the trenches of Yorktown.

LECTURE III.

THE CONGRESS OF THE REVOLUTION.

WE have followed the Revolution through all its phases, from the sowing of the seed to the gathering in of the abundant harvest. We have seen that it began with the Navigation Act of 1660; that it worked slowly and surely, silently too for the most part, though not without occasional indications of its progress, till the Congress of 1754; that it received a new impulse from the old French war; and thenceforward, with the mind of New England prepared for the reception of its doctrines by the contest between monopoly and free labor, more persistently waged there than in the sister Colonies, it broke out in legal resistance to the writs of assistance, in forcible resistance to the Stamp Act, and, spreading through the whole country, received a definite direction from the Congress of 1765; an effective organization in the Committees of Correspondence; deliberate expression in the tea-question; and a natural termination in the Declaration of Independence.

We have traced the war rapidly from the camp

before Boston to the French alliance, and the general acceptance of the supremacy of Washington, — its period of real doubt and real uncertainty, though not the period of greatest suffering, nor, except for a few weeks, of deepest depression; and thence to the immortal campaign of 1781 and the peace of 1783.

In going over a subject of such extent, I have necessarily taken many things for granted; have often been compelled to trust to your previous reading for my justification, and may sometimes have appeared obscure where I studied to be concise. I foresee the same difficulty, though not to the same degree, in the remainder of our course.

Our subject this evening is the Congress of the Revolution; and by the Revolution, as you have already seen, I mean not only the War of Independence, but the change of public sentiment, the alteration in the relations between England and the Colonies, which produced that war. In both of these, Congress bore an important part.

The first Congress, as well as the first essay of union, belong to early colonial history. The first union, as I have already said, was that of New England in 1643. The first Congress was that of New York, in 1690. The suggestion came from Massachusetts, and the place first indicated for the meeting was Rhode Island. But this was subsequently changed to New York; and there, upon a call of the General Court of Massachusetts by circular letters, delegates from Massachusetts, Plymouth, Connecticut, and New York met to prepare a plan of concerted action for the invasion of Canada. And it is worthy of remark that the Massachusetts government, which made the call, was the government which sprang up between the overthow of Andros and the arrival of the new charter, and in which the popular element was more freely mingled; and the New York government which accepted it was the government of Leisler, which sprang directly from an uprising of the people. Thus the earliest utterance of the people's voice was a call for union.

Far more important, however, was the Albany Congress of 1754. Seven Colonies, New York, Pennsylvania, Maryland, and the four Colonies of New England, stronger by the growth, wiser by the experience of another half-century, met in Congress, ostensibly to renew the treaty with the Six Nations, really, to take counsel together about a plan of union and confederacy. In feeling, Virginia was with them also; but the quarrel between her Governor and House of Burgesses rendered it impossible for her to send a legal delegation. The delegates from Massachusetts came with authority to enter at once upon the true subject, and pledge her to the union; for already the Board of Trade had inclined its ears to the suggestions of the royal Governors; and salaries, pensions, and sinecures, for which nothing but taxation could have supplied the means, floated in dazzling visions before the eyes of placemen and courtiers.

No one doubted the importance of union, — the necessity of concerted action. War was at the door; war on the sea-board; war all along their northern and their western frontier. They had men and they had money; but without union neither their men nor their money could be made subservient to the common welfare.

On the 19th of June the delegates met, twenty-five in all, — local celebrities of their day and generation, — earnest and thoughtful men. But wisest of them all, and with a wisdom not of his day and generation alone, but of all ages, that son of a Boston soap-boiler, who was born in Milk Street, and whose serene face looks down upon us, lifelike, in Greenough's bronze, as we go through School Street. It was impossible that what concerned the welfare of the Colonies so nearly should escape the keen eye of Benjamin Franklin. He had thought of it, indeed, long and deeply and wisely, as was his wont; drawing, perhaps, some ideas from Penn's plan of 1697, and Coxe's Corolana, first published in 1722, and republished in 1741. But whatever entered his plastic mind came out again with that mind's impress upon it; and one of the characteristics of that mind was its power of comprehending present wants, and of meeting them, not by palliatives, but by remedies. A judicious employment of the resources of the Colonies for the protection of the Colonies, was the want; union the remedy. This all saw, all felt. But the conditions under which that remedy could best be applied were imperfectly seen and understood, both in England and in America.

Franklin, who cheerfully set his name to the Declaration of Independence in 1776, had no thought of asking for independence in 1754. That it must some day come, that such Colonies would sooner or later grow beyond the control of a small and distant island, he saw plainly; — saw it as the historian Robertson saw it, and wished to put the evil day far off; — as the father of political economy saw it, and felt that both mother and daughter would gain by it. But he felt that the hour was not yet come, and that the truest-hearted American might still be both loyal to England and faithful to the best interests of America.

Therefore the Union that he asked for was a Union in honorable subjection to the crown, leaving the royal prerogative untouched, while it put the rights of the Colonies beyond the reach of further aggression, — a Union which, leaving to England an indefinite enjoyment of her supremacy, should accustom the Colonies to concerted action and collective growth, and thus slowly prepare the way for the inevitable hour of separation.

But the Provincial Assemblies, to whom, after its acceptance by the Congress, it was referred for approval, condemned it as having "too much of the prerogative in it"; while it was condemned in England as having "too much of the democratic." And therefore, thought Franklin, when he came to look back upon it from a distance of thirty years, "it was not far from right."

The immediate object failed; union was not reached; but men from different Provinces, men who had never met before, had passed whole days together talking over their common interests and common desires; saying, perhaps, little about rights, for they were not yet prepared to say all that they felt about wrongs, but drawing confidence from the communication of hopes, and strength from the interchange of opinions. Union thenceforward became an avowed aspiration, a definite subject of thought, and, as a fact, nearer by half a century than it was before the Congress of Albany met.

The next Congress was that of 1765; still with Massachusetts for suggester, and New York — not merely the Province this time, but the city itself — for place of meeting. Other actors were now on the stage, with other questions before them; other enemies at the door, to be met on the threshold and alone. The Massachusetts House of Representatives, deliberating in their June session upon the impending Stamp Act, resolved to ask counsel and aid of their sister Colonies; and in their name, their Speaker, Samuel White, addressed a circular letter to the several assemblies, inviting them "to appoint committees to meet in the city of New York, on the first Tuesday in October next, to consult together on the present circumstances of the Colonies, and the difficulties to which they are and must be reduced by the operation of the acts of Parliament for levying duties on the Colonies, and to consider of a general and united, dutiful, loyal, and humble representation of their condition to his Majesty and the Parliament, and to implore relief." Eight Colonies answered the call. In Virginia and North Carolina the Assemblies were not in session, and delegates could not be appointed without their authorization. Georgia gave in her adherence through the Speaker of her Assembly, but was prevented by her Governor from sending delegates. In New Hampshire there was a strong liberal party, but not yet a strong enough one to hazard so decisive a step.

On Monday the 7th of October, the delegates met, — twenty-seven men from nine Colonies, the chosen representatives of the representatives of the people, brought together by an imperious necessity, with no recognized place in the constitution, and no authority but such as their prudence and their wisdom might give them. Their object was definite, their purpose clearly set forth in the circular letter of the Massachusetts Assembly: they came to consult with each other about their common dangers, and to implore relief of their common sovereign.

If we would form a just estimate of the importance of this Congress, we must go back to 1765; we must rub out all the railroads from our maps; we must imagine sloops instead of steamboats on Narragansett Bay, and Long Island Sound, and the broad bosom of the Hudson; we must see them lying at anchor close under the shore, waiting for the tide to turn before they venture to face the terrors of Hell-Gate or the perils of the Highlands; we must look on that Jersey shore, which six ferry-boats an hour have made a part of New York city, as separated from it by a body of deep and rapid water, which turned woman's cheek pale and often made stout men hesitate; we must see a weekly mail slowly creeping along roads, which, none too good even in summer, in winter were often impassable; we must remember that men had not yet got over wondering that electricity and lightning were the same thing, — that even the wooden telegraph was not yet invented, — and that people, in great emergencies, talked from a distance by beacon fires, and sent expresses which made folks stare when, by killing a horse or two, they succeeded in conveying in twenty-four hours intelligence that we can send along the wires in half a minute.

We must recall all this, if we would understand how those twenty-seven men felt when they found themselves in the streets of the New York of those days, a busy, bustling town, lying comfortably below the Park, with Wall Street for the seat of fashion, and no crowd to prevent strange faces from becoming immediate objects of attention. Then James Otis first took John Dickinson by the hand; the fiery denunciator of the writs of assistance grasping close and binding himself by such firm links to the polished reasoner of the Farmer's Letters, that forty years later, long, long after that spirit which shone so brightly in the opening scenes of the Revolution had passed, through madness, to the grave, the gentler-souled Pennsylvanian still loved to dwell on these days as a pleasing recollection, and "soothe his mind" on the brink of his own grave by bearing "pure testimony" to the worth of his departed friend. Then Lynch and Gadsden and John Rutledge of South Carolina first sat on the same bench with Thomas McKean and Cesar Rodney of the counties that were to become Delaware, and Philip Livingston of New York, and Dyer of Connecticut, to compare feelings and wishes, as, ten years later, when the horizon, now so dark, was already glowing with the swift approach of day, they were to meet and compare them again. If the Congress of '65 had done nothing more than bring such men together, it would still have rendered inestimable service to the common cause. But it did far more.

They met to petition for relief, and they did petition; but in language so firm, with such a strong sense of their rights, such a perfect understanding of their position, such a clear perception of their claim to be heard, for England's sake as well as their own, that their petition became a manifesto.

They reminded the King that they had grown up under governments of their own, governments framed in the spirit of the English constitution; that nurtured by this spirit, and freely spending their blood and treasure, they had added vast domains to the British empire; that they held their connection with Great Britain to be their greatest happiness; but that liberty and justice were the best means of preserving that connection, and that the public faith was pledged for the preservation of their rights. Seldom have such momentous truths been compressed within so narrow a compass as the paragraph in which they remonstrate against the Stamp Act and Admiralty Act, contrasting, with a skill the ablest rhetorician might have envied, the advantages which England might draw from her Colonies properly governed, with the loss she would incur by governing them as Parliament had undertaken to govern them; and characterizing the assumption by the House of Commons "of the right to dispose of the property of their fellow-citizens in America without their consent," in a few grave words whose very calmness gives them all the bitterness of satire, and which furnished Chatham with the substance of one of his most striking bursts of eloquence. Simple, earnest, and almost pathetic in the close, they appeal to the King's paternal love and benevolent desires for the happiness of all his people, and invoke his interposition for their relief. That George the Third should have read this petition unmoved shows how partially they had judged the royal heart, and how imperfectly he had read the heart of the people.

The substance of the memorial to the House of Lords is the same as that of the petition to the King; the language equally sober and simple, but the tone somewhat more elevated, as became the subjects of a constitutional monarchy in addressing their fellow-subjects. In the petition to the Commons they enter more fully into the various bearings of the question, and with a passage or two which, with a very little emphasis on prominent words, would sound wonderfully like deliberate irony. Both in the petition and the memorial they ask to be heard by counsel.

This much for King and Parliament. For the people, telling the English people what they must be prepared to grant and the American people what they must be prepared to assert and defend, they sent forth a declaration of rights and grievances in thirteen clauses, claiming the right of taxing themselves, either personally or by representatives of their own choosing, the right of trial by jury, and the right of petition. Each clause forms part of a continuous chain; each leads to the other as its logical conclusion; there is not a clause too much, not a word too much. Never had state papers spoken a language more decent, more direct, more firm, — freer from conventional forms, professional subtleties, and rhetorical embellishment.

And having done this, the Congress dissolved. The members returned to their homes with minds and hearts strengthened by common deliberations and common labor; with a better knowledge than they had ever had before of the wishes and feelings of their fellow-Colonists, for it was the result of personal intercourse; and a firmer resolution to stand by each other in the impending contest, for they had thrown down the gauntlet together, and pledged themselves to abide the issue.

And now comes the Congress of 1774, the first Continental Congress, not merely to tell England wherein America felt herself wronged, but to tell America what it behooved her to do in order to obtain redress for her wrongs. So strong a hold had the idea of Congress and Union taken of the general mind, that the call came almost simultaneously from different Provinces; Virginia, Pennsylvania, New York, Connecticut, Rhode Island, Massachusetts, taking up the subject within a few days of each other, and acting with a unanimity which, if statesmen had been at the head of affairs in England, would have been accepted as proof that forbearance was fast yielding to indignation. Rhode Island went even a step beyond her sisters, asserting the necessity of a firm and inviolable Union of all the Colonies in counsels and measures for the preservation of their rights and liberties, and proposing annual meetings of Congress as a means of enforcing it. Nor was the idea of a Congress confined to Americans at home, living and acting under the immediate influence of the feelings and passions of the hour. Americans abroad saw the necessity of it, and already, as early as the 2d of April, Arthur Lee had urged it in a letter from London to his brother in Virginia.

Thus, under auspicious influences, and at a moment that called for such a measure of prudence, forecast, firmness, and self-control as has rarely been granted to mortals, did these great men come together.

Of their deliberations and individual opinions, we unfortunately know little. They deliberated with closed doors, and, passing over processes, published only results. There was no gallery of watchful reporters there, to catch every burning word that fell from the lips of Henry, or Adams, or Lee; to tell how cunningly Joseph Galloway strove to mould them to his will; how restless John Adams grew under the sober reasonings of John Dickinson; how George Washington sat, thoughtful, grave, calmly biding his time, prepared for remonstrance, for resistance, for everything but the splendor of his own immortality. We know that there were many doubts, many hesitations, many warm discussions; but we know also that the spirit of an exalted patriotism prevailed over them all, and that when at last their voice was heard it came forth as the utterance of a calm, deep-rooted, and unanimous conviction.

It was Monday morning on the 5th of September that they first met in Carpenter's Hall, Philadelphia; forty-four at the opening, soon to be fifty-two when all the delegates were come in. Like the Congress of 1765, they were still a body unknown to the constitution, and depending solely upon the wisdom of their acts for the confirmation of them. Part of them had been appointed by their Provincial Assemblies, part by County Committees, part by Committees of Correspondence;—a diversity of origin characteristic of the times—for the royal Governors and the Provincial Assemblies were necessarily at variance upon these grave questions—and illustrative also of the readiness with which the people applied the forms of government to measures which government refused to sanction.

Familiar with legislation, they proceeded at once to organize; complimenting, on the motion of Lynch of South Carolina, the first official appearance of the powerful Colony of Virginia among her sisters, by making Peyton Randolph their President; complimenting Pennsylvania, by choosing for Secretary Charles Thompson, formerly a schoolmaster, now a rich man by marriage,—thin, wrinkled, with deep-set, sparkling eyes, and straight, gray hair, not long enough to reach his ears, — "the life of the cause of liberty," Philadelphians said, and whose name, in his own firm, clear hand, looks so familiar, even at this distance of almost a hundred years.

Thus far all ran smoothly, although there had been a slight hesitation about the Secretary on the part of two New-Yorkers, Jay and Duane. But now came the fiery ordeal, for, as they proceeded to make their rules, the question, "How shall we vote?" met them full in the face. There was no avoiding it, no putting it off; for it contained the fundamental principle of their Union, of all unions of unequal elements, — how to preserve the rights of the smaller members without encroaching upon those of the larger members.

"Government is dissolved," said Patrick Henry, in those tones which had often thrilled the Virginia Burgesses. "Where are your landmarks, your boundaries of Colonies? We are in a state of nature, sir. The distinctions between Virginians, Pennsylvanians, New-Yorkers, and New-Englanders are no more. I am not a Virginian, but an American!" And renouncing his first intention of insisting upon a vote by numbers, he declared himself ready to submit, if overruled, and give all the satisfaction in his power. Others, too, had their opinions, — the result of long and earnest meditation; but they knew how to distinguish between the surrender of a principle and the postponement of a discussion; and, making an entry on their journal that the rule was not to be drawn into precedent, they agreed to vote by Colonies, and give each Colony an equal vote.

Then Cushing of Massachusetts moved that Congress should be opened by prayer; and when Jay and Rutledge opposed it, because " they were too much divided in religious sentiment to unite in one form of prayer," the Congregationalist Samuel Adams arose, and, saying that piety, virtue, and love of country were his only tests, moved that the Episcopalian Duché should be asked to read prayers the next morning according to the Episcopal form. And when morning came, Duché, arrayed in his canonical robes, was introduced to the assembly; and read the solemn morning service of the Church, while his clerk gave the responses, and Presbyterians, Anabaptists, Congregationalists, and Quakers, some kneeling, and some standing up, but all mingled and confounded together, listened with decent reverence. When he came to the psalm of the day, the thirty-fifth psalm, David's heart-cry to God for deliverance from his enemies, a sudden thrill went through the assembly; for they called to mind the tidings which had reached them the day before, that the British troops were firing upon Boston, and felt as if God's own finger had pointed out to them the appropriate language of supplication. Then, too, a sudden inspiration warmed the timid heart of the clergyman, and, closing his prayer-book, he broke forth into an extemporaneous prayer for Congress, for the Province of Massachusetts Bay, and especially for the poor devoted town of Boston; and in words so earnest, in such thrilling and pathetic tones, that every heart was stirred, and every eye was wet.

The appointment of the committees followed next; one composed of two delegates from each Province, to draft a Bill of Rights; and another of one delegate from each Province, to report upon the statutes that affected the trade and manufactures of the Colonies. A great concession had already been made by the larger Colonies, and now, as they met with equal voices upon the common ground which they had made for themselves, all knew that in the question before them all other questions were involved. For the enumeration of their rights was the proclamation of their wrongs; and great was the need of weighing well their words, and making their foundations sure. Hardest of all was the part of the delegates from Massachusetts. The sympathy with Boston was universal. Their journey to Philadelphia had seemed more like a royal progress than the journey of the representatives of an oppressed people going to ask for sympathy and succor. Committees from the principal towns met them on their way, and their entrance was hailed by the ringing of bells and firing of cannon. They were invited to lodge in private houses, and feasted with the fat of the land.

But as they drew nigh to their journey's end, they were admonished that doubts of their intentions had gone before them, that they were accused of aiming directly at independence, and that their words would be weighed in a nicer balance than the words of those who had suffered less. Then John Adams reined in his fiery spirit, and Samuel Adams, constraining his nature, was content for a while to follow where he had been accustomed to lead.

But fortunately there were other men there prepared to go resolutely forward, and without attempting to deceive themselves as to whither the path might lead them. "Our rights are built on a fourfold foundation," said Richard Henry Lee; "on nature, on the British Constitution, on charters, and on immemorial usage. The Navigation Act is a capital violation of them"; and he could not see why they should not lay their rights on the broadest bottom, — the law of nature. "There is no allegiance without protection!" said John Jay, "and emigrants have a right to erect what government they please. I have always withheld my assent from the position that every man discovering land does it for the state to which he belongs."

"The Colonies," said Roger Sherman, "are not bound to the King or crown by the act of settlement, but by their consent to it. There is no other legislature over them but their respective assemblies. They adopt the common law, not as the common law, but as the highest reason."

But Rutledge thought that the British constitution gave them a sufficient foundation; and Duane, that the law of nature would be a feeble support. Joseph Galloway talked learnedly of Greece and Rome, of Saxons and Normans, and tried to look bold as he said: "I have ever thought we might reduce our rights to one, an exemption from all laws made by British Parliament since the emigration of our ancestors. It follows, therefore, that all the acts made since are violations of our rights." Adding, — and how his cheeks must have burned as he said it, — "I am well aware that my remarks tend to independency."

"A most ingenious, interesting debate," wrote John Adams in his diary on the evening of the first day. But he soon grew anxious for a conclusion; which, however, was not reached till after many discussions, and in the form of a partial compromise. Still, the great end was attained. The men of twelve Colonies — Georgia was not represented in this Congress — had talked together freely about their obligations and their rights; had brought their duties as subjects to the standard of their rights as men; had counted, one by one, the links in the chain of their allegiance, and found that it did not reach far enough to make them slaves.

There was one grave moment in the general debate, — the moment when Joseph Galloway introduced his insidious plan for a union between Great Britain and the Colonies; a plan so specious and so ingeniously defended, that even the clear-headed Jay was "led to adopt it," and that upon the final trial it failed by only one vote, — but a plan which, like all temporizing with principle, would have merely put off upon the children the work that Heaven had appointed for the fathers; and what such puttings-off lead to, we, not as the children of those brave men of 1776, but as the heirs of the first generation of compromisers, have seen and felt, — have seen with eyes dimmed by tears that will not be stayed, have felt with hearts that cannot be comforted. God forbid that we should entail the curse upon future generations!

By the 26th of October their work was completed. They had prepared a Bill of Rights, and an enumeration of the acts whereby those rights had been violated. They had prepared an address to the King, an address to the people of Great Britain, a memorial to the inhabitants of the British Provinces, an address to the inhabitants of the Province of Quebec, and an association for non-importation.

The Bill of Rights, covering the same ground with the Bill of Rights of the first Congress, starts from a higher point, the immutable laws of nature, and shows, by its fuller development of the principles common to both, that the seed sown in 1765 had not fallen on stony ground. Nothing could be firmer, more manly, or more explicit, than the language of the addresses and memorials; dutiful, respectful, solemnly earnest, to the King; clear, firm, direct, with a mixture of grave exhortation and sober remonstrance, to their fellow-subjects. " When your Lordships look at the papers transmitted to us from America," said Lord Chatham in one of those attempts to awaken his colleagues to a sense of their injustice, which have made his name so dear to Americans, " when you consider their decency, firmness, and wisdom, you cannot but respect the cause and wish to make it your own." The agreement of non-importation, non-exportation, and non-consumption was the same in principle with that which had been tried so successfully against the Stamp Act; although it had proved ineffectual against the later encroachments of England. Like the question of voting, it was a severe test of the sincerity of the desire for union. But many looked to it with full confidence; and with an exception in favor of rice, to propitiate South Carolina, it received the official signature of every member. " Negotiation, suspension of commerce, and war, are the only three things," said John Jay. " War is, by general consent, to be waived at present. I am for negotiation and suspension of commerce."

Then, having also taken care to recommend the calling of a second Congress, the First Continental

Congress dissolved, and John Dickinson could congratulate Josiah Quincy on the hearty union of all America, from Nova Scotia to Georgia, in the common cause. And when the report of their proceedings reached London, Josiah Quincy wrote to his friends: "Permit me to congratulate my countrymen upon the integrity and wisdom with which the Congress have conducted. Their policy, spirit, and union have confounded their foes and inspired their friends."

To crown the triumph of patriotism, it was known that large sums had been sent to New York to bribe the delegates; that this infamous attempt at corruption was openly avowed and vindicated; and that the partisans of the ministers had boasted loudly of their success.

But how did calm and thoughtful men feel as they endeavored to look into the future? how did John Dickinson feel, that sober-minded, sincere, but not sanguine man, who had done so much towards diffusing correct opinions upon the question of taxation by Parliament? "I wish for peace ardently," said he, "but must say, delightful as it is, it will come more grateful by being unexpected. The Colonists have now taken such grounds that Great Britain must relax, or inevitably involve herself in a civil war." Some hoped that she would relax. "Conviction," wrote James Lovel, "must be the consequence of a bare admission of light."

It was soon seen that light was not to reach the eyes of the King, nor to be permitted to reach the eyes of the people; and therefore, on the 10th of May, 1775, a new Congress convened. Already the battle of Lexington had been fought; already an indignant yeomanry had gathered to the siege of the British army in Boston; already defences were rising, men were enrolling throughout the land. Twice had the representatives of the people come together to remonstrate and petition, to appeal to the reason of their fellow-subjects, and invoke the protection of their King. They now met for action; to appeal, if needs be, to the sword, and invoke the protection of their God. Independence lay in their path, and, thick set as that path was with obstacles and dangers, they were not the men to falter or turn aside when the only alternative was slavery.

This time they assembled, not in Carpenter's Hall, the gathering-place of a private association, but, as beseemed the acknowledged representatives of a great people, in the State-House, in that fine old hall which Philadelphia, with a wise gratitude, has carefully preserved from desecration; to which the chairs and tables which they used have been brought back with pious care, and on whose walls, thick-clustering with holy associations, hang the portraits of the founders of our Union, — of the men who, by the great things which they did there, and the wise things that they said there, have made it a temple on whose altars the profoundest statesman may humbly lay down his laurels, and from whose oracles faltering patriots may learn to put their trust in God.

It is impossible to conceive a situation more beset with difficulties, a path more absolutely hedged in with thorns and briers, than that of the Congress which met in Philadelphia on the 10th of May, 1775, and proclaimed the birth of a new nation on the 4th of July, 1776. Builders like to begin on clear ground, where they can see their way from the first, lay their foundations surely, and put every stone in its place, from the corner-stone to the key-stone of the arch. But our builders found themselves in the midst of ruins; and it was only by a careful clearing away of the rubbish that they could reach those solid foundations which still lay unimpaired under the dust and fragments of a transient superstructure. Out of the ruins of royal and parliamentary authority they had to frame a supreme legislature; in place of that dependence upon England which had so long bound them to the fortunes of a single country, they had alliances to form wherever their interests required it. The Act of Navigation was to be thrown aside, and their ports opened to all comers. To protect the commerce which they hoped soon to see growing rapidly up under auspicious influences, they had to build, arm, and man a navy, and provide for its support; and to protect themselves, to protect their cities and their farms, from the wanton violence of a ruthless soldiery, they had to organize an army, and place at its head a man who could guide and control its energy without abusing their confidence. And all this had to be done by general consent, in spite of open and covert opposition, with a powerful enemy all ready to crush them, and an insidious enemy constantly on the watch to turn against them every error of haste, or improvidence, or oversight.

When they first met, fresh from the people, and with vivid recollections of what their own eyes had seen in their own homes, there was an appearance of harmony among them which promised firm, prompt, and united action. But every act on their part was a step towards independence. Whichever way they turned, independence still seemed to meet them at the end of the path. Every road led equally to it. It formed a part of every question, entered directly or indirectly, either as a principle or as an illustration, into every discussion, warming some minds with visions of wealth, and power, and glory, and striking terror into others by images of confiscation and the scaffold.

Some would have begun by assuming all the powers of government, and proceeded at once to open their ports, organize an army, build a navy, prepare themselves to meet the enemy at every point, and thus discuss the question of reconciliation with arms in their hands. Others were willing to arm in order to repel aggression, but they would have carefully avoided every act and every expression which wore the appearance of an intention to change self-defence into attack. Many still continued to flatter themselves with the same hopes by which they had already been so often deluded. They hoped that the King would relent. They hoped that the English people would rise against an oppressive ministry. They hoped that there might still be strength enough in the ties of blood, intelligence enough in the instinct of interest, to bring them all once more together as the children of common ancestors, and members of one great and glorious association.

These hopes were continually fanned by the partisans of England, — ever ready with pretexts and excuses, skilled in all the dangerous arts of retardment, knowing well when to promise and when to threaten. Of especial use to them were the tidings of the appointment of English commissioners, who were speedily to come with an olive-branch in their hands, heal all dissensions, and reinstate the colonies in all their rights.

And this gave to the councils of Congress an appearance of fluctuation which was attended with serious inconveniences. "One day," wrote Samuel Ward, one of the calmest and wisest among them, "measures for carrying on the war were adopted; the next, nothing must be done which would widen the unhappy breach between Great

Britain and the Colonies." Some were seen to turn pale when John Adams, carried away by his ardent temperament and deep convictions, proposed measures that would have brought things to an immediate crisis.

How could it be otherwise with the question of trade before them? for in this question more than in any other were comprehended the question of Independence, and the question of that Union without which independence could neither be won nor worth the winning. To throw open their ports to other nations was to annul the Act of Navigation, a step little short of a declaration of independence, and which must be promptly followed by the organization of State governments and of a central government. John Adams saw this, and urged it expressly with this view. His opponents saw it, and resisted it with equal persistency.

Then, too, men were far from seeing clearly into the economical principles involved in the regulation of trade. The father of political economy had just put the manuscript of his great work into the hands of the printer, and truths which he has made familiar to school-boys had not yet dawned upon the minds of statesmen.

"We ought," said Lee, "to stop our own exports, and invite foreign nations to come and export for us. The provisions of America are needed, and foreigners must come for them." But Willing, a Philadelphia merchant, could not be for inviting foreigners to become their carriers. "Carriage is an amazing revenue. Holland and England have derived their maritime power from it." Livingston, from commercial New York, was for doing away with the non-exportation agreement entirely, except in the articles of lumber and tobacco. Chase was sure that the nation must soon grow rich which exports more than it imports. Edward Rutledge of South Carolina was equally sure that men could be taken from the plough and engaged in manufactures. The Swiss Zubly, who represented Georgia, and who, as he said, having been familiar with a republican government ever since he was six years old, knew that it was little better than a "government of devils," was "for using American virtue as sparingly as possible lest they should wear it out." Livingston's proposition to except lumber and tobacco — the chief staples of three important Colonies — was met by the assertion that it would lead to disunion. Gadsden was for confining the question to one point, — "Shall we shut up our ports and be all on a footing? Mankind act by their feelings; distinctions will divide us; one Colony will be jealous of another."

Equally embarrassing was the question started by the proposal to recommend to the Provincial governments " to arrest and secure every person in their respective Colonies whose going at large might, in their opinion, endanger the safety of the Colony, or the liberties of America."

This was war indeed. Could it be done? Was the time for such a step yet come? Johnson of Virginia confessed that he "saw less and less prospect of a reconciliation each day; still he would not render it impossible." The assistance of France and Spain was mentioned. Zubly fired up: "Some men were for breaking off with Great Britain; men who should propose to his constituents to apply to France and Spain, would be torn in pieces like De Witt."

Rhode Island, which from the beginning had looked upon prompt action as the wisest course, deliberately threw another apple of discord into the assembly; nothing less than a proposition to build a navy. It was received almost with derision. Nobody out of the little phalanx of far-seeing and resolute men, who felt too sure of the future to hesitate about the present, would listen to it. A few were for taking it into consideration as a mark of respect to an independent Province, and then killing it with parliamentary decency. It was put off, by resolve, from week to week, with a fatal loss of time in the actual condition of our military supplies, which could come only by sea. At last, a committee was appointed, and out of the deliberations of that committee grew our glorious American navy, the protector of our commerce, the defender of our flag, the best mediator in our differences with foreign powers, the sight of whose frowning batteries on a distant coast fills the heart of the American traveller with such emotions of confidence and pride, — so honorable, throughout the whole course of its history, to our skill, our enterprise, our daring, to everything but our gratitude.

There was less difficulty in agreeing upon measures for the encouragement of manufactures, agriculture, the arts and sciences; and no serious difficulty, as far as the records show, in forming boards for the administration of the different departments.

But should they again petition the King, whom they had already petitioned in vain? Even this was conceded to the timid, to John Dickinson more especially, whose fluent pen was employed in repeating the thrice-told tale. And the American olive-branch, America's last appeal to the royal heart, was intrusted to John Penn, a grandson of the founder of Pennsylvania.

Thus slowly and cautiously they moved, but still onward. And before many months were passed, they had assumed full authority, executive, legislative, and in some instances even judicial.

They had solemnly laid at England's door the guilt of the first bloodshed. They had met the royal proclamation of the 23d of August, declaring them rebels, and threatening them with the punishment of rebels, by an indignant denial of the accusation, and a bold resolve to meet the punishment by retaliation. They had formed a committee for corresponding with their friends in Europe, and sent Silas Deane to open negotiations for obtaining supplies of arms from France, and preparing the way for commercial intercourse.

They had resolved that no supplies should be furnished the British army or navy, no bills of exchange negotiated for British officers; that no Colonial ships should transport British troops. They had taken the army before Boston into the service of the United Colonies, had made provision for its pay and support, and had given it Washington for commander-in-chief. Every day seemed to make the path of duty clearer. England herself appeared resolved to leave them no pretext for hesitation. It was of the last importance that Congress should not go too fast for the people; that the people should not weaken the influence of Congress by putting themselves in the advance. "The novelty of the thing deters some," wrote Franklin in April, "the doubt of success others, the vain hope of conciliation many. But our enemies take continually every proper measure to remove these obstacles, and their endeavors are attended with success, since every day furnishes us with new causes of increasing enmity, and new reasons for wishing an eternal separation; so that there is a rapid increase of the formerly small party who were for an independent government." "My countrymen," wrote Washington in the same month, and speaking of Virginia, "I know, from their form of government, and steady attachment heretofore to royalty, will come reluctantly into the idea of independence; but time and persecution bring many wonderful things to pass." John Adams, as he tried to curb his impatience, had likened the country to " a large fleet sailing under convoy; the fleetest sailors must wait for the dullest and slowest."

At last, in that same month of April, while Franklin, on his way to Canada as a Congress commissioner, wrote from Saratoga the lines I have read you, and Washington his hopes from Cambridge, John Adams was enabled to write from Philadelphia: " The ports are opened wide enough at last, and privateers are allowed to prey upon British trade. This is not independency, you know. What is? Why, governments in every Colony, a confederation among them all, and treaties with foreign nations to acknowledge us a sovereign, and all that. When these things will be done, or any of them, time must discover. Perhaps the time is near; perhaps a great way off." And a fortnight afterward, for the signs were hourly brightening: " As to declarations of independency, be patient. Read our privateering laws and our commercial laws. What signifies a word?"

At length he saw that the hour was come, and on the 6th of May introduced his resolution for the institution of State governments. On the 10th it was passed, in these most pregnant words: " That it be recommended to the respective assemblies and conventions of the United Colonies, where no government sufficient to the exigence of their affairs hath been hitherto established, to adopt such government as shall, in the opinion of the representatives of the people, best conduce to the happiness of their constituents in particular and America in general." On the 15th, a preamble was added, stating, as the grounds of their resolve, their exclusion, by act of Parliament, from the protection of the crown; the King's refusal to answer their petition; the warlike preparations against them, and the consequent necessity of suppressing the exercise of every kind of authority under the crown.

"When I consider the great events which are passed," wrote John Adams, two days afterwards, "and those greater which are rapidly advancing, and that I may have been instrumental in touching some springs and turning some small wheels, I feel an awe upon my mind which is not easily described. Great Britain has at last driven America to the last step, a complete separation from her; a total, absolute independence, not only of her Parliament, but of her crown; for such is the amount of the resolve of the 15th. There is something very unnatural and odious in a government a thousand leagues off. A whole government of our own choice, managed by persons whom we love, revere, and can confide in, has charms in it for which men will fight."

Five Colonies had already expressly authorized their delegates to vote for independence; and while on that memorable 15th of May, twin birthday of our nation, John Adams was reporting to Congress the comprehensive and energetic preamble to the resolve of the 10th, Virginia was voting instructions to her delegates to unite with their colleagues in the decisive act of separation.

On the 7th of June, says the Journal of Congress, "Certain resolutions respecting independency being moved and seconded, Resolved, that the consideration of them be referred till to-morrow morning, and that the members be ordered to attend punctually at ten o'clock, in order to take the same into their consideration." On that morrow they were discussed in committee of the whole, and a second sitting ordered for Monday the 10th, when, after full discussion, it was resolved, "That the discussion of the first resolution be postponed to Monday, the first day of July next; and in the mean while, that no time be lost, in case the Congress agree thereto, that a committee be appointed to prepare the declaration to the effect of the said first resolution, which is in these words: That these United Colonies are, and of right ought to be, free and independent States; that they are absolved from all allegiance to the British crown; and that all political connection between them and the state of Great Britain is and ought to be totally dissolved." Congress transacted no further business that day.

On the following day the committee was chosen: Jefferson, John Adams, Franklin, Sherman, and Robert R. Livingston. And immediately after it was resolved, "That a committee be appointed to prepare and digest the form of a confederation to be entered into between these Colonies"; and, "That a committee be appointed to prepare a plan of treaties to be proposed to foreign powers."

The 1st of July came. All the delegates but those of New York had now received the instructions of their constituents, and all been authorized to vote for independence. One voice was raised against it, as yet premature; the persuasive voice of John Dickinson, always heard with respect. One voice was raised in its defence, the vehement voice of John Adams. But no discussion was needed. At the request of South Carolina the final vote was postponed to the next day; and then, on Tuesday, the 2d of July, twelve Colonies united in the resolve, "That these United Colonies are, and of right ought to be, free and independent States."

The Declaration of Independence had already been reported from the committee. Another day — the 3d — was partly employed in discussing it. And on the 4th, authenticated by the signatures of John Hancock as President, and Charles Thompson as Secretary, it was sent to the printer. On the 2d of August, fairly engrossed on parchment and made unanimous by the adhesion of

New York, it received the signatures of all the members present as the unanimous "Declaration" of the thirteen United States of America.

And a joyful shout went up from all the land; from inland hamlet and sea-side town; from workshop and field, where fathers could henceforth eat their bread cheerfully, even in the sweat of their brows,— for they knew that their children would inherit the fruit of their labors, and receive and transmit unimpaired the precious birthright of freedom. The solemn words were read at the head of the army drawn out in full array, and welcomed by the waving of banners and the booming of cannon. They were read from the pulpit while heads were bowed reverently in prayer, and hearts glowed as at a visible manifestation of the will of God. They crossed the ocean, waking strange fears in palaces, whispering soothing hopes in hovels, telling the poor and oppressed and down-trodden of every land that an asylum had been opened for them in fertile regions beyond the ocean, where industry was unfettered and thought was uncontrolled.

And still, as we look back to that auspicious day, we bless God that he imparted to our fathers so large a measure of his own wisdom; that he breathed into their councils such a spirit of calm, resolute, and hopeful zeal; that he put into their mouths words of such comprehensive truth that through all time, as each successive generation draws nearer to the law of universal brotherhood, it will but develop more fully the principle by which these United States first took their place among the nations, — "that all men are equally entitled to life, liberty, and the pursuit of happiness."

LECTURE IV.

CONGRESS AND THE STATE GOVERNMENTS OF THE REVOLUTION.

WE have seen that in the history of our country Congress and Union have always gone hand in hand together. We have seen that the Congress of 1690 was convened in order to give a common direction to the energies of the Northern Colonies in an attack upon Canada; that the Albany Congress of 1754 came together with the wish for a more lasting union upon its lips; that the New York Congress of 1765 built its hopes of redress upon the common sense of wrong as expressed in a common remonstrance and appeal; that the Congress of 1774 assumed openly the title of Continental Congress, and spoke as with authority in the name of all the Colonies. We have seen this deliberative body coming directly from the people and with no recognized place in the Constitution, acting in all things in harmony with public sentiment, and assuming, in 1775, executive, legislative, and sometimes even judicial authority, organizing a government and declaring independence. This evening I shall return briefly to the Congress, and endeavor to complete our view of the elements of the civil government of the Revolution by a sketch of the characteristic features of the State governments.

Congress had now accomplished one part of its task, and with a calmness, judgment, and wisdom that confirmed men in their persuasion of its capacity to deal with these delicate questions and bear these grave responsibilities. To the world, too, there was an appearance of unanimity in its counsels which added materially to its authority; for it still deliberated with closed doors, and, publishing its acts, passed silently over its discussions. It was known, however, even then, that there were differences of opinion among its members, though few out of Congress knew their nature or their extent.

Shall we, at this distant day, seek to remove the veil and lay bare the dissensions and personal jealousies which disturbed, although they did not destroy its harmony of resolve, — retarded, although they did not prevent its harmony of action? It seems an invidious and ungrateful task to tell how John Dickinson gave John Adams the cut direct in the streets of Philadelphia; how, one day, as several members were walking together in the lobby, Jay took Richard Henry Lee by the button, and, drawing him towards Jefferson, made him declare he had never denied that Jay wrote the address to the people of England; how Samuel Adams — for though chronologically it comes two years later, yet it belongs in spirit full as much to this as to any other period — how then Samuel Adams turned short upon poor Duponceau, who had addressed him as John Adams, and said, "I would have you to know, sir, that there is a great difference between Samuel Adams and John Adams." Such things are sad, very sad; and it is far pleasanter to think of the author of the "Farmer's Letters" as grasping cordially the hand of the author of "Novanglus" wherever he met him, and the eloquent Lee as rejoicing with a brother's joy in the eloquence of Jay.

But these things are history; stern, impartial, truth-loving history; and it is a wilful rejecting of the most instructive of her lessons arbitrarily to blot the page which reminds us that even the greatest and wisest of men are not altogether exempt from the weaknesses of humanity. I would not dwell upon such things, for they sadden and mortify me. But when I look upon the men of my own day, and hear and read what is said of their errors and weaknesses, I find it a gentle persuasive to charity to remember that weakness and greatness have so often dwelt side by side in the noblest intellects and truest hearts.

Fortunately there was no Horace Walpole in our Congress to distort the picture by bestowing all his finest touches and richest tints upon the worst parts of it. The little that has been preserved in letters and diaries, the little that has crept out through avenues which, however closely guarded, could never be so completely closed but that some secrets would find their way through them, are sufficient for the truth of history; and I gladly turn from them to the contemplation of that pure wisdom and exalted patriotism, in the splendor of whose rays these spots on the bright orbs of our political system are wellnigh lost.

You have already seen that on the 11th of June, immediately after appointing the committee for drafting a "Declaration of Independence," Congress resolved "that a committee be appointed to prepare and digest the form of a Confederation to be entered into between these Colonies," and another to " prepare a plan of treaties to be proposed to foreign powers." The first of these resolves gave us the Confederation; the second I shall return to in a future lecture.*

As we look back upon the Confederation, we are apt to dwell too exclusively upon its errors and deficiencies; to forget that we see it in the light of history, — in the light of the Constitution; that some of its errors were such as time only could reveal, some of its deficiencies were such as nothing but a stern experience could induce us to sup-

* The first movement towards a confederation had been made in July, 1775, by Franklin, ever foremost in the just appreciation of circumstances.

ply. For to supply them required sacrifices, and, in some instances, the sacrifice of habits and prejudices which the popular mind clings to with singular tenacity. A correct estimate of it would require an examination, which we have not time for now, of the ideas which the publicists and statesmen of that day entertained concerning the nature and office of a confederation. A glance, however, I must give, though it will necessarily be a hasty one.

Alliances for particular purposes have been common from an early period of modern history. Du Mont and Rousset and De Martens have filled volumes with the record of minute stipulations made only to be broken, and perpetual friendships that hardly outlived the year of their formation. You have all read to satiety of family compacts, and quadruple alliances, and holy alliances. Of confederations, too, there have been notable examples in ancient and modern times; the Amphictyonic Council and Achæan League in Greece, familiar to the men of our Revolution through Rollin and Millot and Mably; in modern Europe the Germanic system, the United Netherlands, the Hanseatic League, something of confederacy in Poland, in Switzerland much more; all of them, when our Confederation was formed, still objects of living interest, full of suggestions, especially full of warnings. But we must not forget that there were fundamental distinctions between Americans —

even the Americans of that day — and the people of these confederacies, especially of the ancient confederacies.

In ancient society the citizen was absorbed in the state. The legislators of antiquity treated the individual as an element in that collective dignity, power, and grandeur which was called Sparta, or Athens, or Rome. It was not from any consciousness of the dignity of his individual nature, of the dignity of humanity, that the citizen of the victorious Republic repelled insult and injury. But to inflict stripes upon him was to insult the majestic city; to put fetters on his limbs was to bind limbs that ought always to be free for the service of the state.

With Christianity came individual rights, as the necessary consequence of individual responsibilities; the right of deciding and acting for self in civil society, as a necessary consequence of the obligation to answer for self at the bar of God. In the Italian Republics of the Middle Ages, the two ideas stood side by side; the citizen looked upon himself as individually merged in the state; but at brief and regular intervals that state had to be made over again, and he had an equal voice, and an equal hand, in doing it. And thus was established the dependence of the state upon its individual members; the responsibility of every citizen that held office to the citizens by whose votes and for whose protection he held it. The regular return of authority to the source whence it came, the idea of office as a duty to the state and a trust from the individual, was the contribution of those brilliant republics to the cause of political truth.

You can have no difficulty in recognizing this idea, for it is the idea familiar to you all as the sovereignty of the people. Years were still to pass, and a new world to be opened to it, before it obtained solemn acceptance as the corner-stone of all legitimate authority. But that acceptance it found at last in the municipal institutions of New England. To us it is so familiar an axiom that all our political reasonings start from it, all our political theories bring us back to it as their test. In our colonial history, though ever active below the surface, it did not appear so constantly above the surface. But when the Colonies threw off the authority of the King in the name of the people, and asked themselves and one another what and whom they should put in his stead, they were met from the beginning by the fact that the sovereign people was already represented in thirteen distinct individualities; that each State was already an empire in itself. Thus — and it was a natural error — it was not the people that they bound together, but the States; framing a confederacy of collective individuals, with whose elements their common representative had no means of contact; to whose opinions it might appeal, but over whose action it had no control. And thus, instead of commanding, it could only recommend; instead of guiding, it could only advise. It might make the wisest laws, the most advantageous treaties, the most judicious appropriations of the public resources; but it could neither enforce a law, nor guard a treaty from infraction, nor draw out the resources of the country, without the direct and voluntary concurrence of each individual State. "It could declare everything, could do nothing."

It was not till the 15th of November, 1777, that the Articles of Confederation were accepted by Congress, and not till the 1st of March, 1781, that, after many alterations and amendments, they received the adhesion of Maryland, the last of all the States to hesitate upon the brink of Union. During this period Congress continued to exercise the supreme power as it had done in the beginning, governing the army, the navy, the finances, the foreign relations, by committees under the name of Boards; and relying for confirmation upon the confidence of the people. From a deliberative it had become an executive assembly; and when the first impulse of popular enthusiasm was passed, it was exposed to all the searching criticisms with which a free people visits the depositaries of its power and rewards the executors of its will. Without altogether losing its hold upon the popular mind, it lost much of that veneration which had been the chief source of its original strength. King Cong. became a common expression as early as 1777, if not as a term of reproach, still not altogether as a mark of affection. Men felt the presence of the enemy; they saw the distress of the army; but they heard of Congress as living luxuriously in comfortable quarters, while their soldiers and officers were freezing and starving on a bleak hillside. It was accused, and not always unjustly, of procrastination and negligence; of unnecessary delays of decision which led to fatal delays of action. The Commander-in-chief would prepare his plan of campaign; the Quartermaster-General would prepare his estimates; but Congress would put off from day to day and from week to week the concurrent action, without which neither Washington nor Greene could take a step. It was accused, not only of withholding from Washington that full confidence which was essential to the efficient exercise of his authority, but even of opening the door for the misrepresentations of his enemies, and of taking, through several of its members, an active part in the disgraceful cabal for setting up a Gates as his rival, a half-formed Pompey against an impossible Cæsar; the first great blot in our united annals, and which nothing but the more open treason of Arnold could have deprived of its historical prominence as a combination of baseness, cowardice, and treachery. And however great the embarrassments and difficulties of its situation may have been, history will not acquit it of many grave and some wilful errors.

But many of the men who had breathed into its counsels the wise caution and sober courage of 1775 and 1776 were no longer there to foster that rare spirit by their advice and example. As the war advanced, the army became the chief object of attention, upon whose movements men waited with anxious expectation, for all knew that there was no longer any alternative between absolute victory or absolute submission. And that army had found a leader whose character from the first inspired confidence as well as admiration, reverence as well as love. Already known as the hero of Braddock's disastrous campaign, as the man who, when British courage had faltered and British skill was at fault, had saved the remnants of a noble army by prodigies of American courage and skill; known, too, as a man who had sacrificed the enjoyments of a cherished home, and staked a princely fortune upon the issue; he seemed to fill the popular imagination by a happy mixture of the marvellous and the common in his history, of the grave and the impetuous in his character. At the side of such a man no body of men could hold an equal place, for man's inherent love of unity leads him to concentrate his strongest affections upon single objects; and when that object is a worthy one, when judgment approves and goes hand in hand with feeling, those affections become too strong to bear the presence of a rival. Even the Congress of 1776 would have lost somewhat of its halo by the side of the Washington of Trenton and Germantown and Monmouth, — the Washington who had braved the ice of the Delaware, and lived in a log hut amid the snows of Valley Forge. Still less could it keep its hold upon the popular mind when reduced in number and shifting about from place to place; from Philadelphia to Baltimore, to get out of the reach of the Tories; from Philadelphia to Lancaster, to get out of the way of the British army; then farther on, to York; and at last back again to Philadelphia when Washington had opened the way; next to Princeton, threatened by mutineers; and finally to Annapolis, where Washington came once more before it to resign his commission, and perform in its presence what he fondly regarded as the last act of his public life. Franklin, with the weight of seventy years upon him, had again crossed the ocean in 1776 to plead for his country at the court of France, as he had long pleaded for her at the court of her own sovereign. John Adams had followed him in 1778; Jefferson had turned all his energies towards a reform in the civil legislation of his native Province. Others of the original members were also gone; some called away to the more attractive field of State government; some, by private interests; and some, too, to make way for new men. The attendance was often imperfect, sometimes barely sufficient for the transaction of business; and its discussions not being reported, it was shut out from that path to public applause which skill in debate and popular eloquence might still have kept open for it. Yet there were great and good men in it to the last;—still a Morris, a Sullivan, a Schuyler, to impart energy to its counsels; a Jay and a Laurens, to sustain the dignity of the Presidential chair. And although it failed where large bodies must always fail, in executive promptness, decision, and skill, it is none the less entitled to the grateful remembrance of every true American, as the guardian and preserver of civil government through the perilous convulsions of a long and bloody war; receiving its authority from the hands of the people in the midst of a revolution which threatened all the existing forms of society with subversion, and rendering it back to the people untainted when the revolution was completed and new or newly modified forms had everywhere taken the place of the old. Let those who would learn wisdom by example ponder well the history of the Congress of the American Revolution; its merits and its defects; its frailties and its virtues; the much that it accomplished of what it attempted, the little that it left undone of what large assemblies can do.

From the first establishment of the American Colonies the Colonial governments were divided into Provincial governments, directly dependent upon the King; Proprietary governments, immediately dependent upon the proprietary and mediately upon the King as the lord paramount; and Charter governments, in which certain definite rights and privileges were secured to the Colony by letters patent from the King. Thus in every Colony the King was equally the original source of authority; for every Colony was equally founded upon the principle, that the first discoverer of a country not occupied by a civilized or a Christian people discovered for the sovereign to whom he owed allegiance; and thus the sovereign became lord of the soil, with full power to divide and grant it at will, and attach such conditions as he saw fit to the grant.

But, fortunately for our founders, this enormous power was met by another principle peculiar to English law, and no less a clearly settled principle. Every Englishman, carrying his allegiance with him, carried also his rights. The moment that he took possession of a new tract in the name of the crown, English law took possession of it in the name of the Constitution. Thus, wherever Englishmen went, *Magna Charta* went with them. Every right which had been defined in England before they left its shores, was defined for them and their children. Every law which had been made for their government in their old home retained, as far as the difference of circumstances would permit, full control over them in their new home. No longer part and parcel of the realm of Great Britain, they were still, as before, subjects of the crown, bound to such duties as it could constitutionally impose, and possessed of all the rights and immunities which the subject could constitutionally claim.

And fortunately, too, these rights and immunities were of the largest kind; so large, indeed, that their natural development, that development which fundamental principles, whether good or bad, always receive at the hand of time, led by a logical necessity to that full measure of liberty which we ourselves enjoy. And at the same time they were so reasonable, so just, they entered so directly into the domestic life of the people while they acted with such a regular and constant action upon its public life, that they were looked upon as equally essential to the peace of the one and the prosperity of the other.

The first of these rights was the right to participate directly in the government; to have a voice in the making of their laws, in the spending of their money; and, as a guaranty that it would be spent properly, the right of saying when, how, and how much of it they would give.

No less important nor less watchfully guarded was the right of trial by jury; an institution to which Englishmen and the descendants of Englishmen cling so tenaciously, that they are hardly able to conceive of justice in any other form. And side by side with these the right of petition.

Men who carried such rights with them would

necessarily establish a free government wherever they went; a government which, whatever name they might see fit to give it, whatever external form it might bear, would still be essentially free. The absorption of the individual by the state was irreconcilable with such guaranties against the encroachments of the sovereign. The vigorous and healthy life of the state was secured by the constant infusion of vigor and health from every hearth-stone, from every workshop, from every field. And among our fathers the jealous watchfulness of the individual was kept alive by the exigencies of their position; rapid growth constantly calling for new provisions, and starting questions which carried them daily back to fundamental principles.

One form, however, had acquired from early associations a hold upon their affections. They had always been familiar with the idea of a division of powers. They had long been accustomed to see a King, and a House of Lords, and a House of Commons, acting with harmonious interdependence for the common weal. They would have found it difficult to conceive of good laws as emanating from an executive power, or a good executive power as residing in a legislative body. Still less could they have reconciled their conceptions of the due administration of justice with the union of legislative and judicial authority. And as practical freedom consisted for them in the preservation of their civil as well as their political rights, so the forms of freedom consisted in the radical division of the three great functions of government.

Therefore in all the Colonies, in the Provincial and Proprietary as well as in those that were governed by charter, the outlines of the English constitution were more or less accurately preserved. There was a Governor to represent the King, a Council to represent the House of Lords, an elective Assembly to represent the House of Commons. Local peculiarities introduced modifications. A royal Governor in Massachusetts was not in every respect upon the same footing as a royal Governor in Virginia. The Governor of Rhode Island, called from the plough, the workshop, or the counting-room to the executive chair, and going back to his plough, or workshop, or counting-room again, whenever his fellow-citizens thought that another man could serve them better, was a very different person from the needy courtiers who were often sent from the antechambers of royalty to fill their pockets in rich New York. But still in all material things the fundamental distinctions of the English constitution were preserved; the executive, the legislative, and the judicial functions were carefully kept apart.

Hence, when the Revolution came to snap the bands which had so long bound the Colonies to the mother country, it found a people familiar with the functions of government, and strongly attached to certain forms as the best security for their liberties. The Provincial and Proprietary systems, as far as they depended for sanction upon the King, fell of themselves when the King declared the Colonies out of his protection, and they accepted the position; but this was merely a falling of the scaffolding, — the foundations of the great edifice, which a century and a half had been consolidating, remained unshaken. The power returned to whence it came, — the people; and the people were prepared to build up a stronger and more harmonious edifice upon the original foundations. In the Charter governments the change was even less; for the charters were virtually written constitutions, and so much in harmony with public opinion that it was only some twenty years ago that Rhode Island dropped from her statute-book the charter of Charles the Second.

There was, indeed, a critical moment in the passage from the old forms to the new. "O Mr. Adams!" said one of the eager statesman's former clients, a notorious horse-jockey, "what great things have you and your colleagues done for us! We can never be grateful enough to you. There are no courts of justice now in this Province, and I hope there never will be another." John Adams looked grave. It was an interpretation of his iconoclastic labors which had not occurred to him. Other men looked grave, and felt anxious too. They saw that the hour of pulling down was past, and that, if they would build up again, they must begin quickly.

Massachusetts was the first to ask Congress what she should put in the place of the charter which the King and his ministers had tried to force upon her. It was an inconvenient question, for Congress was still talking about loyalty and filial love; and to advise Massachusetts to set up a government of her own would be neither loyal nor filial. But it was a question that must be met. To hesitate would be like casting doubts on its own authority. To refuse an answer would be exposing an important Colony to the perils of anarchy, when circumstances imperiously required the concentrated energy of organized government. She was advised, therefore, to go back as nearly as possible to her old charter.

In October of the same year (1775), New Hampshire came to Congress with the same question. Meanwhile, events had been quickening their motion; the whole fleet, dullest and swiftest alike, were within signal distance, moving fairly on with a wind that promised to blow, like that propitious wind which Apollo sent the Greeks, "full in the middle of their sails." And accordingly Congress spoke out more directly than ever before, advising them, by its resolve of the 3d of November, "to call a full and free representation of the people, and that the representatives, if they think it necessary, establish such a form of government as, in their judgment, will best produce the happiness of the people, and most effectually secure peace and good order in the Province during the continuance of the present dispute between Great Britain and the Colonies."

In January the resolve was acted upon, and a new constitution hastily formed. South Carolina, Virginia, and New Jersey also gave themselves, through their conventions, new constitutions before independence was declared; all of them bearing evident marks of haste. North Carolina was busy early in 1776 with the same questions. All felt alike the necessity of a regular, effective, and legitimate government.

In some of these constitutions grave defects soon became apparent. Massachusetts tired early of her resuscitated charter, and, calling a convention, formed a new constitution in 1780. South Carolina revised hers in 1778. New York, chiefly through the counsels of John Jay, was far more successful in her first effort. Maryland, also, went carefully and deliberately to the work. And thus, with more or less haste, with more or less skill, but all equally earnest and equally bent upon establishing all their rights upon a solid foundation, the thirteen dependent Provinces prepared themselves to enter upon a new career of progress and development as independent States.

And now, in bringing these constitutions together for a collective view, the first circumstance which strikes us is their explicit recognition of the sovereignty of the people. As the Declaration of Independence derived all its authority from the consent of the people, expressed by their acceptance of the new position in which it placed them, so the new constitutions derived all their authority from the consent of the people as expressed by a direct vote of ratification. They accepted them, they chose the representatives who framed them, they named the officers who carried them into execution. In all cases the decision lay with them. The arguments were addressed to their understandings; the appeal was made to their feelings. Familiarity with these things has blunted our sense of their magnitude. History in all her annals has no brighter page, no record so full of promise for every lover of humanity, as that which tells us how, without discord or anarchy, these thirteen Provinces passed through a revolution, and laid anew the foundations of their political existence on the broad basis of the rights, the interest, and the happiness of all.

Another common feature is the preservation in all but two — Pennsylvania and Georgia — of a legislature composed of two Houses, and invested with extensive authority, — an authority reaching in some even to the power of revising the constitution. Thus far we see the influence of English ideas and early associations. But nowhere did the body which took the place of the Colonial Councils come nearer to the House of Lords than by a longer term of office in some instances; and in some instances, also, a different mode of election. They were still the representatives of the people, invested for a stated term with specific powers, which, when that term expired, returned again to the people. The idea of hereditary rights to make laws, like that of hereditary rights to enforce them, took no root in American soil.

Another common feature was the jealousy with which they all looked upon the third element in their government, — the Governor, or, as he was called in some Provinces, the President. If we are to take this as a result of experience, it is a bitter satire upon the Colonial Governors whom they received from the King; if as a speculative conclusion, it shows more circumspection than confidence, a keen perception of possible dangers rather than a just sense of the degree of power which is essential to the usefulness as well as to the dignity of a chief magistrate. Everywhere his hands were tied by a Council, and sometimes tied so tight that it seems wonderful any one should have cared for so powerless a symbol of power.

In their views of religious toleration, also, there were some general features indicative of the point which the struggle between the rights of conscience and the responsibilities of religious conviction had generally reached. The old laws for the keeping of Sunday were retained in every constitution. In some cases, the narrow system of religious tests reappeared. In Delaware, no Unitarian was allowed to hold office. The test of eligibility in Massachusetts and Maryland was belief in the Christian religion, — the inheritors of the land planted by Puritans and the inheritors of the land planted by Catholics meeting upon a common stand-point of intolerance. South Carolina went ostensibly a step further, and declared that no man was fit for the discharge of civil functions who did not believe in a future state of rewards and punishments. Congregationalism still continued to hold the chief place in Massachusetts, New Hampshire, and Connecticut; and, like her sister sects, was still willing to strengthen her hold, and reserve for herself the rewards as well as the duties of the ministry. But Episcopalianism, as if anxious to reverse the terms of James's adage, had shown so decided a leaning towards the royal cause, that her strong hold, Virginia, fell from her, although in New York and New Jersey she still retained the extensive land grants which had been given to her in the day of higher hopes, as earnests of what her well-wishers were ready to do for the extension of her supremacy.

In only five constitutions was education mentioned; and in only two, that of Massachusetts and the second constitution of New Hampshire, were the provisions for schools for general instruction of any practical value.

The question of suffrage, important as it must always be, had not yet attained that degree of importance which it soon attained when the floodgates of emigration were thrown open and a heterogeneous mass of different nations poured in upon our shores. Distinctions had been made at an early period between those to whom the right was extended, and those from whom it was withheld. But here, as elsewhere, the fundamental distinction was a property distinction; and where enormous fortunes were unknown, it was not likely to be great. The highest point was a freehold estate of $250; the lowest, a freehold of $50; and in several States personal property gave the same privileges as real estate. A tribute to primogeniture was paid in Rhode Island and Pennsylvania, the eldest son enjoying a right to vote as the eldest son of a freeholder. In some Colonies voting depended upon the payment of taxes, and every tax-payer was a voter. Suffrage had not yet taken its place as a natural right. Stronger evidence of interest in the public welfare than the mere fact of residence was still required to enable men to say to whom they chose to confide the trust of making and executing their laws.

In only one constitution was there any mention of laws for the transmission of real estate. Georgia abolished entails, and provided for an equal division of property among the children. Nowhere else was the question touched in the beginning;

and in the other States invidious distinctions, derived for the most part from English law, continued to hold their place on the statute-book a few years longer.

It is evident from this brief sketch, that the only material alteration which the Revolution made in the municipal aspect of the Colonies was in the substitution of the people for the King as the visible source of power; for we must still bear in mind that the doctrine of popular sovereignty had been hitherto a revolutionary doctrine, — a principle held in reserve for great emergencies, and never brought prominently forward when any other way of action remained open. But henceforth it became the fundamental principle, the common starting-point, the only basis upon which the builders could construct an edifice fit to stand in the place of that which they had thrown down. And thus every constitution was the production of men especially chosen to make it, — everywhere the work of the people through the delegates of their choice.

It was natural that men should love this work of their own hands. And unfortunately it was equally natural that, in the fervor of this love, they should look suspiciously upon everything which seemed to throw any portion of it into the shade. A good part of their history thus far had been made up of disputes with the crown and the officers of the crown; and they had grown into a sensitive jealousy of possible encroachments, which led them to scrutinize closely every act of their sovereign beyond the ocean. And thus when it became necessary to create another power to act for them all, and confide some of the functions of sovereignty to a sovereign at their own doors, the question that they proposed to themselves was not how much power the common good required them to delegate, but how much it was possible to withhold. Even with that little, the sovereign was an object of jealousy and suspicion. They neither loved nor venerated him, and yet he inspired them with indefinite and unwelcome fears. How could they heartily love and trust King Cong., — they who had wasted so much unrequited affection upon King George?

This jealousy was not long in finding open expression. Even the Congress of 1775, strong in the first glow of patriotic faith from which it sprang, had thought it necessary to explain and apologize to the New York Convention for its resolves against New York Tories. Congress called, but the States did not hear. The whole course of the war is marked by hesitations, doubtings, delays, produced by the consciousness that its authority was an object of suspicion even when its weakness was an object of contempt. In South Carolina, where the State authority had for a season been entirely overthrown, where the legislature could only come together when the Continental army had opened the way for it, the commanding general found it necessary to deal very tenderly with untimely susceptibilities.

You all know how important it is in war to obtain early information of the enemy's plans and movements. Through Colonel Laurens, General Greene had succeeded in securing, within the enemy's lines, the services of some Americans, who, having been prevailed upon in an evil hour to take out protections from the British, were now anxious to make their peace with their countrymen. The information that they gave was important, a full equivalent for the stipulated reward, — pardon and the restoration of their estates. Laurens was killed. General Greene continued to avail himself of the sources of correspondence which Laurens had opened; and, when the proper moment came, felt himself bound to exert all his influence with the legislature in order to obtain for his agents the pardon and restitution that had been promised them. But his representations were received with strong tokens of dissatisfaction. The war was nearly over, and he was no longer needed to stand between the State government and the enemy.

But unfortunately he was soon compelled to return to this delicate ground. Congress had voted a five per cent duty on importations; but the consent of the States was necessary before it could be collected. Eleven States had agreed to it; two had refused, and one of these, I am sorry to say, was Rhode Island. Virginia, after giving her consent, had withdrawn it. South Carolina, it was feared, was about to follow her example. Robert Morris, the Superintendent of Finance, who had counted upon this duty, and built all his hopes of meeting his engagements upon it, was greatly embarrassed. But General Greene, with a victorious, but half-starved, half-naked, and unpaid army depending on him, felt that the question was very grave. Throughout all his Southern campaigns he had kept up a regular correspondence with the Governors of the States comprised in his command; a serious addition to his labors, but essential for keeping the wants of the army and the nature of their own dangers constantly before them. Earnest as his representations had sometimes been, they had always been well received, and by no one more readily than by Thomas Jefferson, when that father of democracy filled the executive chair of Virginia. Rutledge, too, South Carolina's own Governor, had passed weeks in Greene's camp, taking counsel of him, and preparing, with his aid, the measures necessary for the reinstatement of civil government.

And now, although a new Governor held the chair, Greene was unwilling to believe that the candid representations which had always been welcome in the day of trial would be misinterpreted in the day of prosperity. His letter to Governor Guerard was full, earnest, and respectful. He spoke of the embarrassments under which Congress labored; of the little ground that it gave for apprehension; and frankly avowed that he was one of those who thought that independence could only prove a blessing under Congressional influence. He spoke of the army, of the noble proofs which it had given of virtue and patriotism under almost every species of distress and privation. It had done it in the full persuasion that justice would be rendered it in due time. And now that it was in the power of government to take a step towards providing for the fulfilment of its obligations, it was dangerous to drive such men to despair. Many other things he said, and in the same wise and earnest spirit.

The Governor laid the letter before the Assembly, as he was requested to do, but added a letter of his own, strongly dissuading the measures which Greene had advised. As Greene's letter was a-reading, the members could scarcely restrain their impatience. "A Cromwell was dictating to free men, threatening them with a mutinied army, — trying to build up the power of Congress upon the ruin of State rights."

But there was still a step further which this unreasonable jealousy of Congress and their general could go, and Governor Guerard was prepared to take it. The enemy was gone, the State was free; the Governor had once more set up his residence in Charleston. But peace was not yet declared, the army was not yet disbanded, the laws and forms of war were still observed and still necessary. During the occupation of Charleston by the British, a British officer, Captain Kerr, had married an American lady; and now Governor Tonyn of East Florida, having occasion to communicate with General Greene, sent Captain Kerr to Charleston with a flag addressed as usage required to the Commander of the Southern Department. Governor Guerard insisted that the flag should have been addressed to him as Commander-in-chief of the State, and, not satisfied with asserting it, sent the sheriff to seize the vessel which bore the flag, and put the whole party in prison. The astonished Englishman appealed to General Greene. General Greene made a representation of the case to the Governor; Kerr was released, but the crew were detained in custody.

It was a clear case, though a delicate one. General Greene might justly have felt that something was due to him. But he plainly saw what was due to Congress, and he was resolved that the due should be paid. He was not fond of councils of war. Where fighting was to be done, he never called them. But this was a case manifestly within their competency; and, calling his officers together, he told them the story, showed them the letters, and asked them if in their opinion the British officer had violated any of the laws of a flag. They unanimously answered no. Greene instantly took possession of the passes to the city, and ordered that no flag should be admitted without permission from head-quarters. His reputation for thinking before he acted, and holding firmly to his resolutions when he had begun to act, was too well established to admit of any doubt as to what he would do now; and reluctantly, and with very bad grace, the Governor released the men, ordering Captain Kerr, as a salvo for his wounded dignity, to leave the city at once, and the State within three days. Captain Kerr again called upon General Greene for protection. " The order sent you by the Governor," was the reply, "you will pay no attention to. When I am ready to discharge your flag, I will inform you. The time and manner of your leaving the State shall be made as agreeable as possible. . . . . I am exceedingly unhappy at this additional instance of indelicate treatment you have met with. . . . . Nothing but my wishes to preserve the tranquillity of the people, and the respect and regard I have for their peace and quiet, could have prevailed on me to suffer your flag to be treated in the manner it has been."

And reporting the case to General Lincoln, Secretary of War, with a request to him to lay it before Congress, he says that " precedents for such encroachments upon United States authority shall not be founded upon his failure to resist them. This," he adds, " is not one of those cases where the right is doubtful, or public safety the object;

but appears to be a matter of temper, and pursued without regard to either."

And thus ended the first conflict between the government of South Carolina and the government of the United States.

It would be easy to add proof to proof of the feeling with which the new State governments entered upon the possession of their authority. Experience had taught them the value of their municipal institutions, but it had not yet taught them the value of that central institution upon whose preservation they all depended. They had learnt the necessity of combining as States for the protection of their common interests; but they had not learnt the equal necessity of uniting as a people in order to make the union of States firm, effective, and lasting. A short but perilous road was still to be trod before they reached those serene heights whence Washington and Franklin and Hamilton were yet to look hopefully forth upon the future of the country they had loved and served so well.

Yet the men who indulged these untimely jealousies were the men who had displayed so much familiarity with practical government, and so just a comprehension of the principles of theoretical government; men who, knowing that no government can perform its functions without a machinery of its own, had made their State machinery as perfect as they knew how to make it, but had deliberately clogged every wheel and weakened every spring which could give efficiency and vigor to their united strength.

And thus must it ever be with individuals and with States, who, accepting a principle, refuse to accept its consequences. For it is no less sure that every general law of being will sooner or later work itself fully out, than that all society is founded upon law. The law of union is eminently a law of sacrifice. The sacrifice of something that you might freely do while living alone, becomes an imperative condition the moment that you undertake to live with another. And as, in every State, each town, while performing some of the functions of government for itself, and possessing all the machinery which the performance of them required, looked to the State government for the performance of other functions, and cheerfully submitted to the curtailment of municipal authority and the partial subordination which such relations towards the State required; so was it only by the sacrifice of certain rights that the States could build up a central power strong enough to perform for them those indispensable acts of general government which they could not perform for themselves.

Manifest as this truth may now appear to every understanding, the history of the civil government of the Revolution is in a great measure the history of a persistent and bitter struggle with it in almost all its practical applications. Step by step the ground was contested, — step by step the ground was won. Yet how many steps were still required to bring our fathers to the Constitution which made us a powerful nation! How many more must yet be taken, before we reach the full consequences of that sublime Declaration which made us an independent people!

LECTURE V.

FINANCES OF THE REVOLUTION.

IN the sketches which formed the subject of my last two Lectures, you doubtless observed that I confined myself to general views and statements, without attempting to enter into a full study of any of the various classes of acts which statesmen are called upon to perform. This evening I propose to give you a fuller view of Congress in action; and in action upon one of the most complex and difficult subjects of legislation. Resistance once resolved on, it became necessary to provide the means of rendering it effective. There were men enough in the country to fill up the army, there was money enough in the country to feed, pay, and clothe them; but how were these men and that money to be reached? We shall see hereafter what was done to bring out the physical resources of the country, and how unwisely it was done. This evening I shall confine myself to a review of the efforts which were made earnestly and persistently, from the beginning of the war to the end of it, to bring out its pecuniary resources.

And here, on the threshold, let me remind you that, in all historical studies, you should still bear in mind the difference between the point of view from which you look at events, and that from which they were seen by the actors themselves. We all act under the influence of ideas. Even those who speak of theories with contempt are none the less the unconscious disciples of some theory, none the less busied in working out some problems of the great theory of life. Much as they fancy that they differ from the speculative man, they differ from him only in contenting themselves with seeing the path as it lies at their feet, while he strives to embrace it all, starting-point and end, in one comprehensive view. And thus in looking back upon the past we are irresistibly led to arrange the events of history, as we arrange the facts of a science, in their appropriate classes and under their respective laws. And thus, too, these events give us the true measure of the intellectual and moral culture of the times, of the extent to which just ideas prevailed therein upon all the duties and functions of private and public life. Tried by the standard of absolute truth and right, grievously would they all fall short, and we, too, with them. Judged by the human standard of progressive development and gradual growth, — the only standard to which the man of the beam can venture, unrebuked, to bring the man of the mote, — we shall find much in them all to sadden us, and much also in which we can sincerely rejoice.

In judging, therefore, the political acts of our ancestors, we have a right to bring them to the standard of the political science of their own age, but we have no right to bring them to the higher standard of ours. Montesquieu could give them but an imperfect clew to the labyrinth in which they found themselves involved; and yet no one had seen farther into the mysteries of social and political organization than Montesquieu. Hume had scattered brilliant rays on dark places, and started ideas which, once at work in the mind, could never rest till they had evolved momentous truths and overthrown long-standing errors. But no one had yet seen (Adam Smith's great work was just going to the press), that labor was the original source of every form of wealth, — that the farmer, the merchant, the manufacturer, were all equally the instruments of national prosperity, — or demonstrated as Smith does, that nations grow rich and powerful by giving as they receive, and that the good of one is the good of all. The world had not yet seen that fierce conflict between antagonistic principles which she was soon to see in the French Revolution; nor had political science yet recorded those daring experiments in remoulding society, those constitutions framed in closets, discussed in clubs, accepted and overthrown with equal demonstrations of popular zeal, and which, expressing in their terrible energy the universal dissatisfaction with past and present, the universal grasping at a brighter future, have met and answered so many grave questions, neither propounded nor solved in any of the two hundred constitutions which Aristotle studied in order to prepare himself for the composition of his "Politics." The world had not yet seen a powerful nation tottering on the brink of anarchy, with all the elements of prosperity in her bosom, — nor a bankrupt state sustaining a war that demanded annual millions, and growing daily in wealth and strength, — nor the economical phenomena which followed the reopening of Continental commerce in 1814, — nor the still more startling phenomena which a few years later attended England's return to specie-payments and a specie-currency, — nor statesmen seating themselves gravely before the map of Europe to distribute its kingdoms and peoples according to their own conceptions of the balance of power, but finding all the results of their combined wisdom set at nought by the inexorable development of the fundamental principle which they had refused to recognize.

But we have seen these things, and, having seen them, unconsciously apply the knowledge derived from them to events to which we have no right to apply it. We condemn errors which we should never have detected without the aid of a light which was hidden from our fathers, and will still be dwelling upon shortcomings which nothing could have avoided but a general diffusion of that wisdom which Providence never vouchsafes except as a gift to a few exalted minds. Every schoolboy has his text-book of political economy now; but many can remember when these books first made their appearance in schools; and so late as 1820 the Professor of History in English Cambridge publicly lamented that there was no work upon this vital subject which he could give to his classes.

When, therefore, our fathers found themselves face to face with the complex questions of finance, they naturally fell back upon the experience and devices of their past history; they did as in such emergencies men always do, — they tried to meet the present difficulty without weighing maturely the future difficulty. The present was at the door, palpable, stern, urgent, relentless; and as they looked at it, they could see nothing beyond half so full of perplexity and danger. They hoped, as in the face of all history and all experience men will ever hope, that out of those depths which their feeble eyes were unable to penetrate, something might yet arise in their hour of need to avert the peril and snatch them from the precipice. Their past history had its lessons of encouragement, some thought, and, some thought, of warning. They seized the example, but the admonition passed unheeded.

Short as the chronological record of American history then was, that exchange of the products of labor which so speedily grows up into commerce had already passed through all its phases, from direct barter to bank-notes and bills of exchange. Men gave what they wanted less to get what they wanted more; the products of industry without doors for the products of industry within doors; and it was only when they wished to add to their stock of luxuries or conveniences from a distance that they felt the want of money. Prices naturally found their own level, — were what, when left to themselves they always are, the natural expression of the relations between demand and supply. Tobacco stood the Virginian instead of money long after money had become abundant, procuring him corn, meat, raiment. More than once, too, it procured him something still better. In the very same year in which the Pilgrims landed at Plymouth, history tells us, ninety maidens of "virtuous education and demeanor" landed in Virginia; the next year brought sixty more; and, provident industry reaping its own reward, he whose busy hands had raised the largest crop of tobacco was enabled to make the first choice of a wife. And it must have been an edifying and pleasant spectacle to see each stalwart Virginian pressing eagerly on towards the landing, with his bundle of tobacco on his back, and walking deliberately home again with an affectionate wife under his arm.

But already there was a pernicious principle at work, — protested against by experience wherever tried, and still repeatedly tried anew, — the assumption by government of the power to regulate the prices of goods. The first instance carries us back to 1618, and thinking men still believed it possible in 1777. The right to regulate the prices of labor was its natural corollary, bringing with it the power of creating legal tenders, and the various representatives of value, without any correspondent measures for creating the value itself, or, in simpler words, paper-money without capital. And thus, logically as well as historically, we reach the first issue of paper-money in 1690, that year so memorable as the year of the first Congress.

New England, encouraged by a successful expedition against Port Royal, made an attempt upon Quebec. Confident of success, she sent forth her little army without providing the means of paying it. The soldiers came back soured by disaster and fatigue, and, not yet up to the standard of 1776, were upon the point of mutinying for their pay. To escape the immediate danger, Massachusetts bethought her of bills of credit. They were issued, accepted, and redeemed, although the first holders suffered great losses, and the last holders, or the speculators, were the only ones that found them faithful pledges. The flood-gates once opened, the water poured in amain. Every pressing emergency afforded a pretext for a new issue. Other Colonies followed the seductive example. Paper was soon issued to make money plenty. Men's minds became familiar with the idea, as they saw the convenient substitute passing freely from hand to hand. Accepted at market, accepted at the retail store, accepted in the counting-room, accepted for taxes, everywhere a legal tender, it seemed adequate to all the demands of domestic trade. But erelong came undue fluctuations of prices, depreciations, failures, — all the well-known indications of an unsound currency. England interposed to protect her own merchants, to whom American paper-money was utterly worthless; and Parliament stripped it of its value as a legal tender. Men's minds were divided. They had never before been called upon to discuss such questions upon such a scale or in such a form. They were at a loss for the principle, still enveloped in the multitude and variety of conflicting theories and obstinate facts.

One fact, however, was clearly established, — that a government could, in great need, make paper fulfil, for a while, the office of money; and if a regular government, why not also a revolutionary government, sustained and accepted by the people? Here, then, begins the history of Continental money, — the principal chapter in the financial history of the Revolution, — leading us, like all such histories, over ground thick-strown with unheeded admonitions and neglected warnings, through a round of constantly recurring phenomena, varied only here and there by modifications in the circumstances under which they appear.

It is much to be regretted that we have no record of the discussions through which Congress reached the resolves of June 22, 1775: "That a sum not exceeding two millions of Spanish milled dollars be emitted by the Congress in bills of credit for the defence of America. That the twelve confederated Colonies" (Georgia, it will be remembered, had not yet sent delegates) "be pledged for the redemption of the bills of credit now to be emitted." We do not know positively that there was any discussion. If there was, it is not difficult to conceive how some of the reasoning ran, — how each delegate had arguments and examples from his own Colony; how confidently Pennsylvanians would speak of the security which they had given to their paper; how confidently Virginians would assert that even the greatest straits might be passed without having recourse to so dangerous a medium; how all the facts in the history of paper-money would be brought forward to prove both sides of the question, but how the underlying principle, subtile, and impalpable, might still elude them all, as it long still continued to elude wise statesmen and thoughtful economists; how, at last, some impatient spirit, breaking through the untimely delay, sternly asked them what else they proposed to do. By what alchemy would they create gold and silver? By what magic would they fill the coffers which their non-exportation resolutions had kept empty, or bring in the supplies which their non-importation resolutions had cut off? What arguments of their devising would induce a people in arms against taxation to submit to tenfold heavier taxes than those which they had indignantly repelled? Necessity, inexorable necessity, was now their lawgiver; they had adopted an army, they must support it; they had voted to pay their officers, they must secure the means of giving their vote effect; arms, ammunition, camp-equipage, everything was to be provided for. The people were full of ardor, glowing with fiery zeal; your promise to pay will be received like payment; your commands will be instantly obeyed. Every hour's delay imperils the sacred cause, chills the holy enthusiasm; action, prompt, energetic, resolute action, is what the crisis demands. Men must see that we are in earnest; the enemy must see it; nothing else will bring them to terms; nothing else will give us a lasting peace; and in such a peace how easily, how cheerfully, shall we all unite in paying the debt by which so inestimable a blessing was won!

It would have been difficult to deny the force of such an appeal. There were doubtless men in Congress who believed firmly in the virtue of the people, — who thought that after the proof which the people had given of their readiness to sacrifice the interests of the present moment to the interests of a day and a posterity that they might not live to see, it would be worse than scepticism to call it in question. But even they might hesitate about the form of the sacrifice they called for, for they knew how often the world is governed by names, and that men's minds might revolt at the idea of a formal tax, although they would submit to pay it fifty-fold under the name of depreciation. Even at this day, with all our additional light, — the combined light of science and of experience, — it is difficult to see what else they could have done without strengthening dangerously the hands of their domestic enemies. Nor let this be taken as a proof that they engaged rashly in an unequal contest, even though it was necessarily in part a war of paper against gold. They have been accused of this by their friends as well as by their enemies; they have been accused of sacrificing a positive good to an uncertain hope, — of suffering their passions to hurry them into a war for which they had made no adequate preparation, and had not the means of making any; that they wilfully, almost wantonly, incurred the fearful responsibility of staking the lives and fortunes of those who were looking to them for guidance upon the chances of a single cast. But the accusation is unjust. As far as human foresight could reach, they had calculated these chances carefully. They knew the tenure by which they held their authority, and that, if they ran counter to the popular will, the people would fall from them, — that, if they should fail in making their position good, they would be the first, almost the only victims, — that, then as ever, "the thunderbolts on highest mountains light." Charles Carroll added "of Carrollton" to his name, so that, if the Declaration he was setting it to should bring forfeiture and confiscation, there might be no mistake about the victim. Nor was it without a touch of sober earnestness that Harrison, bulky and fat, said to the lean and shadowy Gerry, as he laid down his pen, — "When hanging-time comes, I shall have the advantage of you. I shall be dead in a second, while you will be kicking in the air half an hour after I am gone." But they knew also, that, if there are dangers which we do not perceive till we come full upon them, there are likewise helps which we do not see till we find ourselves face to face with them, — and that in the life of nations, as in the life of individuals, there are moments when all that the wisest and most conscientious can do is to see that everything is in its place, every man at his post, and resolutely bide the shock.

While this subject was pressing upon Congress, it was occupying no less seriously leading minds in the different Colonies. All felt that the success of the experiment must chiefly depend upon the degree of security that could be given to the bills. But how to reach that necessary degree was a perplexing question. Three ways were suggested in the New York Convention: that Congress should fix upon a sum, assign each Colony its proportion,

and the issue be made by the Colony upon its own
responsibility; or that the United Colonies should
make the issue, each Colony pledging itself to redeem the part that fell to it; or, lastly, that, Congress issuing the sum, and each Colony assuming
its proportionate responsibility, the Colonies should
still be bound as a whole to make up for the failure of any individual Colony to redeem its share.
The latter was proposed by the Convention as
offering greater chances of security, and tending
at the same time to strengthen the bond of union.
It was in nearly this form, also, that it came from
Congress.

No time was now lost in carrying the resolution
into effect. The next day, Tuesday, June 23, the
number, denomination, and form of the bills were
decided in a Committee of the Whole. It was
resolved to make bills of eight denominations, from
one to eight, and issue forty-nine thousand of each,
completing the two millions by eleven thousand
eight hundred of twenty dollars each. The form
of the bill was to be, —

Continental Currency.

No. *Dollars.*

This bill entitles the bearer to receive ———
*Spanish milled dollars or the value thereof in gold
or silver, according to the resolutions of the Congress held at Philadelphia on the 10th day of May,*
A. D. 1775.

In the same sitting a committee of five was appointed "to get proper plates engraved, to provide paper, and to agree with printers to print the above bills." Both Franklin and John Adams were on this committee.

Had they lived in 1862 instead of 1775, how would their doors have been beset by engravers and paper-dealers and printers! What baskets of letters would have been poured upon their tables! How would they have dreaded the sound of the knocker or the cry of the postman! But, alas! paper was so far from abundant that generals were often reduced to hard straits for enough of it to write their reports and despatches on; and that Congressmen were not much better off will be believed when we find John Adams sending his wife a sheet or two at a time under the same envelope with his own letters. Printers there were, as many, perhaps, as the business required, but not enough for the eager contention which the announcement of government work to be done excites among us in these days. And of engravers there were but four between Maine and Georgia. Of these four, one was Paul Revere of the midnight ride,* the Boston boy of Huguenot blood, whose self-taught graver had celebrated the repeal

* A name sure, henceforth, of its true place in our history; for, thanks to Longfellow, it has taken a firm place in our poetry. Would that others' names equally deserving might be equally fortunate.

of the Stamp Act, condemned to perpetual derision the rescinders of 1768, and told the story of the Boston Massacre, — who, when the first grand jury under the new organization was drawn, had met the judge with, "I refuse to *sarve*,"— a scientific mechanic, — a leader at the Tea-party, — a soldier of the old war, — prepared to serve in this war, too, with sword, or graver, or science, — fitting carriages, at Washington's command, to the cannon from which the retreating English had knocked off the trunnions, learning how to make powder at the command of the Provincial Congress, and setting up the first powder-mill ever built in Massachusetts.

No mere engraver's task for him, this engraving the first bill-plates of Continental Currency! How must he have warmed over the design! how carefully must he have chosen his copper! how buoyantly must he have plied his graver, harassed by no doubts, disturbed by no misgivings of the double mission which those little plates were to perform, — the good one first, thank God! but ah! how fatal a one afterward! but resolved and hopeful as on that April night when he spurred his horse from cottage to hamlet, rousing the sleepers with the cry, long unheard in the sweet valleys of New England, "Up! up! the enemy is coming!"

The paper of these bills was thick, so thick that the enemy called it the pasteboard money of the rebels. Plate, paper, and printing, all had little in common with the elaborate finish and delicate texture of a modern bank-note. To sign them was too hard a tax upon Congressmen already taxed to the full measure of their working-time by committees and protracted daily sessions; and therefore a committee of twenty-eight gentlemen not in Congress was employed to sign and number them, receiving in compensation one dollar and a third for every thousand bills.

Meanwhile loud calls for money were daily reaching the doors of Congress. Everywhere money was wanted, — money to buy guns, money to buy powder, money to buy provisions, money to send officers to their posts, money to march troops to their stations, money to speed messengers to and fro, money for the wants of to-day, money to pay for what had already been done, and still more money to insure the right doing of what was yet to do: Washington wanted it; Lee wanted it; Schuyler wanted it; from north to south, from sea-board to inland, came one deep, monotonous, menacing cry, — "Money, or our hands are powerless!"

How long would these two millions stand such a drain? Spent before they were received, hardly touching the Treasury-chest as a starting-place before they flew on "the wings of all the winds" to gladden thousands of expectant hearts with a brief respite from one of their many cares. Relief there certainly was; neither long, indeed, nor lasting, but still relief. Good Whigs received the bills, as they did everything that came from Congress, with unquestioning confidence. Tories turned from them in derision, and refused to give their goods for them. Whereupon Congress took the matter in hand, and told them that they must. It was soon seen that another million would be wanted, and in July a second issue was resolved on. All-devouring war had soon swallowed this also. Three more millions were ordered in November. But the war, men said, was to end soon, — by June, '76, at the latest. All expenditures were calculated upon this supposition; and wealth flowing in under the auspices of a just and equable accommodation with their reconciled mother, these millions which had served them so well in the hour of need would soon be repaid by a happy and grateful people from an abundant treasury.

But early in 1776 reports came of English negotiations for foreign mercenaries to help put down the rebellion, — reports which soon took the shape of positive information. It was evident that no immediate end of the war was to be looked for now; already, too, independence was looming up on the turbid horizon; already the current was bearing them onward, deep, swift, irresistible; and thus seizing still more eagerly upon the future, they poured out other four millions in February, five millions in May, five millions in July. The Confederacy was not yet formed; the Declaration of Independence had nothing yet to authenticate it but the signatures of John Hancock and Charles Thompson; and the republic that was to be was already solemnly pledged to the payment of twenty millions of dollars.

Thus far men's faith had not faltered. They saw the necessity and accepted it, giving their goods and their labor unhesitatingly for a slip of paper which derived all its value from the resolves of a body of men who might, upon a reverse, be thrown down as rapidly as they had been set up. And then whom were they to look to for indemnification? But now began a sensible depreciation, — slight, indeed, at first, but ominous. Congress took the alarm and resolved upon a loan, — resolved to borrow directly what it had hitherto borrowed indirectly, the goods and the labor of its constituents. Accordingly, on the 3d of October, a resolve was passed for raising five millions of dollars at four per cent; and in order to make it convenient to lenders, loan-offices were established in every Colony, with a commissioner for each.

Money came in slowly, but ran out so fast that, in November, Congress ordered weekly returns from the Treasury, not of sums on hand, but of what parts of the last emission remained unexpended. The campaign of 1777 was at hand; how the campaign of 1776 would end was uncertain. The same impenetrable veil that as yet hid

Trenton and Princeton from all eyes concealed also the disasters of Fort Washington and the Jerseys. Men still looked hopefully to the lower line of the Hudson. It was resolved, therefore, to make an immediate effort to supply the Treasury by a lottery to be drawn at Philadelphia.

A lottery, — does not the word carry you back, a great many years back, to other times and other manners? The Articles of War were now on the table of Congress for revision; and in the second and third of those articles, officers and soldiers had been earnestly recommended to attend divine service diligently, and to refrain, under grave penalties, from profane cursing or swearing. And here legislators deliberately set themselves to raise money by means which we have deliberately condemned as gambling. But years were yet to pass before statesmen, or the people rather, were brought to feel that the lottery-office and the gaming-table stand side by side on the same broad highway.

No such thoughts troubled the minds of our forefathers, well stored as those minds were with human and divine lore; but, going to work without a scruple, they prepared an elaborate scheme, and fixed the 1st of March for the day of drawing, — "or sooner, if sooner full." It was not full, however, nor was it full when the subject next came up. Tickets were sold; committees sat; Congress returned to the subject from time to time; but what with the incipient depreciation of the bills of credit, the rising prices of goods and provisions, and the incessant calls upon every purse for public and private purposes, the lottery failed to commend itself either to speculators or to the bulk of the people. Some good Whigs bought tickets from principle, and, like many of the good Whigs who took the bills of credit for the same reason, lost their money.

In the same November, the Treasury was directed to make preparations for a new issue; and in order to meet the wants of the retail trade, it was also resolved to issue five hundred thousand dollars in bills of two thirds, one third, one sixth, and one ninth of a dollar. Evident as it ought now to have been that nothing but taxation could save public credit, men could not bend their minds to the necessity. "Do you think, gentlemen," said a member of Congress, "that I will consent to load my constituents with taxes, when we can send to our printer and get a wagon-load of money, one quire of which will pay for the whole?" It was so easy a way of making money, that men seemed to be getting into the humor of it.

The campaign of 1777, like the campaign of 1776, was fought upon paper-money without any material depreciation. The bills could never be signed as fast as they were called for. But this could not last. The public mind was growing anxious. Extensive interests, in some cases whole fortunes, were becoming involved in the question of ultimate payment. The alarm gained upon Congress. Burgoyne, indeed, was conquered; but a more powerful, a more insidious enemy, one to whom Congress itself had opened the gate, was already within the works and fast advancing towards the heart of the citadel. The depreciation had reached four for one, and there was but one way to prevent it from going lower. The deliberations were long and anxious. Thus far the public faith had supported the war. But, it was said, the quantity of the money for which this faith stood pledged already exceeded the demands of commerce, and hence its value was proportionably reduced. Add to this the arts of open and secret enemies, the avidity of professed friends, and the scarcity of foreign commodities, and it seemed easy to account for the depreciation. "The consequences were equally obvious and alarming," — "depravity of morals, decay of public virtue, a precarious supply for the war, debasement of the public faith, injustice to individuals, and the destruction of the safety, honor, and independence of the United States." But "a reasonable and effectual remedy" was still within reach; and therefore, "with mature deliberation and the most earnest solicitude," Congress recommended the raising by taxes on the different States, in proportion to their population, five millions of dollars in quarterly payments, for the service of 1778.

But having explained, justified, and recommended, its power ceased. Like the Confederation, it had no right of coercion, no machinery of its own for acting upon the States. And, unhappily, the States, pressed by their individual wants, feeling keenly their individual sacrifices and dangers, failed to see that the nearest road to relief lay through the odious portal of taxation. Had the mysterious words that Dante read on the gates of hell been written on it, they could not have shrunk from it with a more instinctive feeling: —

"Lasciate ogni-speranza voi ch' entrate."
"All hope abandon, ye who enter in!"

Some States paid, some did not pay. The sums that came in were wholly insufficient to relieve the actual pressure; and that pressure, unrelieved, grew daily more severe. Congress had tried the regulating of prices, — it had tried loans, — it had tried a lottery; and now it was forced back again to its earliest and most dangerous expedient, paper-money. New floods poured forth, and the parched earth drank them greedily up. One may almost fancy, as he looks at the tables, that he sees the shadowy form of a sickly Credit tottering feebly forth to catch a gleam of sunshine, a breath of pure air, while myriads of little sprites, each bearing in his hand an emblazoned scroll with "Depreciation" written upon it in big yellow letters, dance merrily around him, thrusting the bitter record in his face, whichever way he turns, with gibes and taunts and demoniac laughter. But his course was almost ended; the grave was nigh, an unhonored grave; and as eager hands heaped the earth upon his faded form, a stern voice bade men remember that they who strayed from the path as he had done, must sooner or later find a grave like his.

It was not without a desperate struggle that Congress saw the rapid decline and shameful death of its currency. The ground was fought manfully, foot by foot, inch by inch. The idea that money derived its value from acts of government seemed to have taken deep hold of men's minds, and their policy was in perfect harmony with their belief. In January, 1776, it had been solemnly resolved that everybody who refused to accept the Continental bills, or did anything to obstruct the circulation of them, should, upon due conviction, "be deemed, published, and treated as an enemy of his country, and be precluded from all trade or intercourse with the inhabitants of these Colonies." And to enforce it, there were Committees of Inspection, whose power seldom lay idle in their hands, whose eyes were never sealed in slumber. In this work, which seemed good in their eyes, the State Assemblies, and Conventions, and Committees of Safety, joined heart and hand with Congress. Tender-laws were tried, and the relentless hunt of creditor after debtor became a flight of the recusant creditor from the debtor eager to wipe out his responsibility for gold or silver with a ream or two of paper. Limitation of prices was tried, and produced its natural results, — discontent, insufficient supplies, heavy losses. Threatening resolves were renewed, and fell powerless. It was hoped that some relief might come from the sales of confiscated property; but property changed hands, and the Treasury was none the better off; just as in France, a few years later, the whole landed property of the kingdom changed hands, and left the government assignats what it found them, — bits of waste paper.

Meanwhile speculation ran riot. Every form of wastefulness and extravagance prevailed in town and country; nowhere more than at Philadelphia, under the very eyes of Congress; luxury of dress, luxury of equipage, luxury of the table. We are told of one entertainment at which eight hundred pounds were spent in pastry. As I read the private letters of those days, I sometimes feel as a man might feel if permitted to look down upon a foundering ship whose crew were preparing for death by breaking open the steward's room and drinking themselves into madness.

An earnest appeal was made to the States. The sober eloquence and profound statesmanship of John Jay were employed to bring the subject before the country in its true light and manifold bearings; the state of the Treasury, the results of loans and of taxes, and the nature and amount of the obligations incurred. The natural value and wealth of the country were held up to view as the foundations on which Congress had undertaken to construct a system of public finances, beginning with bills of credit, because there was no nation they could have borrowed of, coming next to loans, and thus "unavoidably creating a public debt; a debt of $159,948,880, in emissions; $7,545,196$\frac{67}{90}$, in money borrowed before the 1st of March, 1778, with the interest payable in France; $26,188,909, money borrowed since the 1st of March, 1778, with interest due in America; about $4,000,000, of money due abroad." The taxes had brought in only $3,027,560; so that all the money supplied to Congress by the people was but $36,761,665$\frac{67}{90}$.

"Judge, then, of the necessity of emissions, and learn from whom and from whence that necessity arose. We are also to inform you that on Wednesday, the first day of September instant, we resolved that we would on no account whatever emit more bills of credit than to make the whole amount of such bills two hundred million dollars; and as the sum emitted and in circulation amounted to $159,948,880, and the sum of $40,051,120 remained to complete the two hundred million above mentioned, we, on the third day of September instant, further resolved that we would emit such part only of the said sum as should be absolutely necessary for public exigencies before adequate supplies could otherwise be obtained, relying for such supplies on the exertions of the several States."

Coming to the depreciation, he reduces the causes to three kinds: natural, or artificial, or both. The natural cause was the excess of the supply over the demands of commerce; the artificial cause was a distrust of the ability or inclination of the United States to redeem their bills; and assuming that both causes have combined in producing the depreciation of the Continental money, he proceeds to prove that there can be no doubt of the ability of the United States to pay their debt, and none of their inclination. Under the head of inclination he divides his argument into three parts: —

First, Whether, and in what manner, the faith of the United States has been pledged for the redemption of their bills.

Second, Whether they have put themselves in a political capacity to redeem them.

Third, Whether, admitting the two former propositions, there is any reason to apprehend a wanton violation of the public faith. The idea that Congress can destroy the money, because Congress made it, is treated with scorn.

"A bankrupt, faithless republic would be a novelty in the political world. . . . . The pride of America revolts from the idea; her citizens know for what purposes these emissions were made, and have repeatedly plighted their faith for the redemption of them; they are to be found in every man's possession, and every man is interested in their being redeemed. . . . . Provide for continuing your armies in the field till victory and peace shall lead them home, and avoid the reproach of permitting the currency to depreciate in your hands, when by yielding a part to taxes and loans, the whole might have been appreciated and preserved. Humanity as well as justice makes this demand upon you; the complaints of ruined widows and the cries of fatherless children, whose whole support has been placed in your hands and melted away, have doubtless reached you; take care that they ascend no higher! . . . Determine to finish the contest as you began it, honestly and gloriously. Let it never be said that America had no sooner become independent than she became insolvent."

But it was not only the Continental money that was blocking up the channels through which a sound currency would have carried vigor and health. The States had their debts and their paper-money too, — wheel within wheel of complicated, desperate insolvency. The two hundred millions had been issued and spent. There was no money to send to Washington for his army, and he was compelled for a while to support them by seizing the articles he needed, and giving certificates in return. The States were called upon for specific supplies, beef, pork, and flour, — a method so expensive, irregular, and partial, that it was soon abandoned. One chance remained: to call in the old money by taxes, and burn it as soon as it was in; then to issue a new paper, — one of the new for every twenty of the old; and when the whole of the old was cancelled, to issue only ten millions of the new, — four millions of it subject to the order of Congress, and the remaining six to be divided among the States: the whole redeemable in specie within six years, and bearing till then an interest of five per cent, payable in specie annually, or on redemption, at the option of the holder. By this skilful change of base it was hoped that a bold front could still be presented to the enemy, and the field, which had been so long and so obstinately contested, be finally won.

But the day of expedients was past. The zeal which had blazed forth with such energy at the beginning of the war was fast sinking to a fitful, smouldering flame. Individual interests were again taking the precedence of general interests. The moral sense of the people had contracted a deadly taint from daily contact with corruption. The spirit of gambling, confined in the beginning and lost to the eye, like Le Sage's Devil, had swollen to its full proportions, and, in the garb of speculation, was undermining the foundations of society. Rogues were growing rich; the honest men, who were not already poor, were daily growing poor. The laws that had been made in the view of propping the currency, had served only to countenance unscrupulous men in paying their debts at a discount ruinous to the creditor. The laws against forestallers and engrossers, who, it was currently believed, were leagued against both army and country, were powerless, as such laws always are. Even Washington wished for a gallows as high as Haman's to hang them on; but the army was kept starving none the less.

The seasons themselves — God's visible agents — seemed to combine against our cause. The years 1779 and 1780 were years of small crops. The winter of 1780 was severe far beyond the common severity even of a northern winter. Provisions were scarce, suffering universal. Farmers, as if forgetting their dependence on rain and sunshine, had planted less than usual, — some from disaffection, some because they were irritated at having to give up their corn and cattle for worthless bills, and certificates which might prove equally worthless. Some, who were within reach of the enemy, preferred to sell to them, for they paid in silver and gold. There were riots in Philadelphia, and they were put down at the point of the sword. There was mutiny in the army, and this, too, was put down by the strong hand, — though the fearful sufferings which had caused it almost justified it in the eye of sober reason.

It is easy to see why farmers should have been loath to raise more than they needed for their own use, and why merchants should have been unwilling to lay in stores which they might be compelled to sell at prices so truly nominal that the money which they received would often sink to half they had taken it for before they were able to pass it. But it is not so easy to see why this wretched substitute for values should have circulated so freely to the very last. Even at two hundred for one, with the knowledge that the next twenty-four hours might make that two hundred two hundred and fifty, or even more, without the slightest hope that it would ever be redeemed at its nominal value, it would still buy everything that was to be bought, — provisions, goods, houses, lands, even hard money itself. Down to its last gasp there were speculations afoot to take advantage of the differences in the degree of its worthlessness at different places, and buy it up in one place to sell it at another, — to buy it in Philadelphia at two hundred and twenty-five for one, and sell it in Boston at seventy-five for one. It was possible, if the ball passed quickly from hand to hand, that some might gain; it was very manifest that some must lose; and here outcrops that pernicious doctrine, that true, life-giving, health-diffusing commerce consists in stripping one to clothe another.

And thus we reach the memorable year 1781, the great, decisive year of the war. While Greene was fighting Cornwallis and Rawdon, and Washington was watching eagerly for an opportunity to strike at Clinton, Congress was busy making up its accounts. One circumstance told for it. There was no longer the same dearth of gold and silver which had embarrassed commerce so much at the beginning of the war. A gainful intercourse was now opened with the West Indies. The French army and the French fleet were here, and hard money with them. Louis-d'ors and livres, and Spanish dollars, — how welcome must their pleasant faces have looked, after this long, long absence! With what a thrill must the hand which for years had touched nothing but Continental bills have closed upon solid gold and silver! It is easy to conceive that a new spirit must soon have manifested itself in the wide circle of contractors and agents, — that shopkeepers must speedily have discovered that their business was shifting its ground as they obtained a reliable standard for counting their losses and gains, — that every branch of trade must have felt a new vigor diffusing itself through its veins. But it is equally evident, that, while the gold and silver which flowed in upon them from these sources strengthened the people for the work they were to do and the burdens they were to bear, the comparisons they were daily making between fluctuating paper and steadfast metal were not of a nature to strengthen their faith in money that could be made by a turn of the printing-press and a few strokes of the pen.

Another circumstance told for Congress, too. The accession of Maryland had fulfilled the conditions for the acceptance of the Confederation so long held in abeyance, and the finances were taken from a board, and intrusted to the hands of a skilful and energetic financier. Robert Morris, who had protested energetically against the tender-laws, made specie payments the condition of his acceptance of office; and on the 22d of May, though not without a struggle, Congress resolved "that the whole debts already due by the United States be liquidated as soon as may be to their specie value, and funded, if agreeable to the creditors, as a loan upon interest; that the States be severally informed that the calculations of the expenses of the present campaign are made in solid coin, and therefore that the requisitions from them respectively, being grounded on those calculations, must be complied with in such manner as effectually to answer the purpose designed; that, experience having evinced the inefficacy of all attempts to support the credit of paper money by compulsory acts, it is recommended to such States, where laws making paper bills a tender yet exist, to repeal the same."

Another public body, the Supreme Executive Council of Pennsylvania, dealt paper another blow, fixing the ratio at which it was to be received in public payments at one hundred and seventy-five for one. Circulation ceased. In a short time the money that had been carted to and fro in reams disappeared from the shop, the counting-room, the market. All dealings were in hard money. Gold and silver resumed their legitimate sway, and men began to look hopefully forward to a return of economy, frugality, and invigorating commerce.

The Superintendent of Finance entered seriously upon his task. One great obstacle had been removed; one great and decisive step had been made towards the restoration of that sense of security without which industry and enterprise are powerless. As a merchant, he was familiar with the resources of the country; as a member of Congress, he was familiar with the wants of government. His resources were taxes and loans; his obligations, an old debt and a daily expenditure. Opposed as he was to the irresponsible currency which had brought the country to the brink of ruin, he was a believer in banks and bills resting on a secure basis. One of his earliest measures was to prepare, with the aid of his Assistant-Superintendent, Gouverneur Morris, a plan of a bank, which soon after, with the sanction of Congress, went into operation as the Bank of North America. Small as the capital with which it started was, — only four hundred thousand dollars, — its influence was immediately felt throughout the country. It gave an impulse to legitimate enterprise which had long been wanting, and a confidence to buyer and seller which they had not felt since the first year of the war. In his public operations the Superintendent used it freely, and, using it at the same time wisely, was enabled to call upon it for aid to the full extent of its ability without impairing its strength.

Henceforth the financial history of the Revolution, although it loses none of its importance, loses much of its narrative-interest. No longer a hand-to-hand conflict between coin and paper, — no longer the melancholy spectacle of wise men doing unwise things, and honorable men doing things which, in any other form, they would have been the first to condemn as dishonorable, — it still continues a long, a wearisome, and often a mortifying struggle; still presents the sad spectacle of men knowing their duty and refusing to do it; knowing consequences, and yet blindly shutting their eyes to them. I will give but one example.

After a careful estimate for the operations of 1782, Congress had called upon the States for eight millions of dollars. Up to January, 1783, only four hundred and twenty thousand had come into the Treasury. Four hundred thousand Treasury-notes were almost due; the funds in Europe were overdrawn to the amount of five hundred thousand by the sale of drafts. But Morris, waiting only to cover himself by a special authorization of Congress, made fresh sales upon the hopes of the Dutch loan and the possibility of a new French loan, and still held on — as cautiously as he could, but ever boldly and skilfully — his anxious way through the rocks and shoals that menaced him on every side. He was rewarded, as faithful servants too often are, by calumny and suspicion. But when men came to look closely at his acts, comparing his means with his wants, and the expenditure of the Treasury Board with the expenditure of the Finance Office, it was seen and acknowledged that he had saved the country thirteen millions a year in hard money.

And now, from our stand-point of the Peace of 1783, let us give a parting glance at the ground over which we have passed. We see thirteen Colonies, united by interest, divided by habits, association, and tradition, engaging in a doubtful contest with one of the most powerful and energetic nations that ever existed; we see them begin, as men always do, with very imperfect conceptions of the time it would last, the length to which it would carry them, or the sacrifices it would impose; we see them boldly adopting some measures, timidly shrinking from others, — reasoning justly about some things, reasoning falsely about things equally important, — endowed at times with singular foresight, visited at times with incomprehensible blindness; boatmen on a mighty river, strong themselves and resolute and skilful, plying their oars manfully from first to last, but borne onward by a current which no human science could measure, no human strength could resist.

They knew that the resources of the country were exhaustless; and they threw themselves upon those resources in the only way by which they could reach them. Their bills of credit were the offspring of enthusiasm and faith. The enthusiasm grew chill, the faith failed. With a little more enthusiasm, the people would cheerfully have submitted to taxation; with a little more faith, the Congress would have taxed them. In the end, the people paid for the shortcomings of their enthusiasm by seventy millions of indirect taxation, — taxation through depreciation; the Congress paid for the shortcomings of its faith by the loss of confidence and respect. The war left the country with a Federal debt of seventy million dollars, and State debts of nearly twenty-six millions.

Could this have been avoided? Could they have done otherwise? It is easy, when the battle is won, to tell how victory might have been bought cheaper, — when the campaign is ended, to show what might perhaps have brought it to an earlier and more glorious close. It is easy for us, with the whole field before us, to see that from the beginning, from the very first start, although the formula was *Taxation*, the principle was *Independence;* but before we venture to pass sentence upon the shortcomings of our fathers, ought we not to pause and dwell awhile upon our own, — we who, in the fiercer contest through which we are passing, have so long failed to see, that, while the formula is *Secession*, the principle is *Slavery?*

LECTURE VI.

THE DIPLOMACY OF THE REVOLUTION.

WHEN a European speaks about the American Revolution, he speaks of it as the work of Washington and Franklin. These two names embody for his mind all the phases of the contest and explain its result. The military genius of Washington, going hand in hand with the civil genius of Franklin, fill the foreground of his picture. He has heard of other names and may remember some of them: but these are the only two which have taken their place in his memory, at the side of the great names of European history.

In part this is owing to the importance which all Europeans attach to the French alliance as one of the chief causes of our success. For then, as now, France held a place among the great powers of the world which gave importance to all her movements. With direct access to two of the principal theatres of European strife and easy access to the third, she never raised her arm without drawing immediate attention. If less powerful than England on the ocean, she was more powerful there than any other nation; and even England's superiority was often and sometimes successfully contested. The adoption by such a power of the cause of a people so obscure as the people of the "Thirteen Colonies" then were, was, in the opinion of European statesmen, decisive of its success. The fact of our actual poverty was known to all; few, if any, knew that we possessed exhaustless sources of wealth. Our weakness was on the surface; palpable, manifest, forcing itself upon attention; our strength lay out of sight, in rich veins, which none but eyes familiar with their secret windings could trace. Thus the French alliance, as the European interpreted it, was the alliance of wealth with poverty, of strength with weakness; a magnanimous recognition of efforts which, without that recognition, would have been vain. What, then, must have been the persuasive powers, the commanding genius of the man who procured that recognition?

Partly, also, this opinion is owing to the personal character and personal position of Franklin. Franklin was pre-eminently a wise man, wise in the speculative science and wise in the practical art of life. Something of the maturity of age seems to have tempered the liveliest sallies of his youth; and much of the vivacity of youth mingles with the sober wisdom of his age. Thoughtful and self-controlling at twenty, at seventy his ripe experience was warmed by a genial glow. He entered upon life with the feeling that he had a part to perform, and the conviction that his happiness would depend upon his performing it well. What that part was to be was his earliest study; and a social temperament, combining with a sound judgment, quickly taught him that the happiness of the individual is inseparably connected with the happiness of the species. Thus life became his study as a condition of happiness; man and nature, as the means of obtaining it. He sought to control his passions as he sought to control the lightning, that he might strip them of their power to harm. Sagacious in the study of causes, he was still more sagacious in tracing their connection with effects; and his speculations often lose somewhat of their grandeur by the simple and unpretending directness with which he adapts them to the common understanding and makes them minister to the common wants of life. The ambition which quickened his early exertions met an early reward. He was ambitious to write well, and he became one of the best writers in our language. He was ambitious of knowledge, and he laid it up in such stores that men sought his conversation in order to learn from him. He was ambitious of pecuniary independence, and he accumulated a fortune that made him master of his time and actions. He was ambitious of influence, and he obtained a rare control over the thoughts and the passions of men. He was ambitious of fame, and he connected his name with the boldest and grandest discovery of his age.

Living thus in harmony with himself, he enjoyed the rare privilege of living in equal harmony with the common mind and the advanced mind of his contemporaries. He entered into every-day wants and feelings as if he had never looked beyond them, and thus made himself the counsellor of the people. He appreciated the higher wants and nobler aspirations of our nature, and thus became the companion and friend of the philosopher. His interest in the present, and it was a deep and active interest, did not prevent him from looking forward with kindling sympathies to the future. Like the diligent husbandman of whom Cicero tells us, he could plant trees without expecting to see their fruit. If he detected folly with a keen eye, he did not revile it with a bitter heart. Human weakness, in his estimate of life, formed an inseparable part of human nature, the extremes of virtue often becoming the starting-points of vice; better treated, all of them, by playful ridicule than by stern reproof. He might never have gone with Howard in search of abuses; but he would have drawn such pictures of those near home, as would have made some laugh and some blush and all unite heartily in doing away with them. With nothing of the ascetic, he could impose self-denial and bear it. Like Erasmus, he may not have aspired to become a martyr; but in those long voyages and journeys, which, in his infirm old age, he undertook in his country's service, there was much of the sublimest spirit of martyrdom. His philosophy, a philosophy of observation and induction, had taught him caution in the formation of opinions, and candor in his judgments. With distinct ideas upon most subjects, he was never so wedded to his own views as to think that all who did not see things as he did must be wilfully blind. His justly tempered faculties lost none of their serene activity or gentle philanthropy by age. Hamilton himself, at thirty, did not labor with more earnestness at the formation of the Constitution, than Franklin at eighty-one; and as if in solemn record of his own interpretation of it, his last public act, with eternity full in view, was to head a memorial to Congress for the abolition of the slave-trade.

That such a man should produce a strong impression upon the excitable mind of France must be evident to every one who knows how excitable that mind is. But to understand his public as well as his personal position, not so much at the French court as at the court of French opinion, we must go back a dozen years and see what that opinion had been since the peace of 1763.

The treaty of Paris, like all treaties between equals founded upon the temporary superiority of one over the other, had deeply wounded, not the vanity only, but the pride of France. Humbled in the eyes of her rival, humbled in the eyes of Europe, she was still more profoundly humbled in her own. A barbed and venomous arrow had been haughtily left to rankle in the wound. For high-minded Frenchmen, it was henceforth the wisdom as well as the duty of France to prepare the means and hasten the hour of revenge. It was then that the eyes of French statesmen were first opened to the true position of the American Colonies. It was then that they first saw how much the prosperity of the parent state depended upon the sure and constant flow of wealth and strength from this exhaustless source. Then, too, they first saw that in obedience to the same law by which they had grown into strength, these Colonies, in due time, must grow into independence; and in this independence, in this severing of ties which they foresaw English pride would cling to, long after English avidity had stripped them of their natural strength, there was the prospect of full and sweet revenge.

Scarce a twelvemonth had passed from the signing of the treaty of Paris, when the first French emissary, an officer of the French navy, was already at his work in the Colonies. Passing to and fro, travelling here and there, moving from place to place as any common traveller might have done, his eyes and his ears were ever open, his note-book was ever in his hand, and, without awakening the suspicions of England, the first steps in a work to which the Duke of Choiseul looked forward as the crowning glory of his administration were wisely and surely taken. They were promptly followed up. The French Ambassador in England established relations with Colonial agents in London, which enabled him to follow the progress of the growing discontent and anticipate the questions which must soon be brought forward for decision. Franklin's examination before the House of Commons became the text of an elaborate despatch, harmonizing with the report of his secret agent, and opening a prospect which even the weary eyes of Louis XV. could not look upon without some return of the spirit that had won for his youth the long forfeited title of the Well-beloved! It was not the first time that the name of the great philosopher had been heard in the council-chamber of Versailles. But among the secret agents of France, we now meet for the first time the name of De Kalb, a name consecrated in American history by the life that he laid down for us on the fatal field of Camden. Scarce a step was taken by the English ministry that was not instantly communicated by the Ambassador in London to the French Minister at Versailles, with speculations, always ingenious, often profound, upon its probable results. Scarce a step was taken in the Colonies without attracting the instant attention of the French agent. Never were events more closely studied or their character better understood. When troops were sent to Boston, the English ministry was not without serious apprehensions of resistance. But when the tidings of their peaceful landing came, while the English were exulting in their success, the French Ambassador rejoiced that the wisdom of the Colonial leaders had withheld them from a form of opposition for which they were not yet ready. The English ministry was preparing to enter upon a system of coercion at the point of the bayonet. " If the Colonists submit under the pressure," said Choiseul, " it will only be in appearance and for a short time."

Meanwhile his active brain was teeming with projects: the letters of his agents were teeming with suggestions. Francès counsels caution, dreads the effects of hasty measures; for the Colonists have not yet learnt to look upon France as a friend, and premature action might serve only to bind them more firmly to England. Du Châtelet proposes that France and Spain, sacrificing their old colonial system, should open their colonial ports to the products of the English colonies; thus inflicting a fatal blow upon England's commerce, while they supplant her in the affections of the Colonists. A clerk in the department of commerce goes still further, advocating a full emancipation of the French colonies, both to throw off a useless burden and to increase the irritation of the English colonies by the spectacle of an independence which they were not permitted to share.

There is nothing in history more humiliating

than to see on what small hinges great events sometimes turn. Of all the disgraceful intrigues of a palace filled with intrigues from the day of its foundation, there is none half so disgraceful as the overthrow of the Duke of Choiseul in 1770. And yet vile as it was both by its motive and by its agents, it marks an important point in the progress of American independence. A bow more, a sarcasm less, might have confirmed the power of a man, whose deep-rooted hatred of England was fast hastening to its natural termination, an open rupture; and a premature rupture would have brought the Colonists into the field, either as the subjects of England or as the allies of France. To secure the dependence of the Colonies, England would have been compelled to make large concessions; and timely concessions might have put off the day of separation for another century. To secure the alliance of the Colonies, France would have been compelled to take upon herself the burden of the war; a French general might have led our armies; French gold might have paid our troops; we might have been spared the sufferings of Valley Forge, the humiliation of bankruptcy; but where would have been the wise discipline of adversity? and, if great examples be as essential to the formation of national as of individual character, what would the name of independence have been to us, without the example of our Washington?

French diplomacy had little to do with the

American events of the next five years. England, unconscious how near she had been to a new war with her old enemy, held blindly on in her course of irritation and oppression; the Colonies continued to advance by sure steps from resistance by votes and resolves to resistance by the sword. When Louis XVI. ascended the throne in 1774, and Vergennes received the portfolio of foreign affairs, domestic interests pressed too hard upon them to allow of their resuming at once the vast plans of the fallen minister. Unlike that minister, Vergennes, a diplomatist by profession, preferred watching and waiting events to the hastening or anticipating them. But to watch and wait events like those which were then passing in the Colonies without being drawn into the vortex was beyond the power of even his well-trained and sagacious mind. In 1775, a French emissary was again taking the measure of American perseverance; French ambassadors were again bringing forward American questions as the most important questions of their correspondence. That expression which has been put into so many mouths as a summing up of the value of a victory was applied in substance by Vergennes to the battle of Bunker Hill, — "Two more victories of this kind, and the English will have no army left in America."

And while thus tempted by this proof of American strength, his wavering mind was irritated by the apprehension of some sudden outbreak of

English arrogance; for the Ambassador wrote that Whigs and Tories might yet unite in a war against France in order to put an end to the troubles in the Colonies, — and no Frenchman had forgotten that England began the war of 1755 by an open violation of international law, by seizing three hundred French merchant ships and casting into prison ten thousand French sailors, before the declaration of hostilities. Thus events prepared the way for American diplomacy; and, more powerful than the prudence of Vergennes or the pacific longings of Louis XVI., compelled them to decide and act, when they would still gladly have discussed and waited.

And, moreover, a new element had been introduced into the councils of statesmen, or, rather, an element hitherto circumscribed and resisted had begun to act with irresistible force. Public opinion speaking through the press by eloquent pens, through coffee-houses and saloons by eloquent voices, called loudly for action in the name of humanity and in the still more exciting name of French honor. Little as most Frenchmen knew about America, they knew enough about England to believe that in her disputes with other nations she was apt to be in the wrong; and if with other nations, why not with her own colonies? The longing for revenge which ever since the treaty of Paris filled some corner of every French heart, grew stronger at the near approach of so abundant a harvest; nor did it lose any of its sweetness from the reflection that their enemy himself was doing what they could never have done alone to prepare it for them.

But humanity, too, was a powerful word. Men could not read Rousseau without being led to think more earnestly, if not always more profoundly, upon the laws of social organization. They could not read Voltaire without a clearer perception of abuses and a more vigorous contempt for the systems which had put the many into the hands of the few to be butchered or butchers at their will. They could not read Montesquieu without feeling that there was a future in store for them for which the long past had been patiently laboring, and longing, as they read, to hasten its coming. In that future, mankind were to rise higher than they had ever risen before; rulers and ruled were to act in fruitful harmony for their common good; the brightest virtues of Greece, the purest virtues of Rome, were to revive in some new form of society, not very definitely conceived by the understanding, but which floated in magnificent visions before the glowing imagination.

I hasten reluctantly over this part of my subject; for the formation of public opinion in France and its action upon government, even while all the forms of an almost absolute monarchy were preserved, is an important chapter in the history of European civilization. But hasten I must, merely calling attention to the existence of this element, and reminding my reader that, chronologically, of the two parts which composed this opinion, hatred for England had been at work ever since 1763, while sympathy with the Colonists was rather an individual than a public feeling till late in 1776.

It was at Versailles and not at Paris that action began. Vergennes's first step was to send another agent, no longer merely to observe and report, but to ascertain, though without compromising the French government, how far the Americans were prepared for French intervention. English suspicions were already awakened. Already the English Minister had informed the French Ambassador, upon the authority of a private letter of General Lee to General Burgoyne, that the Americans were sure of French aid. It was not without great difficulty that the new agent, De Bonvouloir, could find a safe conveyance. But by December he was already in Philadelphia, and, though still pretending to be a mere traveller, was soon in full communication with the Committee of Secret Correspondence.

The appointment of this committee on the 29th of November, 1775, is the beginning of the history of our foreign relations. Then began our attempts to gain admission into the great family of nations as an independent power,— attempts not always judiciously directed, attended in some instances with disappointment and mortification, but crowned at last with as full a measure of success as those who understood monarchy and Europe could have anticipated. Two of its members, Franklin and Dickinson, were already known abroad, where, at a later day, Jay also was to make himself an enduring name. The other two, Johnson and Harrison, enjoyed and merited a high Colonial reputation.

There can be but little doubt that Franklin's keen eye quickly penetrated the veil under which De Bonvouloir attempted to conceal his real character. It was not the first time that he had been brought into contact with French diplomacy, nor the first proof he had seen that France was watching the contest in the hope of abasing the power of her rival. While agent in London for four Colonies, — a true Ambassador, if to watch events, study character, give timely warning and wise counsel, is the office of an ambassador, — he had lived on a friendly footing with the French legation and profited by it to give them correct views of the character and feelings of the Colonies. And now, reducing the question to these simple heads, he asked, —

"How is France disposed towards us? if favorably, what assurance will she give us of it?

"Can we have from France two good engineers, and how shall we apply for them?

"Can we have, by direct communication, arms and munitions of war, and free entrance and exit for our vessels in French ports?"

But whatever reliance they may have placed on the French emissary, the committee were unwilling to confine themselves to this as the only means of opening communication with European powers. During a visit to Holland, Franklin had formed the acquaintance of a Swiss gentleman of the name of Dumas: a man of great learning and liberal sentiments, and whose social position gave him access to sure sources of information. To him he now addressed himself with the great question of the moment: "If we throw off our dependence upon Great Britain, will any court enter into alliance with us and aid us for the sake of our commerce?"

Such then, was the starting-point of our diplomatic history; the end and aim of all our negotiations; alliance and aid for the sake of our commerce.

But we should greatly mistake the character of the times if we suppose that this point was reached without many and warm debates. When the question was first started in Congress, that body was found to be as much divided upon this as upon any of the other subjects which it was called upon to discuss. With Franklin, one party held that, instead of asking for treaties with European powers, we should first conquer our independence, when those powers, allured by our commerce, would come and ask us; the other, with John Adams, that as our true policy and a mark of respect from a new nation to old ones, we ought to send ministers to every great court of Europe in order to obtain the recognition of our independence and form treaties of amity and commerce. Franklin, who had already outlived six treaties of "firm and lasting peace" and now saw the seventh swiftly approaching its end, might well doubt the efficacy of those acts to which his young and impetuous colleague attached so much importance. But in Congress the majority was with Adams, and for a while there was what Gouverneur Morris called a rage for treaties.

The Committee of Secret Correspondence, as I have already said, was formed in November, 1775. One of its first measures was to appoint agents, Arthur Lee for London, Dumas for the Hague, and, early in the following year, Silas Deane for France. Lee immediately opened relations with the French court by means of the French Ambassador in London; and Deane, on his arrival in France in June, followed them up with great intelligence and zeal. A million of livres was placed by Vergennes in the hands of Beaumarchais, who assumed the name of Hortalez & Co., and arranged with Deane the measures for transmitting it to America in the shape of arms and supplies.

And now the Declaration of Independence came to add the question of recognition to the question of aid. But recognition was a declaration of war, and to bring the French government to this deci sive pass required the highest diplomatic skill supported by dignity and weight of character. There was but one man in the new Republic in whom these qualities were combined, and that man was Franklin.

The history of diplomacy, with its long record of solemn entrances and brilliant processions, its dazzling pictures of thrones and courts, which make the head dizzy and the heart sick, has no scene half so grand as the entrance of this unattended, unushered old man into France in December, 1776. No one knew of his coming until he stood among them: and then, as they looked upon his serene yet grave and thoughtful face, — upon his gray hairs which carried memory back to the fatal year of Ramillies and the waning glories of the great Louis, — on the right hand which had written words of persuasive wisdom for prince and peasant, which had drawn the lightning from its home in the heavens, and was now stretched forth with such an imperial grasp to strip a sceptre they all hated of its richest jewel, — a feeling of reverential awe came over them, and they bowed themselves before him as, in the secret depths of their hearts, they had never bowed to emperor or king. "He is at Nantes. He is on the road," was whispered from mouth to mouth in the saloons of the capital, as his landing became known. Some asserted confidently that he had already reached Paris, others that he might be hourly expected. Then came the certainty: he had slept at Versailles the night of the 21st, had come to Paris at two the next afternoon, and now was at his lodgings in the Rue de l'Université.

No one, perhaps, was more surprised than Franklin to find himself the object of such universal attention. But no one knew better than he how to turn it to account for the accomplishment of his purpose. In a few days he withdrew to the quiet little village of Passy, at easy distance both from the city and the court; and, without endeavoring to increase the public curiosity by an air of mystery or seclusion, kept himself sufficiently in the background to prevent that curiosity from losing its stimulant by too great a familiarity with its object. Where men of science met for the discussion of a new theory or the trial of a new experiment, he was to be seen amongst them with an unpretending air of intelligent interest, and wise suggestions, never indiscreetly proffered, never indiscreetly withheld. Where humane men met to discuss some question of practical benevolence, or philosophers to debate some principle of social organization, he was always prepared to take his part with apt and far-reaching illustrations from the stores of his meditation and experience. Sometimes he was to be seen in places of amusement, and always with a genial smile, as if in his sympathy with the enjoyment of others he had forgotten his own perplexities and cares. In a short time he had drawn around him the best minds of the capital, and laid his skilful hand on the public pulse with an unerring accuracy of touch, which told him when to speak and when to be silent, when to urge and when to leave events to their natural progress. Ever active, ever vigilant, no opportunity was suffered to escape him, and yet no one whose goodwill it was desirable to propitiate was disgusted by injudicious importunity. Even Vergennes, who knew that his coming was the signal of a new favor to be asked, found in his way of asking it such a cheerful recognition of its true character, so considerate an exposition of the necessities which made it urgent, that he never saw him come without pleasure. If he had been a vain man, he would have enjoyed his position too much to make good use of it for the cause he came to serve. If he had been a weak man, he would have fallen under the control of the opinion which it was his office to guide. If he had not possessed a pure and genuine sympathy with human nature, he would not have been able, at the age of seventy, to enter into the feelings of a people so different from those among whom he had always lived. And if he had not been stimulated by earnest convictions, and governed by high principles, he would not have been able to withstand the frequent and insidious attempts that were made to shake his fortitude and undermine his fidelity. But in him, as in Washington, there was a rare predominance of that sound common-sense which is man's surest guide in his relations with events, and that firm belief in the progress of humanity which is his best reliance in his relations with men.

Congress had given him two associates in his commission to France, Silas Deane of Connecticut, and Arthur Lee of Virginia. Deane had been a member of Congress, was active, enterprising, and industrious; but his judgment was not sound, his knowledge of men not extensive, his acquaintance with great interests and his experience of great affairs insufficient for the important position in which he was placed. Lee had lived long in England, was an accomplished scholar, a good writer, familiar with the character of European statesmen and the politics of European courts; but vain, jealous, irritable, suspicious; ambitious of the first honors, and disposed to look upon every one who attracted more attention than himself as his natural enemy. Deane, deeply impressed with the importance of Franklin's social position for the fulfilment of their common duties, although energetic and active, cheerfully yielded the precedence to his more experienced colleague. Lee, conscious of his own accomplishments, regarded the deference paid to Franklin as an insult to himself, and promptly resumed in Paris the war of petty intrigue and secret accusation, which, a few years before, he had waged against him in England. In this vile course Congress soon unwittingly gave him a worthy coadjutor, by appointing, as Commissioner to Tuscany, Ralph Izard of South Carolina; who, without rendering a single service, without even going near the court to which he was accredited, continued for two years to draw his salary and abuse Dr. Franklin.

When Franklin reached Paris, he found that Deane had already made himself a respectable position; and that, through Caron de Beaumarchais, the brilliant author of Figaro, the French government had begun that system of pecuniary aid which it continued to render throughout the whole course of the war. Vergennes granted the commissioners an early interview, listened respectfully to their statements, asked them for a memorial to lay before the King, assured them of the personal protection of the French court, promised them every commercial facility not incompatible with treaty obligations with Great Britain, and advised them to seek an interview with the Spanish Ambassador. The memorial was promptly drawn up and presented. A copy of it was given to the Spanish Ambassador to lay before the court of Madrid. Negotiations were fairly opened.

But Franklin soon became convinced that the French government had marked out for itself a line of policy, from which, as it was founded upon a just appreciation of its own interests, it would not swerve; that it wished the Americans success, was prepared to give them secret aid in arms and money, and by a partial opening of its ports; but that it was compelled by the obligations of the family compact to time its own movements in a certain measure by those of Spain, and was not prepared to involve itself in a war with England by an open acknowledgment of the independence of the Colonies, until they had given fuller proof of the earnestness of their intentions and of their ability to bear their part in the contest. Nor was he long in perceiving that the French government was giving the Colonies money which it sorely needed for paying its own debts and defraying its own expenses; and thus, that however well-disposed it might be, there were certain limits beyond which it was not in its power to go. It was evident, therefore, to his just and sagacious mind, that to accept the actual policy of France as the gage of a more open avowal under more favorable circumstances, and to recognize the limits which her financial embarrassments set to her pecuniary grants, was the only course that he could pursue without incurring the danger of defeating his own negotiations by excess of zeal. Meanwhile there was enough to do in strengthening the ground already gained, in counteracting the insidious efforts of English emissaries, in correcting erroneous impressions, in awakening just expectations, in keeping up that public interest which had so large a part in the formation of public opinion, and in so regulating the action of that opinion as to make it bear with a firm and consistent and not unwelcome pressure upon the action of government. And in doing this he had to contend not only with the local difficulties of his position, but with the difficulty of uncertain communications, months often intervening between the sending of a despatch and the receiving of an answer. Thus newsmongers had abundant opportunities for idle reports and unfounded conjectures, and enemies ample scope for malicious falsehoods.

It was a happy circumstance for the new state that her chief representative was a man who knew when to wait with dignity, and when to act with energy; for it was this just appreciation of circumstances that gave him such a strong hold upon the mind of Vergennes, and imparted such weight to all his applications for aid. No sooner had Congress begun to receive money from Europe, than it began to draw bills upon its agents there, and often without any certainty that those agents would be in a condition to meet them. Bills were drawn on Mr. Jay when he was sent to Spain, and his already difficult position made doubly difficult and humiliating. Bills were drawn on Mr. Adams in Holland, and he was unable to pay them. But such was the confidence of the French court in the representations of Dr. Franklin, that he was not only enabled to honor all the drafts which were made upon him directly, but to relieve his less fortunate colleagues from the embarrassments in which the precipitation of their own government had involved them.

And thus passed the first twelve months of his residence in France, cloudy and anxious months, more especially during the summer of 1777, when it was known that Burgoyne was coming down by Lake Champlain, and Howe preparing for a great expedition to the northward. Then came the tidings that Howe had taken Philadelphia. "Say rather," said Franklin, with that air of conviction which carries conviction with it, "That Philadelphia has taken Howe." Men paused as they repeated his words, and suspended their judgment; and when the news of the battle of Germantown and the surrender of Burgoyne followed, they felt deeper reverence for the calm old man who had reasoned so wisely when all others desponded. It was on the 4th of December that these welcome tidings reached Paris, and the commissioners lost no time in communicating them to the court. The second day after, the secretary of the King's Council came to them with official congratulations. Negotiations were resumed and carried on rapidly, nothing but a desire to consult the court of Madrid being allowed to retard them; and on the 6th of February, 1778, the first treaty between the United States and a foreign power was signed with all the formalities which custom has attached to these acts. On the 20th of March, the commissioners were presented to the King.

Nor was it mere curiosity which filled the halls of the royal palace with an eager throng on that eventful day. These were the halls which had witnessed the gathering of powerful men and of great men to the footstool of the haughtiest of French kings; which had seen a Condé and a Turenne lay down their laurels at the royal feet; a Bossuet and a Boileau check the flow of independent thought to bask them in the beams of the royal smile; a Fénélon retiring with saddened brow to record for posterity the truths which he was not permitted to utter to the royal ear; a Racine, shrinking from the cold glance of the royal eye, and going home to die of a broken heart. Here Louis had signed the decree which sent his dragoons to force his Protestant subjects to the mass and the confessional. Here he had received with a smile of triumph the tidings that the Pope himself had been compelled to yield to his arrogant pretensions; and here he had listened in haughty state when one of the last of the glorious republics of the Middle Ages, the city of Columbus and Andrew Doria, which had once covered the Mediterranean with her ships, and sent forth her hardy mariners as from a nursery of brave men to impart their skill and communicate their enterprising genius to the rest of Europe, humbled herself before him through her Doge, as, bowing his venerable head, the old man asked pardon in her name, not for the wrongs that she had committed, but for the wrongs that she had borne.

And now, up those marble stairs, through those

tapestried halls, came three men of humble birth, two of whom had wrought for their daily bread and eaten it in the sweat of their brows, to receive their recognition as the representatives of a power which had taken its place among the nations, not by virtue of the divine right of kings, but in the name of the inalienable rights of the people. Happy would it have been for the young King who sat in Louis's seat if he could have understood the full meaning of his act, and recognized at the same moment the claims of his own people to participate in that government which, deriving its strength from their labor, could have no security but in their love.

Nothing could have demonstrated more clearly the wisdom of Franklin's confidence in the sincerity of the French government, than the generous and liberal terms of the treaty. No present advantage was taken of the dependent condition of their new ally; no prospective advantage was reserved for future contingencies. Only one condition was stipulated, — and that as much in the interest of the Colonies as of France, — that they should never return to their allegiance. Only one reciprocal obligation was assumed, that neither party should make peace with England without the knowledge and consent of the other. All the rest was full and free reciprocation in the future, and the assurance of efficient aid in the present; no ambiguities, no doubtful expressions, no debatable ground for interpretation to build upon and weave the mazes of her subtile web; but clear, distinct, and definite; a mutual specification of mutual duties and mutual rights; equal could not have treated more firmly with equal than this new power, as yet unrecognized in the congress of nations, treated with the oldest monarchy of Europe.

I have already alluded to the rage for treaties which prevailed for a while in Congress. It was this that sent William and Arthur Lee upon their bootless errands to Vienna and Berlin; Francis Dana to St. Petersburg; John Jay to encounter embarrassment and mortification at Madrid; and gave Ralph Izard an opportunity to draw an unearned salary, through two successive years, from the scanty funds of the Congressional banker at Paris.

Jay's situation was peculiarly trying. He had been Chief Justice of New York, President of Congress, had written some of the most eloquent state papers that were issued in the name of that body whose state papers were ranked by Chatham among the best that ever were written, and, at a personal sacrifice, had exchanged a position of honor and dignity at home for a doubtful position abroad. A clear-headed, industrious, decided man, he had to contend, for more than two years, with the two qualities most alien to his nature, — habitual dilatoriness and diplomatic reticence.

Spain, like France, had marked out a path for herself, and it was impossible to move her from it.

He obtained some money to help him pay some of the drafts of Congress, but neither treaty nor recognition. "They have taken four years," wrote Franklin, "to consider whether they would treat with us: I would give them forty, and let us mind our own business." And still viewing the question as he had viewed it in the beginning, he wrote in his diary in May, 1782: "It seems to me that we have, in most instances, hurt our credit and importance by sending all over Europe, begging alliances and soliciting declarations of our independence. The nations, perhaps, from thence seemed to think that our independence is something they have to sell, and that we do not offer enough for it."*

The most important European event in its American bearings, after the recognition by France, was the armed neutrality of the Northern powers; a court intrigue in Russia, though a sober act in Spain, — and which was followed in December, 1780, by the addition of Holland to the open enemies of England.

Attempts had already been made to form a treaty with Holland; first through William Lee, with such prospect of success as to induce Congress to send Henry Laurens to the Hague to continue the negotiations. Laurens was captured by an English cruiser, and soon after John Adams was directed to take his place. At Paris, Adams had

---

* Franklin's Works, Vol. IX. p. 284, Sparks's edition.

failed singularly as a negotiator; lending a ready ear to Lee, hardly attempting to disguise his jealousy of Franklin, and enforcing his own opinions in a manner equally offensive to the personal feelings of the minister and the traditional usages of the court. But at the Hague he found a field better suited to his ardent temperament, and, backed by the brilliant success of the campaign of 1781, and the votes of the House of Commons in favor of reconciliation, succeeded in obtaining a public recognition in the spring of 1782, and concluding a treaty in the autumn.

All these things were more or less upon the surface, — done and doing more or less openly. But under the surface the while, and known only to those directly concerned therein, were covert attempts on the part of England to open communications with Franklin by means of personal friends. There had been nothing but the recognition of our independence that England would not have given to prevent the alliance with France; and now there was nothing that she was not ready to do to prevent it from accomplishing its purpose. And it adds wonderfully to our conception of Franklin to think of him as going about with this knowledge, in addition to the knowledge of so much else in his mind; this care, in addition to so many other cares, ever weighing upon his heart. Little did jealous, intriguing Lee know of these things; petulant, waspish Izard still less. A mind less sagacious than Franklin's might have grown suspicious under the influences that were employed to awaken his distrust of Vergennes. And a character less firmly established would have lost its hold upon Vergennes amid the constant efforts that were made to shake his confidence in the gratitude and good faith of America. But Franklin, who believed that timely faith was a part of wisdom, went directly to the French Minister with the propositions of the English emissaries, and frankly telling him all about them, and taking counsel of him as to the manner of meeting them, not only stripped them of their power to harm him, but converted the very measures which his enemies had so insidiously, and, as they deemed, so skilfully prepared for his ruin, into new sources of strength.

Of the proffers of mediation in which first Spain and then Russia and the German Emperor were to take so important a part, as they bore no fruit, they may safely be passed over in silence; simply observing, as we pass, how little European statesmen understood the business in which they were so ready to intermeddle, and what a curious spectacle Catharine and Kaunitz present, seeking to usher into the congress of kings the first true representative of that great principle of popular sovereignty which was to make all their thrones totter and tremble under them. And observing, too, that it furnished that self-dependence of John Adams which too often degenerated into arrogance an occasion to manifest itself in a nobler light; for he refused to take part in the discussions in any other character than as the representative of an independent power.

Meanwhile, events were hastening the inevitable termination. In Europe, England stood alone, without either secret or open sympathy. In June, 1779, a war with Spain had followed the French war of 1778. In July, 1780, the "armed neutrality" had defined the position of the Northern powers adversely to her maritime pretensions. War was declared with Holland in December of the same year. In America, the campaign of 1781 had stripped her of her Southern conquests, and effaced the impression of her early victories. At home her people were daily growing more and more restless under the pressure of taxation; and even the country gentlemen, who had stood by the ministry so long in the hope of transferring their own burden to the shoulders of their American brethren, began to give evident tokens of discontent. It was clear that England must consent to peace. And yet she still stood bravely up, presenting a bold front to each new enemy; a grand spectacle in one light, for there is always something grand in indomitable courage; but a sad one in the true light, and one from which, a hundred years hence, the philosophic historian will turn with a shudder, when summing up all these events, and asking what all this blood was shed for, he shows that the only principle at stake on her part was that pernicious claim to control the industry of the world which, had she succeeded, would have dried up the sources of prosperity in America, as it is fast drying them up in Ireland and in India.*

Nor was peace less necessary to her rival. The social revolution which the two last reigns had rendered inevitable, was moving with gigantic strides towards its bloody consummation. The last well-founded hope of reforms that should probe deep enough to anticipate revolution had disappeared with Turgot. The statesmanship of Vergennes had no remedy for social disease. It was a statesmanship of alliances, and treaties, and wars, — traditional and sometimes brilliant, — but all on the surface, leaving the wounded heart untouched, the sore spirit unconsoled. The financial skill of Necker could not reach the evil. It was mere banking skill, and nothing more; very respectable in its time and place, filling a few mouths more with bread, but failing to see, although told of it long ago by one who never erred, that "man does not live by bread alone." The finances were in hopeless disorder. The resources of the country were almost exhausted. Public faith had been strained to the utmost. National forbearance had been put to humiliating tests under the last reign by the partition of Poland and the peace of Kaïnardji; and

---

* I cannot deny myself the pleasure of referring in this connection to Mr. Carey's admirable exposition of this fact in his "Principles of Political Science."

the sense of self-respect had not been fully restored by the American war. And although no one yet dreamed of what seven swift years were to bring forth, all minds were agitated by a mysterious consciousness of the approaching tempest.

In 1782, the overtures of England began to assume a more definite form. Franklin saw that the time for decisive action was at hand, and prepared himself for it with his wonted calm and deliberate appreciation of circumstances. That France was sincere he could not doubt, after all the proofs she had given of her sincerity; nor could he doubt that she would concur heartily in preparing the way for a lasting peace. He had the instructions of Congress to guide him in what America would claim; and his own mind was quickly made up as to what England must yield. Four points were indispensable,— a full recognition of independence; an immediate withdrawal of her troops; a just settlement of boundaries, those of Canada being confined, at least, to the limits of the act of 1774; and the freedom of the fisheries. Without these there could be no treaty. But to make the work of peace sure, he suggested, as equally useful to both parties, four other concessions, the most important of which were the giving up of Canada, and securing equal privileges in English and Irish ports to the ships of both nations. The four necessary articles became the real basis of the treaty.

John Adams, John Jay, and Henry Laurens

were joined with him in the commission. Jay was first on the ground, reaching Paris in June; Adams came in October; Laurens not till November, when the preliminary articles were ready for signature. They all accepted Franklin's four articles as the starting-point. But unfortunately they did not all share Franklin's well-founded confidence in the sincerity of the French government. Jay's mind was embittered by the tergiversations of Spain. Adams had not forgotten his former disagreements with Vergennes, and hated Franklin so bitterly that he could hardly be prevailed upon to treat him with the civility which his age and position demanded, much less with the consideration which the interest of his country demanded. Both Jay and Adams were under the influence of that hostility to France which prevailed as extensively in the Colonies as in the mother country, — a hostility which neither of them was at sufficient pains to conceal, although neither of them perhaps was fully conscious of it. It was this feeling that kept them both aloof from the French Minister, and made them so accessible to English influences. And it was a knowledge of this feeling which three years later suggested to George III. that well-known insinuation about Adams's dislike to French manners, which would have been a scathing sarcasm if it had not been an inexcusable impertinence.

The English agents availed themselves skilfully

of those sentiments; sowing suspicions, fostering doubts, and not shrinking, there is strong reason to suppose, from gross exaggeration and deliberate falsehood. The discussion of articles, like all such discussions, was protracted by the efforts of each party to make the best terms, and the concealing of real intentions in the hope of extorting greater concessions. But England was really prepared to yield all that America was really prepared to claim. France, in spite of the suspicions of Adams and Jay, was really sincere; and on the 30th of November, 1782, the preliminary articles were signed.

Franklin's position was difficult and delicate. He knew the importance of peace. He knew that the instructions of Congress required perfect openness towards the French Minister. He believed that the Minister deserved, both by his past kindness and present good intentions, to be treated with perfect openness. But both his colleagues were against him. What should he do? Refer the difference to Congress, and meanwhile hold the country in painful and expensive suspense? What could he do but submit, as he had done through life, to the circumstances which he could not control, and give the appearance of unanimity to an act which the good of his country required to be unanimous?

He signed the preliminaries, and submitted to the reproach of personal and public ingratitude as he had submitted to the taunts of Wedderburn.

History has justified his confidence; the most careful research having failed to bring to light any confirmation of the suspicions of his colleagues. And Vergennes, though nettled for the moment, understood Franklin's position too well to lay the act at his door as an expression of a real opinion. Much time and long discussions were still required to convert the preliminaries into a final treaty; for the complicated interests of England, France, and Spain were to be taken into the account. But each party longed for peace; each party needed it; and on the 3d of September, 1783, another treaty of Paris gave once more the short-lived though precious boon to Europe and America.

During Franklin's residence at the court of France, and mainly through his influence, that court had advanced to Congress three millions of livres a year as a loan, had increased it to four millions in 1781, had the same year added six millions as a free gift to the three millions with which she began, and become their security for the regular payment of the interest upon a loan of ten millions to be raised in Holland.*

Nor will it be inappropriate to add that before he sailed upon his mission to France, he called in all the money he could command in specie (between three and four thousand pounds in all), and put it into the public treasury as a loan; and that

* In all, eighteen millions as a loan, and nine millions as a free gift.

while the young men, Adams and Jay, were provided with competent secretaries of legation, he, though bowed down by age and disease, and with ten times their work to do, was left to his own resources, and, but for the assistance of his grandson, would have been compelled to do it all with his own hand.

It has been said that a soldier accustomed to conquer with Claverhouse, when, under a new leader, he saw victory wavering at the decisive moment, exclaimed in his indignation, "O for one hour of Dundee!" Might not we, as we look at the clouds which lower so ominously on our eastern horizon, exclaim with equal reason, O for **one hour of Franklin?**

LECTURE VII.

THE ARMY OF THE REVOLUTION.

THE army of the Revolution! What remembrances this name awakens! What fireside tales, charms of childhood, stimulants of youth, fanning the flame of young ambition, kindling the glow of early patriotism, come crowding upon our memories as we utter these words. Many of us grew up in the midst of men who could tell us all about that army; who could tell us how the redcoats looked as they marched with measured tread, to the note of bugle and drum, up the grassy slope of Bunker Hill, and what a gleam of exultation flashed along the American line, when, through the veil of smoke, the broken ranks were seen rushing madly towards the shore, to the sharp, quick ring of the American guns; who remembered the sad march through the Jerseys; who had felt the keen December blasts of Trenton, and the keener tooth of hunger on the bleak hillside of Valley Forge; who had looked upon the face of Washington in gloom, and peril, and triumph. These, for many of us, were the old men of our youth, men with a wooden leg, or a single arm, or a single eye; some of them with a deep scar on their faces; all with something about them that gave them a mysterious power over our young imaginations, and bore witness to their tales of hardship and danger. But now that questions crowd upon us there are none left to answer them. Now, when often a single word would solve perplexing doubts and set a whole controversy at rest, the thousand lips that once might have uttered it are sealed forever. Gone, nearly all gone! the few that remain, eight or ten at the utmost, already more than half hidden by the deepening shadows of the grave. Temper the chilling darkness of those shadows while yet you may, those of you, if any there be, who live where kind offices can do it; temper it with soothing words, and gentle acts, and that reverence which is so grateful to age; for generation after generation may pass away before the world shall look upon such men again.

One of the most pernicious errors concerning America into which the English government was led by its ill-informed informers, was, that there was no material there out of which an army could be made. A Colonel Grant, forgetting how the regulars had run at the Monongahela, while a Virginia volunteer was vainly endeavoring to rally them and Virginia militiamen were holding the enemy at bay, kept Parliament on a roar with ludicrous pictures of American cowardice. Voice after voice took up the welcome tale, still believed by British soldiers when they marched to Concord, and not fully disbelieved till they had marched up Bunker Hill. No country, indeed, ever possessed better materials for an army than the thirteen Colonies; hardy yeomen, robust mechanics, bold sailors, accustomed from boyhood to the use of the gun, accustomed through half their lives to long journeys on foot or on horseback, at all seasons and in all weathers. Hundreds of them had fought by the side of English soldiers in the old French war; hundreds more had fought the Indians alone in frontier wars. Tales of hair-breadth escapes, of perilous marches, of patient ambuscades, of all the forms of primitive warfare, were as familiar to their winter-evening firesides as Homer's tale of Troy to a Greek banquet. Washington's name had reached the royal closet. Putnam was already the hero of many stirring legends. Prescott had brought back from the French war a high reputation for gallantry. Gridley had made himself a name at Louisburg as an engineer of rare attainments. Pomroy had taken his place with Ward and Stark; while scattered over the country were hundreds less known than they, but heroes, each of them, of his own village circle. There was not a well-fought field to which some American could not point with pride. There were dishonorable fields on which none but Americans had preserved their honor. It was from materials like these that United America was to form her army. It was with a full knowledge that these materials existed and could be reached, that the leaders of our Revolution began the war.

One grave doubt may have occurred to some of them. Could these men, admirable as they were for frontier soldiers, become regular soldiers? Did not their habits of social equality unfit them for the nice distinctions and inflexible lines of military subordination? Would they obey, as a soldier must obey, the man who had worked by their sides in the cornfield or in the workshop, and who owed his epaulets to their votes?

Here, indeed, was a difficulty inherent in the nature of the people, interwoven with their virtues, deep rooted in their manners and customs, their modes of action and their modes of thought; acting unequally in different parts of the country, it is true; stronger in the Eastern States than in the Middle or Southern States; but strong enough in all to awaken serious anxiety in those who saw from the beginning that the war was to be fought with trained masses, — the victory to be won, if won at all, by that firm, patient, and resolute intrepidity which nothing but discipline can inspire.

But no sooner had it become evident that force would enter into the dispute than the people had begun to prepare themselves for their part by forming independent companies and organizing the militia. Some of these independent companies were drilled by British deserters; and it is not one of the least characteristic traditions of the period that a young Rhode Island Quaker, who had joined one of them, not being able to procure a musket at home, came to Boston under the pretext of collecting an old debt, attended the morning and evening drills and parades of the British troops till his eye had become familiar with their evolutions, and carried back with him an English sergeant as drill-master for his company, and an English musket to drill with. The whole country was astir; everywhere musterings and trainings, everywhere the sound of fife and drum, everywhere the hum of preparation.

Massachusetts organized her militia in October, 1774, and out of her militia came those bands of minute-men who did such good service during these anxious days. A name well known afterwards throughout the length and breadth of the land, the name of Timothy Pickering, meets us for the first time, in connection with a plan for drilling these minute-men in battalions and paying them out of the public treasury. Their drill was a social and religious exercise, followed almost always by a sermon and sometimes by a banquet. It is almost impossible to read how the three were mingled and not think of the solemn banquets of Homer's Greeks auspicated by sacrifice and libation and prayer, and followed by an impetuous rush upon the enemy. The minister descended from the pulpit to take his place at the head of his company or even in the ranks. In the company of minute-men of Danvers the deacon was captain and the minister lieutenant; for none, in those days, seemed to doubt that duty to God comprised duty to the state which secured them the privilege of worshipping God according to their own interpretation of his word. And thus it came to pass that when the alarm was sounded on the night of the 18th of April, thousands answered the call.

Already, ten days before the battle of Lexington, the Provincial Congress of Massachusetts had resolved that an army ought to be raised, and had appointed delegates to ask New Hampshire, Rhode Island, and Connecticut to co-operate with them in raising it. And meeting again as soon as they could after the battle, children of the Puritans as they were, the knowledge that it was Sunday did not prevent them from setting themselves earnestly to their work. The army was fixed at 30,000 men; the Massachusetts contingent at 13,600.

But already the army was gathering. Already from every town and village men of strong hearts and stern resolve were crowding the roads to Boston. The plough was left in the furrow, the plane on the work-bench. Father and son marched side by side; the preacher in the midst of his flock. "Numbers passed our river yesterday at the upper ferry," says a colonel of Newburyport, writing for orders. "Four companies went through this town on their way to you: we have a party of men from this town; upwards of one hundred on their march to you." And not from Massachusetts only. "The ardor of our people is such that they cannot be kept back," writes the Committee of Correspondence from Connecticut.

The fight was still going on when the tidings that the British were out reached Rhode Island. In the placid little hamlet of East Greenwich the Kentish Guards were instantly mustered, and, pushing forward, had already reached the banks of the Pawtucket, when an order from the Tory Governor, Wanton, called them back. Two of them, recent outcasts from the Quaker meeting, held on, and arrived at Roxbury in time to see the inpouring of the yeomanry, and hear lips, still stern with the excitement of battle, describe the disastrous flight of the British and the eager pursuit of the Americans. By the 21st, twenty thousand men were assembled.

O for a warning voice, a voice from history, a voice from philosophy, a voice from some one read in the contradictions of the human heart, to say to their leaders, "now is your time: make sure of them all for the war, the whole war, in this, the moment of fiery enthusiasm; for too surely will the moment of discouragement follow, when the stout-hearted will hesitate, the faint-hearted will turn back." But no such voice was heard. "If I have not enlisting orders immediately," writes Ward on the 24th, "I shall be left alone." The orders came: the enlistments began; the rolls were filled; but not for the war.

Here, then, is the first, the fundamental error: an error never to be repaired. You will readily understand why men fell into this error. They did not believe that the war would last. They did not see whither the road they had entered on would necessarily lead them. "A few acts of firmness," said the King and his ministers, "and the Colonists will submit."* "A resolute, unanimous resistance," said the Colonists, "and the King and his ministers will give way." Equal short-sightedness, equal infatuation on both sides, and an eight years' war for illustration and commentary.†

Who should command this motley army, was one of the first questions that presented itself; who should clothe and feed it, was another. Congress had not yet adopted it. Massachusetts had called for it: but still it was the army of Massachusetts, with the equally independent armies of New Hampshire, of Connecticut, and of Rhode Island, for voluntary auxiliaries. Gradually, as the necessity of a single head came to be felt, General Ward, the Massachusetts general, was accepted as com-

---

* Washington to Bryan Fairfax (Works, Vol. V. p. 248).

† See particularly a letter of R. H. Lee to Washington (Sparks's Correspondence of the Revolution, I. 52).

mander-in-chief. But each Colony continued to provide for its own men.

It soon became evident that something more was required to infuse a spirit of unity into elements like these. There could be no strength without union, and of union the only adequate representative was the Continental Congress. To induce the Congress to adopt the army in the name of the United Colonies was one of the objects towards which John Adams soon directed his attention. With the question of adoption came the question of commander-in-chief; and here personal ambition and sectional jealousies manifest themselves in ways whereon it would be useful to dwell.

Washington's was, of course, the first name that occurred to Northern and Southern men alike; for it was the only name that had won a continental reputation. But some New-England men thought that this New-England army would do better service under a New-England commander; and some Southern men were not prepared to see Washington put so prominently forward. Then New England was divided against herself. Ward had warm advocates, and John Hancock had aspirations for the high place which were not always concealed from the keen eyes of his colleagues. Among Washington's opponents were some " of his own household," Pendleton of Virginia being the most persistent of them all. At last John Adams moved to adopt the army, and appoint a general;

and a few days after — Thursday, the 5th of June, the interval having been actively used to win over the little band of dissenters — Washington was chosen by a unanimous vote.

The next day the organization of the army was reduced to a definite plan, two major-generals, eight brigadiers, with an adjutant-general, a quartermaster-general, a paymaster-general, and a chief engineer. On the 19th, the number of major-generals was raised to four.

It was not without new heart-burnings that these lists were filled up. Ward, though propitiated with the first place on the roll of major-generals, could not forget that he once cherished aspirations to a place still higher. John Hancock is said never to have felt cordially towards John Adams after the day which had nipped his hopes of military glory so remorselessly in the bud. Spencer was unwilling to make way for Putnam; Thomas, for Pomroy. Similar pretensions and similar piques displayed themselves as the work of organization went on. There were discontented colonels as well as discontented generals; captains who would have been colonels, and lieutenants who thought it hard that they were not made captains. Harder still was it for a Massachusetts soldier to serve under an officer from Rhode Island; a New-Hampshire soldier under an officer from Connecticut.* Hardest of all, when, at a later day, New-

* Washington to Reed, November 8, 1775 (Sparks, III. 151); also, December 25, 1775 (Ibid., III. 214).

Yorkers and Pennsylvanians and the aristocratic Marylanders, with their smart uniforms and soldierly bearing, found themselves mixed up with the plain democratic farmers of New England.

It was at two o'clock in the afternoon of the 2d of July, that Washington reached Cambridge. You all know where his head-quarters were.* You all know what rich associations have been added to the associations which his nine months going in and out thereat have given those doors. You all know that words of classic eloquence have been written under that hallowed roof; that Washing-

---

* Who will gather the mosses from this old manse, and tell us the story of the Colonial days of the wealthy Vassal, — of the siege of Boston days, with Washington for the central figure, — of the early days of the Republic, when Craigie sat at the head of the board, and Talleyrand was his guest, — of the later day, when Everett collected his little class of advanced Grecians around him in the southeast room on the first floor, Emerson among them, — when Sparks, first of our true laborers, set himself to the illustration of our Revolutionary history by documents, and wrote the life of Washington in the very place in which Washington had passed some of its most memorable hours, — and, last of all, of the days of "Hyperion," and "Evangeline," and "Hiawatha," days of earnest thought and deep feeling, which have found expression in imperishable verse, and of genial intercourse which gives us pleasant glimpses of Hawthorne and Felton and Agassiz and the two Sumners — now, alas! but one — and Lowell and Holmes and Curtis and Read and Norton and Fields, and of pilgrims, too, from afar off in our own broad land and from still farther beyond the sea, who have come to look upon the great poet in his home and thank him for the noble words he has written for the cheering and consolation of his brother man?

ton's own words and the record of Washington's acts have come thence in enduring forms to take their place at the head of the monuments of our history; and that in the still watches of the night, voices of tender melody have borne from it soothing to the sorrowful, strength to the weak, heavenward aspirations to those who had looked too steadfastly upon earth; lessons that have mingled harmoniously with the kindred teachings of Wordsworth and Tennyson; which have been welcomed by ears familiar with the lines of Goethe and Schiller; and ever true to the universal language of the heart, retain their power to purify and inspire in the tongue of Dante and Petrarch.

Washington's first call was for the returns of his army. They gave him 16,770 in all; fit for duty, 13,743. Never had their spirits been higher. Officers and men seemed to catch a new enthusiasm from his presence; for men know when they have a man at their head, and no one doubted but what there was a man there now. Every day he was among them on his mettled charger, his commanding form towering above every other in its blue and buff, with rich epaulets on each shoulder, a cockade in his hat, and by his side a sword already tried in battle. War had not yet put on all its terrors. There were some men killed from time to time; there were some wounded; breastworks and redoubts blocked up the fields and highways; and here and there cannon looked down from their embrasures with a frown, and muskets gleamed menacingly above a parapet. But it was the opening of a noble epic, when the feelings are yet calm enough to allow the eye to dwell thoughtfully upon the novel beauty of the scene.

The hills lay all round the beleaguered city as they lie there now. Thousands of trees that have long since disappeared mingled their luxuriant foliage in grateful shades. The green grass was springing abundantly; and as the English looked out from their prison-house, they saw village spires, and cottage-roofs, and those sweet aspects of nature which fill the heart with longings for peace and rest. But all over those enamelled fields, and all over those green hillsides, were thousands of little fabrics suddenly called into life by the wants of the hour; huts decked with boughs and branches; huts formed of interwoven branches and thatched with leaves; huts of logs, board, stone, turf, brush; — melting into the landscape as if they had always formed a part of it, but with now and then a flash of steel, or a tap of a drum, or a blast of bugle from among them, which reminded you startlingly of the purpose for which they were there. In one part, too, ranged in the measured lines of a regular encampment, were real tents and real *marquees*, where the Rhode-Islanders were fast making themselves real soldiers under the eye of their Quaker general.

Is it hard to divine the feelings with which the

Americans looked on their devoted town, as they called to mind all that she had done for their holy cause, all that she had suffered rather than yield? And as the morning gun waked the echoes of the hills, and trumpet and drum frightened the birds from their early song, may not some indignant son of the Puritans have added a war-hymn to his prayers, in words, perhaps, like these? —

> O never, never, never,
>   Shall you bend us to your will;
> Though your giant arm may crush us,
>   We will scorn and hate you still!
>
> The souls that we inherit
>   Fear not the conqueror's chain;
> However firm your fetters,
>   We will tear them off again!
>
> Where'er a mountain rears its head
>   We'll fight like mountaineers;
> Where'er a valley opes its arms,
>   We'll gird it with our spears.
>
> On every river-bank we'll rear
>   A bulwark of the slain;
> And fire and sword shall guard our homes,
>   Till we come back again.
>
> On, then, to Freedom's battle!
>   Gray sires and striplings, — all!
> Free homes shall welcome those who live,
>   And angels those who fall.

Summer wore away. Autumn came with chilling, precursory blasts, soon to grow chiller as they flew over the snow. The leaves withered on window and doorway; the thatch fell from the roof. Men's hearts fainted within them. They remembered their cheerful firesides, their huskings and merry-makings; how pleasant it had been in other days to fill up the barn and crib till the corn and the grain ran over; how the cider had flowed in rivulets from their apple-presses. They bethought them too of the wives and children that looked to them for food and protection, and they sighed for home. Had there been battles and marches to vary the scene, they might have found relief in the excitement. But this dull monotony of camp-life fell with double weight upon men accustomed to work all day in the occupations of their choice, and go home at night to a cheerful fire and abundant table. The poetry was gone; the hard, stern prose was there, never harder, never sterner, than when strong men suffer want and privation together. As winter advanced their sufferings increased. They suffered from want of clothing, and still more from want of wood. Trees were cut down, fences pulled up, everything that could be made to burn was converted into fuel; and still, hundreds were compelled to eat their food raw. And to complete the picture, I must reluctantly add that those who had wood, or clothing, or provisions to sell, asked the highest prices and demanded the promptest payment.

From the beginning Washington had called the

attention of Congress to the condition of the army, and as winter approached his calls grew more urgent. He had found it impossible to induce either officers or soldiers to subscribe the Articles of War. He had been compelled to assume the responsibility of settling the rank of the officers, and numbering the regiments. The terms of enlistment of the Rhode Island and Connecticut troops expired on the 1st of December. None were bound beyond the 1st of January. Yet it was not till the middle of October that a committee of Congress came to Cambridge and set itself seriously to the task of reorganization. The subject had already been considered in a council of war, and the council and committee agreed in fixing the number of regiments at twenty-six, exclusive of riflemen and artillery; each regiment to consist of eight companies, and the whole to compose an army of 20,372 men to face the English in Boston.

It was evident that a portion of the new army must be drawn from the old. But would men with such experience of war as our soldiers were now going through be willing to go through it again?

It was equally evident that every enlistment ought to be made for the war, and every nerve strained to form a permanent army. "If Congress had given a large bounty, and engaged the soldiery during the war," wrote General Greene in December, "the continent would be much securer, and the measure cheaper in the end." But Congress was still groping in the dark, wasting time and energy in discussions and half-measures, — the unconscious victim of two fatal errors, — sectional jealousies and the dread of a standing army. An army raised, paid, clothed, fed, disciplined, and governed in the name of Congress, seemed to some a dangerous encroachment upon State rights; to others, a dangerous weapon in the hands of a successful general. "If our enemies prevail, which our dissensions may occasion," wrote Governor Trumbull of Connecticut, "our jealousies will then appear frivolous, and all our disputed claims of no value to either side." "The fate of kingdoms depends upon the just improvement of critical moments," wrote General Greene. . . . "The temper and feelings of men can be wrought up to a certain pitch, and then, like all transitory things, they sicken and subside. This is the time for a wise legislator to avail himself of the advantage which the favorable disposition of the people gives him, to execute whatever sound policy dictates. It is not in the province of mortals to reduce human events in politics to a certainty. It is our duty to provide the means to obtain our ends, and leave the event to Him who is the all-wise governor and disposer of the universe." Many, too, were terrified at the expense. "What signifies our being frightened at the expense?" wrote General Greene; "if we succeed, we gain all; if we are conquered, we lose all." And speaking of Colonial jealousies, "It grieves me that such jealousies should prevail. If they are nourished, they will sooner or later sap the foundations of the Union and dissolve the connection. God in mercy avert so dreadful an evil."

But while some clearer minds saw things in their true light, the public mind had not yet been thoroughly awakened to a perception of duties or responsibilities, and Congress seldom ventured far in advance of the public mind. Therefore the new army, like the old, was enlisted for a limited period.

Fortunately, the feeling in the country was still strong. In December, when the Connecticut troops went home "by shoals," the people on the road refused to give them food or shelter. Many of the old soldiers were ready to enlist for another year, but asked a short furlough before they returned to duty. Never were Washington and his generals less to be envied than during the autumn and winter of 1775, with an old army to disband and a new army to enroll within point-blank shot of an enemy perfectly armed and disciplined, and led by experienced officers.* Howe's blindness is almost incredible. But Washington's calm self-possession is sublime.

All through October and November the work of

---

* For some of the difficulties referred to, see Washington's letter to the President of Congress. (Sparks, III. 156; Correspondence of Rev., I. 82.)

enlistment went on; sometimes so briskly as to awaken strong hopes; sometimes so slowly as to excite serious apprehensions. Dissatisfied officers discouraged enlistments. Important as it was to conciliate the good will of the old troops, the dearth of arms was so great, that on dismissing the men it was found necessary to retain their arms without regard to the distinction between public and private property. Often, too, the price set upon them by the public appraisers fell below the original cost. And of the arms thus hardly got, half were mere fowling-pieces of different bores, and nearly all of them without bayonets.

At last December came. The militia was called in to take the place of the disbanded troops. Everything was confusion and disorder. But in spite of confusion and disorder and discouragement, Washington went calmly on, the old army was dissolved, and by the beginning of the year a new army had taken its place.

And thus ended the first army of the Revolution. Hurriedly formed in an hour of intense excitement, composed principally of farmers and mechanics, men of some means and accustomed to labor, it had never acquired much skill of evolution or much exactness of discipline; it had fought no battles after Bunker Hill, had made no marches or expeditions; but it had kept a veteran army, supported by a large fleet, closely penned up for eight months within the limits of a small town; had effectually cut off their supplies and rendered their superiority of equipments and discipline useless; and when it passed away, it contributed a large body of its best and ablest men as a nucleus for the formation of the army of 1776.

This army of '76, with reinforcements of militia and additional regiments from the Middle States, was the army with which Washington made his wonderful retreat from Long Island and fought the battle of White Plains. Sickness, battle, detachments, desertion, expiration of service, had sadly thinned its ranks when it made its memorable retreat through the Jerseys. But it surprised the Hessians at Trenton; defeated the British at Princeton; and accomplished those brilliant movements which, even without Yorktown, would have been sufficient to establish Washington's claim to military genius of the highest order. Nor should it be forgotten that at the most critical moment of the campaign, when the terms of service of the New-England regiments was about to expire, instead of marching off as they might have done "to the music of the enemy's cannon," they engaged for six weeks of winter service and stood by their General until he had taken up his strong position at Morristown and the enemy had gone into winter quarters.

During the whole of this momentous year Washington had been exerting all his influence to convince Congress of the impossibility of carrying on such a war as that which they were engaged in, by means of militia and troops enlisted for so short a period as to make them almost as unsusceptible of discipline and as unfit for the execution of extensive plans as the militia itself. Forty-seven thousand Continentals and twenty-seven thousand militia had been in service during the year; and yet on the 2d of January, 1777, when he began his night march upon Princeton, five thousand men, more than half of them militia, were all that he could muster. It seems strange to us, as we look back upon these events, that, with such work before it, Congress could have hesitated a moment about the proper way of doing it. The British regulars were now backed by German regulars, men trained in the strictest school of military discipline. It was only by disciplined men that such men could be met upon equal terms; and discipline is the work of time. When the American recruits came in, they had barely time to learn their places in the ranks before they were called upon for active service. And by the time that they had made themselves familiar with the duties of a camp and learnt the first rudiments of military evolutions, their term of enlistment was ended. The militia brought with them not only the ignorance of recruits, but an aversion to every form of restraint. Accustomed at home to come and go as they pleased, they could not see why their freedom of action should be restrained in camp. Accustomed to use their own powder freely, they made free with the powder of Congress. Inexperienced in the details of camp life, they consumed more food and wasted more supplies than would have supported twice their number of regular troops for twice the time. And when their time was out, they seldom hesitated to sacrifice the most important public interests to their individual rights. Uncertain in battle, fighting at times with the boldness of veterans, running at times before they came within gunshot of the enemy, they were equally unreliable for complicated movements or bold assaults; nor was it the least of their defects that in serving with regulars they communicated to them the contagion of their own irregular and improvident habits. If there is a lesson perpetually inculcated in the letters of Washington and his best officers, it is the folly and extravagance, the waste of property and the waste of life, of carrying on a war by means of temporary levies and raw recruits.

Congress saw its error, but saw it too late. The favorable moment was past, and past beyond recall. The new committee came prepared to adopt all Washington's plans, — but these plans could no longer be carried out. They resolved to raise an army of 66,000 men; divided not by regiments, but battalions; and shortly afterwards, at Washington's earnest request, sixteen battalions of foot, with three regiments of artillery, three thousand light horse, and a corps of engineers, were added. It was also resolved that the enlistments should be made for the war, and to hasten them, a bounty of twenty dollars on enlisting, and a grant of a hundred acres of land at the close of the war, were offered to privates, and proportionate grants of land to officers. But it was soon found that men were unwilling to enlist for the war, and accordingly an optional term of three years without the hundred acres of land was agreed upon. But now three years seemed long. The rolls filled up slowly, very slowly, and this grand army was little more than an army upon paper.

It was found necessary to take men upon their own terms. The army still continued to be a body of men brought together for unequal periods, some for nine months, some for three, some for a year, some for three years, and a few for the war; with a discipline so imperfect, that to eyes accustomed to Prussian discipline it seemed anarchy; with such irregularity of administration, that it was impossible to form any idea of its numbers from its muster-rolls or the reports of its officers; so imperfectly clad, that out of 9,000 men there were at one time 3,989 unable to go upon duty for want of clothing; and so imperfectly armed, that "muskets, carbines, fowling-pieces, and rifles were to be seen in the same company," and these too for the most part "covered with rust, and with many" from which not a single shot could be fired with safety.* A regiment might contain any number of platoons, from three to twenty-one; sometimes it was stronger than a brigade; and one instance is recorded in which there were but thirty men in a regiment, and one man in a company, and that man a corporal. Manœuvres were out of the question. The whole drill consisted of the manual exercise, and for this every colonel had a system of his own. The only point upon which they were all agreed was on marching in Indian file.

But if the changes made by Congress failed to reach these evils, they were, with the exception of the deep-rooted evil of short enlistments, and deficient clothing, all reached and all corrected by the knowledge and energy of one man. Of this man, Baron Steuben, I shall have occasion to speak more fully in another lecture. But his name meets us here as the author of that decisive revolution which converted the motley band that had crouched more like beasts than like men in the huts of Valley Forge into the trained soldiers who manœuvred and fought with the precision and firmness of veterans on the bloody field of Monmouth. The spring of 1778 was the decisive epoch in the history of the American army. All the objections that had been drawn from the nature of our institutions and the habits of our people were fully met. It was seen that they could

---

* Important details upon this subject may be found in Kapp's Life of Steuben.

submit to discipline without sacrificing their independence, and learn to move like machines without impairing their energy of will. "You say to your soldier," wrote Steuben to a Prussian officer, "Do this, and he doeth it. But I am obliged to say to mine, This is the reason why you ought to do that, and then he does it." Henceforth we begin to find uniformity of discipline, uniformity of drill, uniformity of manœuvres; a system of reports which enabled a commander to see at once how many men he could count upon for active service; a system of inspection which saved the country $600,000 in arms and accoutrements alone. The ranks, it is true, still remained thin. The army in the field still fell far short of the army voted by Congress. The men were still badly clothed. Officers might still, perhaps, be seen, as they had been seen at Valley Forge, "mounting guard in a dressing-gown made of an old woollen blanket or bed-cover!" But officers and men knew their duty and did it. Without ceasing to be citizens, they became soldiers; proud of their regiment, attached to their profession; accepting without a murmur the "iron despotism" which Washington himself had declared to be the only system by which an army could be governed; and so thoroughly trained, even in complicated manœuvres, that Steuben, the severest of judges, declared himself willing to put them, in every thing but clothing, side by side with the veterans of France.

The whole number of continental soldiers employed during the war was 231,971, of whom Massachusetts alone furnished 67,907. The whole number of militia called into service has been estimated at 56,163, although there are good grounds for believing that it was somewhat larger.

I have already alluded to the privations and sufferings of the army of the Revolution. It is difficult to speak of them without, at least, an appearance of exaggeration: and yet the testimony is so uniform, the details are so minute and so authentic, that the strongest coloring would fall short of the dark reality. These sufferings began with the beginning of the war, and continued to the end of it. During the first winter, soldiers thought it hard that they often had nothing to cook their food with; but they found before its close that it was harder still to have nothing to cook. Few Americans had ever known what it was to suffer for want of clothing; but thousands, as the war went on, saw their garments falling by piecemeal from around them, till scarce a shred remained to cover their nakedness. They made long marches without shoes, staining the frozen ground with the blood from their feet. They fought battles with guns that were hardly safe to bear a half-charge of powder. They fought, or marched, or worked on intrenchments, all day, and laid them down at night with but one blanket to three men. And thus in rags, without shoes, often without bread, they fought battles and won campaigns. They marched from the banks of the Hudson to the banks of the Brandywine, — hung upon the flank of the victorious British; and when the enemy thought themselves firmly in possession of Philadelphia, fell suddenly upon their right wing at Germantown, and nearly cut off half their army. They marched from the Hudson to the southern extremity of Virginia, and took Cornwallis prisoner in Yorktown. They crossed rivers on the ice of northern winters, and made campaigns under the sun of southern summers. In the beginning, they had been paid with some degree of regularity; but as financial embarrassments increased, they found it almost impossible to get their pay even in the almost worthless continental paper. As they looked forward to the continuation of the war, how often must their hearts have sunk within them at the anticipation of all the suffering it would bring with it. As they looked forward to the return of peace, what fears and misgivings must have assailed them at the thought of going pennyless, and often, too, with constitutions undermined by privation and disease, to look for new homes and new means of support in a world to which they had become strangers.

The condition of the officers was scarcely better than that of the men. They, too, had suffered cold and hunger; they, too, had been compelled to do duty without sufficient clothing; to march and watch and fight without sufficient food. We are told of a dinner at which no officer was admitted who had a whole pair of pantaloons; and of all the invited there was not one who did not fully establish his claims to admission.

And yet the history of this army contains the record of only three partial mutinies: the revolt of the Pennsylvania line in January, 1781, followed in a few days by that of the New Jersey line; and the attempt to coerce Congress by another body of Pennsylvanians in 1783;— for the transient outbreaks of one or two regiments can hardly be termed a mutiny. The Pennsylvania line claimed their pay and discharge upon the ground that they had enlisted for three years, and that the three years had expired; and, even in the heat of the revolt, denounced and gave up the emissaries whom the British commander had sent among them to buy them back to England. All of these revolts were repressed without actual collision. The spirit of subordination to an authority of their own creating was too deeply rooted in the American mind to be forgotten long, even when men felt themselves most aggrieved.

Not that there were not vices and vicious men in the army: not that drunkenness, and profanity, and the other forms of evil which prevail where many men are gathered together and the purifying influences of domestic life suspended, were not to be found in some measure among these men also: but neither could they have borne what they bore, or done what they did, if by far the greater part of them had not been as sound at heart as they were strong in will.

To the officers, Congress, after much discussion and delays that savored equally of impolicy and ingratitude, had voted half-pay for life. It is painful to think of the long opposition to the claims of men who, besides risking their lives in battle and their health in the hardships of camp, were necessarily cut off, during their most vigorous years, from every other method of providing for themselves or their families. To some minds the army seems always to have presented itself as an object of apprehension. In strengthening it against the enemy they were still disturbed by the fear of strengthening it against the people. Forgetting that the men who composed it came directly from the body of citizens, and must sooner or later return to it, they feared that the ties by which long service would bind them to their officers might prove stronger than the ties by which they were bound to their families. History troubled them with visions of Cæsars and Cromwells; and like too many who misapply her lessons, they failed to see how utterly unlike were the "Thirteen Colonies" to the dregs of Romulus or the England of Charles the First. They erred where sensible men daily err, by applying to one class of circumstances the principles which they have deduced from a class radically different. The idea of building up a standing army in a country of vast extent, thinly peopled, sturdily independent, too strongly attached to their local institutions to be willing to sacrifice them to the certain prospect of immediate advantage and under the stimulant of immediate danger, accustomed to self-government, and jealously sensitive to the least encroachment upon their rights, ought never to have found admission into a sound mind. Yet it not only found admission to some, but took such deep root therein as to make them systematically unjust towards the best and most faithful advocates of their common liberties. It was, in a great measure, this feeling, combined with a morbid attachment to State rights, or rather an imperfect conception of the vital importance of a real union, that delayed the formation of an army for the war till the moment for forming it cheaply and readily was past. It was this feeling which, under the plausible show of strengthening the dependence of the army upon Congress, kept the officers in much feverish anxiety about the rules of promotion. It was this feeling which led John Adams to talk seriously about an annual appointment of generals; and both the Adamses to draw nigh to Gates as a man who, in some impossible contingency, was to be set up against Washington.

It is not surprising, therefore, that to minds tinged with these suspicions, the idea of half-pay for life should seem fraught with serious danger, or that the men who entertained them should have opposed, as an invasion of popular rights, what in the light of impartial history seems a mere act of justice. It was not till the terrible winter of Valley Forge had been passed through, and when Washington saw himself upon the point of losing many of his best and most experienced officers, that a promise of half-pay for seven years to all who should serve through the war was wrung from a reluctant Congress. It took two years more of urgent exhortation and stern experience to overcome the last scruples and secure a vote of half-pay for life.

But the opponents of this measure were not disposed to submit tamely to their defeat. The question was soon revived, both in Congress and out of Congress, in the army and in the country. The letters of the time are filled with it, and the nearer the approach of peace, the more anxiously did the army watch the movements of their adversaries. The great underlying question of a strong central government, or virtually independent State governments, came out more and more clearly. Hamilton, now in Congress, and taught by his long experience as Washington's aid the weakness of relying for justice upon the action of individual States, was for funding the whole public debt and making just provisions for the payment of the army. The advocates of State rights were for throwing the army upon their respective States.

A new idea was gaining ground; the commutation of half-pay for life for five years' full pay, which many of the officers preferred, as giving them something in hand to enter upon the world with anew. It was while all minds were agitated by these exciting questions, and thoughtful men were glancing anxiously towards the future, that that stirring appeal to the army appeared which is known in history as the "Newburg Letters." You all know the history of this grave event. You all know how adroitly and how wisely Washington parried the blow, and drew from men smarting under a sense of past and present wrongs a declaration of unshaken confidence in the justice of Congress.

And now Congress, resolving to be just, voted to commute the half-pay for life for five years' full pay, and secure it by certificates bearing interest at six per cent. When the sum was calculated it was found to amount to five millions of dollars. But of these five millions, "the price," as Washington called it, "of their blood and your independence," the officers themselves, pressed by urgent need to part with their certificates for whatever they would bring, received in the end but a small part; the greater part going, as usual, to those who had been making money for themselves while these men had been fighting for their country.

And now, too, the army was to be disbanded; not indeed, solemnly, as became a grateful people, but stealthily and by degrees, as if the nation were afraid to look their deliverers in the face. All through the spring and summer of 1783, furloughs were granted freely, and the ranks gradually thinned. Then, on the 18th of October, a final proclamation was issued, fixing the 3d of November "for their absolute discharge." On the 2d of November, Washington issued his final orders to his troops from Rocky Hill, near Princeton. On the 3d they were disbanded. There was no formal leave-taking. Each regiment, each company, went as it chose. Men who had stood side by side in battle, who had shared the same tent in summer, the same hut in winter, parted never to meet again. Some still had homes, and therefore definite hopes. But hundreds knew not whither to go. Their four months' pay, the only part of their country's indebtedness which they had received, was not sufficient to buy them food or shelter long, even when it had not been necessarily pledged before it came into their hands. They had lost the habits of domestic life, as they had long foregone its comforts. Strong men were seen weeping like children; men who had borne cold and hunger in winter camps, and faced death on the battle-field, shrunk from this new form of trial. For a few days the streets and taverns were crowded. For weeks soldiers were to be seen on every road, or lingering bewildered about public places like men who were at a loss what to do with themselves. There were no ovations for them as they came back toil-worn before their time, to the places which had once known them; no ringing of bells, no eager opening of hospitable doors. The country was tired of the war, tired of the sound of fife and drum, anxious to get back to sowing and reaping, to buying and selling, to town meetings and general elections. Congress was no longer King, no longer the recognized expression of a common want, the venerated embodiment of a common hope. Political ambition looked for advancement nearer home. Professional ambition returned to its narrow circle. Everything that belonged to the State resumed its importance; everything that belonged to the general government lost its importance. The army shared the common fate, gradually melting into the mass of citizens, some going back to the plough, some to the workbench; all, but those whom disease and wounds had utterly disabled, resuming by degrees the habits and avocations of peace. But in many a town and country inn you would long have found men with scars and mutilated limbs seated around the winter fire, and telling stories of the war. In many a farm-house you might long have seen an old musket on the hooks over the mantel-piece, or an old sword hanging by its leathern belt from the wall. In many a field, and by many a wayside, there were mounds and crumbling ruins; in many a churchyard there were little green hillocks with unsculptured stones at head and foot, to tell the new generation where their fathers had fought, had encamped, had buried their dead.

It was long before the country awoke to a consciousness of its ingratitude towards these brave men. The history of our pension bills is scarcely less humiliating than the history of the relations between the army and the Congress of the Revolution. Their claims were disputed inch by inch. Money which should have been given cheerfully as a righteous debt, was doled out with reluctant hand as a degrading charity. There was no possible form of objection that was not made by men who owed the opportunity of discussing the soldiers' claims to the freedom which these soldiers had won for them with their blood. Never did Daniel Webster display a higher sense of the responsibilities of legislation, than in his defence of the bill for the relief of the survivors of the army of the Revolution. Thank God that something was done for these men before they had all passed away! Thank God that some portion of the stain was effaced from our annals! Heaven grant that the feeling whence it sprang may be forever rooted out from our national character, and that, when the question of national gratitude which the present war is preparing for us shall be brought to the door of our national council, it may be met in a manner more worthy of a just and enlightened people!

LECTURE VIII.

CAMPAIGNS OF THE REVOLUTION.

"THE success of a war," says one of the greatest masters of the art, "depends in a great measure upon the ability of the general, upon his knowledge of the country, and the skill with which he takes advantage of the ground, both by preventing the enemy from taking favorable positions, and by choosing for himself those which are best suited to his designs." "The talent of a general," says Jomini, "consists in two things very different in themselves: to know how to judge and combine operations; and to know how to carry them out."

And thus the history of a war becomes, to a certain extent, an individual history, — the history of the genius and success, or of the errors and failures, of successful and unsuccessful generals. In the second Punic war Hannibal fills more than half the canvas. In the Seven Years' War we pass hastily over every other name to concentrate our attention upon Frederic. And in the long European wars from 1796 to 1815, — from the battle of Montenotte to the battle of Waterloo, —

we instinctively refer every great event to the genius and the ambition of Napoleon.

The war of our Revolution forms no exception to this tendency of the human mind to make individuals the representatives of ideas and events. As the page of our history fills up, names that were once familiar are cast into the shade; and acts in which the concurrence of many hands and many minds was required, gradually become associated with the master minds which inspired and directed them all. Washington is the first name that occurs to us in connection with our military history, as it is the first in our civil history; and wherever our history comes in as a chapter in that of the world, it will, for the period to which it belongs, be almost the only one. Next, for the importance of the events with which they are associated, though with very different degrees of merit, come Gates and Greene. Thus, whenever we see the main army, we find Washington directing all its movements. The great historical importance of the Northern army was derived from the defeat of Burgoyne; and with this, Gates has succeeded in connecting his name, almost to the exclusion of Schuyler and Arnold, by whom most of the real work was done. The reconquest of the South in the brilliant campaign of 1780–81 belongs exclusively to Greene.

If we would form a correct estimate of the military genius of Washington, we must study his eight campaigns as a connected and harmonious whole; the result of a careful study of his own situation, a just appreciation of the character and resources of his enemy, and a thorough knowledge of those fundamental principles which, though not yet set forth in any treatise upon the art of war, had inspired the combinations of every great commander from Cæsar to Frederic. I know that it has been common to underrate Washington as a soldier; to speak of him as a man of sound sense surrounded by men better inspired than himself, whose advice he always took before he ventured to act. I know that the original suggestion of his most brilliant movements has been claimed for other men, and that he has often been represented as deliberating and discussing under circumstances which admitted of no deliberation and called for no discussion. But history teaches us that, in situations like his, none but great men know how to take counsel, and that the mind which gathers around it the master minds of its age, and through a series of years, and under great diversities of circumstances, uses their best faculties as its own, must, in some things, be superior to them all.

I know, too, that the campaigns of the Revolution have none of that physical grandeur which overwhelms the imagination in the movements of vast masses. The loss of the allied armies at the battle of Leipsic, was greater than twice the population of New York city in 1744; and the French lost fifteen thousand more than they. But there is a moral grandeur about Trenton with its two officers and two or three men wounded, and two frozen to death, which gives a glow — or, as the poet terms it, a "kindling majesty" — to our conceptions, which none but moral causes can awaken. And even as illustrations of the art of war, we shall find that the principles applied in these campaigns — the principles which for seven years kept open the communication between the Eastern and Middle Provinces by the line of the Hudson, which kept an ill-armed and half-organized army year after year within striking distance of the enemy, harassing where it could not openly attack, retarding and embarrassing where it could not openly oppose, and often attacking and opposing with a skill and vigor which astonished its adversaries and revived the drooping spirits of its friends — are the same principles by which all great armies have been moved and all the most brilliant achievements of war's most brilliant masters performed. Never did a general change his line of operations more promptly or with more effect than Washington changed his between sunset and midnight of the 2d of January, 1777. Never was an enemy more effectually deceived by skilful manœuvring than Clinton in New York, or more effectually taken in the snare than Cornwallis in Yorktown in the autumn of 1781. There is a way of doing things upon a small scale which reveals the existence of capacity to do them upon a large scale, as plainly as the action itself would have done. And the general who carried a nation of less than three millions through a successful contest of eight years with the most powerful nation of modern times, may justly claim a place among great generals.

The campaign of 1775 was a campaign of preparation and organization. Much of Washington's time was necessarily given to the study of his materials. He had the character of his officers to study, — strangers, almost all of them, and most of them with the barest tincture of military science. He had the character of the people to study, and to find the way of establishing himself firmly in their confidence and affections. He had the country itself to study, in order to form a calm estimate of its spirit and its resources, and to devise the most effectual way of guiding the one and drawing out the other. And, meanwhile, he had to keep close watch upon his enemy, harass him, annoy him, cut off his supplies, weary him with false alarms, and by a menacing aspect keep up the appearance of strength even when most wanting in all the elements of which military strength consists. His army was what Frederic has described as one with which a general will hardly dare to look his enemy in the face, — badly exercised and badly disciplined.

There was no room here for the display of enterprise. Prudence, caution, self-control, were what the situation required. An eagle eye to watch, but a strong will to keep down impatience and wait for the moment of action. To confine the English army within the limits of Boston and Charlestown until he should be able to compel it to surrender or evacuate, — such was the problem.

The first part of the solution filled the summer and winter of 1775 – 76, and was accomplished by blockade. With less than fifteen thousand efficient men, he held over ten miles of circumvallation. It was long before he could get cannon or mortars enough to fire upon the enemy's works; in August he had only powder enough to furnish twenty-five rounds to a man, and not enough to serve his small park of artillery a day. He lacked sadly, too, good engineers, men who could make up by science for the want of strength, and turn every favorable feature of the ground to the best advantage.

But the ground was used to the best advantage. The access to the city was cut off by a connected line of works. The approaches to the works were carefully guarded. Ploughed Hill, Winter Hill, Prospect Hill, were covered with intrenchments. From the Mystic to Dorchester Neck, men kept close guard from morning to night, from night to morning, behind breastworks and redoubts, from which every gun could have been aimed with the same deadly precision which had twice broken the ranks of England's best soldiers from the half-finished redoubt of Bunker Hill. Gage looked out upon them from Beacon Hill, and feared to repeat the bloody experiment of the 17th of June. Howe looked upon them and felt that he could not afford the blood it would require to take them.

Every day Washington was on the lines, among the men, gradually infusing the spirit of order and subordination by showing them that his eye was ever upon them. From time to time there was cannonading from the nearest points; now and then the surprise of a picket, or a menace of attack. From time to time detachments met on the islands of the bay, — the English coming for hay or cattle, the Americans to prevent them. To soldiers like ours, these skirmishes had all the appearance of real battles, and a successful skirmish inspirited them as much as a great victory. " Heap up small successes," says Frederic, " and their sum will be a great success." More than once Washington would have ventured upon a general attack, but his officers thought the hazard too great, and the time had not yet come for overruling the decision of a council of war. At last, when all his preparations were completed and he felt himself strong enough to strike a decisive blow, he took possession of Dorchester Heights and fortified them in a single night. When the English admiral saw the American guns looking down upon his ships, he saw that unless Howe could drive the Americans from their post, the fleet would be driven from the bay. Howe resolved to make the trial. A day of storm gave Washington time to strengthen his works, till Howe, remembering how much the single redoubt of Bunker Hill had cost, gave up the attempt and evacuated the city. And thus the blockade of Boston, sustained for ten months by a judicious use of the ground, was decided without a battle by the judicious occupation of a favorable position at the proper moment. The man who wrote that the "success of a war depends in a great measure upon a choice of positions," would have found in this campaign something to study and much to praise; and that man was Frederic the Great, when he sat down to write the history of his Seven Years' War.

The same skilful choice of positions characterized the summer campaign of 1776. That he would be compelled to give ground before his disciplined adversary, Washington knew from the first; but he was resolved to dispute every foot of it where it could be disputed to advantage. He fortified Brooklyn and New York, and only gave them up when any further attempt to hold them would have imperilled the whole army. For we must constantly bear in mind that the loss of Washington's army would have involved the loss of the war, and that all his measures were controlled by political as well as by military considerations. Could he have followed Greene's advice, — and there can be but little doubt that his own opinion went with it, — he would have burned New York.

But Congress ordered him to protect and preserve it. And thus the enemy — for to keep it from them was impossible — obtained a sure base of operations for the whole war; a base which enabled them to use their fleet at will.

See for a moment his position the second day after the battle of Long Island. The battle was irretrievably lost. To defend the works at Brooklyn was impossible, for the enemy's fleet could in a few hours be brought against them on one side while the enemy's army attacked them on the other. How promptly was the plan of retreat formed! how promptly was it carried into execution! In a single afternoon boats of all kinds were brought together from a range of fourteen miles. In a single night nine thousand men, with all their tents, baggage, and field-artillery, were conveyed from within earshot of the enemy across a rapid river three quarters of a mile wide. The English lay down at night with the Americans in their toils; they arose in the morning to see them safely landing on the opposite shore. The last to embark was Washington himself. He had been forty-eight hours without closing his eyes, and most of the time in the saddle.

And now half of the army that his skill had saved deserted him. The militia went off, — I use his own words, — "in some instances almost by whole regiments, in many by half ones, and by companies at a time." The regulars, if any part of this irregular body deserved the name, were "infected by their example." "With the deepest concern," says he, in words almost pathetic from the simplicity with which they unveil the secret struggle of his heart, "with the deepest concern I am obliged to confess my want of confidence in the generality of the troops." It was then that Congress, yielding to his remonstrances, voted that army of eighty-eight battalions for the war, which, as we saw in our last lecture, was never much more than an army on paper.

And now see how, with these remnants of a demoralized army, Washington continued to retard the enemy's advance, and control his movements. It was Howe's aim to cut off his communications with the Eastern States, and, shutting him up on York Island, compel him to fight at a disadvantage. It was Washington's aim to gain time by disputing the ground where it could be disputed, and protracting the campaign while Congress was maturing its plans and raising a new army. The battle of Long Island was fought on the 27th of August; but it was not till the 15th of September that the enemy got possession of New York. A strong position enabled him to fight the brilliant skirmish at Harlaem, which cost the enemy over a hundred men, and went far towards restoring the Americans to the confidence they had lost in the defeat of Long Island. A well chosen position enabled him to make his stand at the White Plains, and hold his ground till the British general was compelled to renounce the hope of forcing him to a general action at a disadvantage, on the left bank of the Hudson. Foiled therefore in this, Howe crossed over into the Jerseys, and Washington began that memorable retreat, in which, by contesting every inch of ground that could be contested, by breaking down bridges, and throwing every possible obstacle in the enemy's path, he made less than seventy miles of level country cost them nineteen days, and succeeded not only in putting the broad Delaware betwixt his army and theirs, but effectually secured the command of the river by sinking or destroying all the boats from Philadelphia upwards, for seventy miles.

Now, thought Howe, the campaign is over; we have secured New York; we have overrun New Jersey; all that remains to do is to hold our ground by detachments, and go quietly into the comfortable winter-quarters that we have won for ourselves. Lord Cornwallis, who had been foremost in all these movements, asked leave of absence, and prepared to make a visit to England.

Washington had crossed the Delaware on the 8th of December, with less than three thousand men fit for duty. He had readily divined the enemy's plan of keeping down the Whigs by spreading their men over a large tract of country. "And now," said he, "is the time to clip their wings when they are so spread." On Christmas night he recrossed the river, knowing that the enemy would keep dull watch mid their Christmas carols. The weather was so cold that of the four or five men lost, two at least were frozen to death; but in spite of the ice, which delayed him till near daybreak, before the next daybreak he was safe again on the Pennsylvania shore with nine hundred and nine prisoners, and all their arms and equipments. Nothing but the ice saved the troops at Bordentown from a similar fate.

Cornwallis, giving up all thoughts of England for that winter, hurried back to Brunswick, and, gathering in his forces, marched rapidly upon Trenton, which Washington, following up his blow, had reoccupied on the 30th of December. By four in the afternoon of the 2d of January, Cornwallis was upon him with a superior force. By the 5th, Washington was securely encamped at Pluckemin; the enemy had been baffled by a bold change of line of operations; the battle of Princeton had been won, and nothing left to the English general of his conquests in the Jerseys but Brunswick and Amboy.

Frederic himself could not, under similar circumstances, have chosen a better winter-post than that which Washington now took at Morristown; strength, command of supplies, security of communications, accessibility to reinforcements, convenience for watching the enemy and harassing him at every opening, were all combined. Henceforth, a cloud like that which lowered so ominously before the eyes of Hannibal, when Fabius was watching him from the mountains, met the eyes of Howe whenever he turned them towards the west. He advanced, he retreated, he threatened, now on one side, now on another; he exhausted all' the manœuvres of his art in efforts to bring the American to an engagement, and open for himself a land route to Philadelphia; and, thwarted in all, suddenly withdrew to New York, and, embarking his troops, put to sea.

Whither? An anxious question, which Washington anxiously revolved. From the north, Burgoyne was advancing towards Albany. A corresponding advance from New York might break the line of the Hudson, and cut off the communication between the Middle and the Eastern States. All that he could do to prevent it, Washington had already done. But on what point of the long line of the American coast this new blow would fall, it was impossible to foresee. Philadelphia seemed the most probable, and, holding himself ready to move at a moment's warning, he prepared for a desperate struggle.

At last the veil was lifted. The British fleet was in the Chesapeake; the British army was landing at the head of Elk. Washington hurried his motley battalions southward, looking hopes which he hardly felt, and trying to rouse the courage of Philadelphia by marching in full array through the city. Political motives called loudly for a battle, and he fought the battle of the Brandywine. Erroneous information concerning the movements of Cornwallis, a circumstance utterly beyond his control, was brought him just as he was upon the point of crossing the river to attack Knyphausen, and cut off the English line of retreat, — a suggestion of the same daring genius which suggested the advance upon Princeton, and which could hardly have failed of the same brilliant success. Defeated, he secured his retreat, saved his army, was ready for another battle. A violent storm coming on just as both sides were preparing to engage, separated them on that day, and when the storm ceased, the Americans, ill-provided for such contingencies, found that their ammunition was wet. Marching, countermarching, manœuvring followed. Howe had but thirty miles between him and Philadelphia; thirty miles through an open country in which every stream was fordable; but so judicious were Washington's manœuvres, so unremitting his watchfulness, so skilful his employment of his unequal force, that fifteen days were consumed in marching those thirty miles.

Philadelphia fell; but hardly were the English established in their quarters, when Washington darted upon their advance at Germantown, and, though foiled in his attempt to cut them off, struck a blow that was felt at once by the American Commissioners in Paris. "Nothing," said Count Vergennes, "has struck me so much as General

Washington's attacking and giving battle to General Howe's army; to bring an army raised within a year to this, promises everything." A continued struggle of six weeks for the command of the Delaware followed, and November was near its end before Howe could truly call Philadelphia his own. But the cloud was still on the horizon, ominous, full of menace. He could not rest tranquilly in his pleasant quarters till he had seen what those menaces meant. Opposite the range of hills on which the American army lay, was the range of Chestnut Hill, equally strong. From this Howe tried once more to draw his enemy into an engagement on unfavorable ground. Washington was willing to fight on ground of his own choice, but not on that of his enemy's choosing. Three days the English general manœuvred; three days the American general stood prepared for an attack. Neither party was willing to give up the advantage of ground; and Howe, on the afternoon of the third day, confessing himself once more vanquished in the contest of skill, marched his fourteen thousand veterans back to Philadelphia, leaving fifteen thousand Americans, not a thousand of whom had seen a year's service, and more than three thousand of whom were militia, in undisputed possession of the field.

Then came that terrible winter at Valley Forge, which our fathers could never speak of without a shudder. The general was once more merged in the organizing, administrating statesman. And when, in the summer of 1778, he led his new army down upon the traces of Clinton, — flying traces I might almost call them, so hurried was his passage through the once conquered Jerseys, — it was an army into which Steuben had infused a spirit of order and discipline which no American army had possessed before. Do you remember Monmouth? Washington's positive orders to fight? Lee's unwillingness to obey them? Have you not seen Washington standing with his arm on his horse's neck, waiting for tidings from the advance, — the burst of indignation with which he received the tidings that Lee was retreating,— how he sprang into the saddle, spurred to the front, checked by his presence the retreat, though almost a flight, issued his rapid orders, restored the confidence of men and officers, and snatched a victory from the eager grasp of his experienced and skilful adversary? No time that for deliberation and counsel, but for lightning thoughts and words that should send every man to the right place, resolved to do the duty assigned him or die in trying to do it.

No great movements marked the next two years. To preserve the line of the Hudson, to secure the passes of the Highlands, to straiten the enemy in his quarters, and inflict upon him some of that distress for food in summer, and food and fuel in winter, which fell so heavily upon his own troops, was almost all that Washington could do with his skeleton of an army. But he planned expeditions and directed them, saved Connecticut by sending Wayne to storm Stony Point, and still made himself everywhere felt as the inspiring and commanding spirit. But I hasten to 1781, the great year of the war, and to Yorktown, where Washington heard for the last time that whistling of bullets, in the sound of which he had found something so charming when he first heard it at the "Great Meadows," twenty-seven years before.

Cornwallis was in Virginia. Clinton had weakened New York by detachments. In conjunction with Rochambeau, Washington planned a blow at this stronghold from whence so many fatal expeditions had been sent forth since it first fell into the hands of the enemy. Preparations were made upon a scale commensurate with the object. The combined armies advanced close to the old ground of the autumn campaign of 1776. But the reinforcement which had been called for weeks before did not come, and at the most critical moment a strong reinforcement reached the English. Just at this moment, too, came tidings that a French fleet might soon be expected in the Chesapeake. Between daybreak and breakfast, Washington decided to carry the war into Virginia, and, if he could not cut off Clinton, to deprive him at least of his right arm, Cornwallis.

Admitting none to his councils but those with whom immediate co-operation was required, he made all his preparations with profound secrecy and marvellous despatch. Every appearance of a design upon New York was carefully kept up, — a camp was marked out in the Jerseys as if for operations from that quarter, and false intelligence prepared and allowed to fall into the enemy's hands. Even trusted officers were held till the last moment in ignorance of their destination; Washington knowing well, and again I use his own words, that "when the imposition does not completely take place at home, it can never sufficiently succeed abroad." The American army was already on the banks of the Delaware before Clinton suspected whither it was going. On the 20th of August, it began to cross the Hudson; by the 25th of September, it was before Yorktown. How skilfully the siege was conducted, how gloriously it ended, I need not tell an audience of Americans. Need I tell them that, in the formation and carrying out of this decisive plan, Washington had displayed a promptness of conception, a power of combination, and a completeness of execution, which, when combined with the knowledge of character, force of will, and personal intrepidity which have never been denied him, entitle him to a place among the greatest of generals?

The first campaigns of the Northern army derive their historical importance from their having deprived the Colonies of two provinces which might have become useful members of the Union, and having left the enemy in possession of a strong base of operations on the northern frontier. The last, from the enemy's attempting to use that base, and losing a large and well-appointed army in the attempt. Two episodes, one brilliant and one sad, have preserved the memory of the first campaign with peculiar freshness; and we still speak of Arnold's march through the wilderness, and Montgomery's death, as we speak of the occurrences of last year. If history were always just, there would be a brilliant page in those northern annals for Sullivan too, whose masterly retreat in the face of overwhelmning obstacles, was one of the great events of the war. But success, which too often lends as false a coloring to our judgments of the past as to our opinions of the present, has in spite of the indignant protests of contemporaries, and the unanswerable demonstrations of impartial investigators, given the honor of the closing campaign to a man who, of all those who bore a part in these events, had the smallest share in preparing the causes, and hardly a greater one in directing the measures which led to that glorious consummation.

The Northern campaign of 1777 ought to have been for England the last campaign of the war. Secure in the possession of Canada, an advance by Lake George to Albany, supported by a corresponding advance from New York, would have cut off the communication between the Eastern and Middle States, and reduced each section to its unassisted resources. But to accomplish this, Burgoyne should have been twice as strong, Howe and Clinton twice as active. When Burgoyne began his advance, Schuyler was in command of the Northern army. The experience of two campaigns on the same ground had prepared him for the difficult task of disputing step by step the advance of an enemy greatly his superior in appointments and discipline. And never was ground disputed more resolutely, never were obstacles accumulated more persistently, in an enemy's path. At every step the British general was compelled to pause in order to remove some obstruction which his skilful adversary had put in his way. The farther he advanced, the more did his embarrassments increase. If there was labor in front, there was danger on the flank, and still greater danger in the rear. The diversion in the Mohawk by St. Leger, which at one moment promised him important aid, was defeated by the watchfulness of Schuyler, and the energy of Arnold. A desperate attempt to get supplies from Vermont had cost him seven hundred men at Bennington. He counted the miles behind him and the miles before; he counted his supplies, and saw no escape from starvation but in a rapid advance, or a still more rapid retreat. And he could do neither without opening or securing his way by an overwhelming victory. When Gates took command of the American army on the 19th of August, the toils were so far laid around the English general, that a child's hand might have drawn them. Two brilliant battles were fought, but neither at Stillwater nor at Bemis's Heights was the American general under fire. On the 17th of October, the English laid down their arms.

Why did not the army at New York save them?

The original plan of the campaign had comprised an advance by Howe along the line of the Hudson, and an irruption into New England. Instead of this, he turned southward, as we have already seen, and directed all his efforts against Philadelphia. Burgoyne's advance from Canada was well known, and in all Howe's army there were but two men who did not wonder at the sudden change in his well-devised plan of co-operation. These two, Cornwallis and Grant, had doubtless been admitted to his secret counsels; and we now know, what they alone then knew, that another plan of operations had been proposed to the British commander by Charles Lee.

Lee was then a prisoner in New York, — a disappointed and embittered man; signally foiled, hitherto, in his selfish ambition, and still revolving schemes of selfish revenge in his morose and gloomy mind. In a long letter to the Howes, — the General and the Admiral, — he proposed the crushing of the rebellion by a movement to the southward; and they accepted the suggestion, though, happily for us, in a modified form. And thus Burgoyne was left to make his way to Albany by his own exertions; the feeble and tardy co-operation of Clinton producing no result beyond the burning of two flourishing villages, and the destruction of some valuable stores. To Howe's contemporaries his change of plan was a mystery; and history has classed it, thus far, among those actions which she is so often compelled to record without being able to explain them. But six years ago, eighty years, that is, after the event, Lee's original letter, with the indorsement of Howe's secretary, was brought to light, removing all doubts, not only as to Howe's motives in 1777, but as to his own motives also in the autumn of 1776, and two years later at the battle of Monmouth. The whole story is so singular a one, so important in its bearing upon three capital events in our history, and so important, too, as showing to the warning of bad men, and the comfort of the good, that sooner or later historical truth, like murder, will out, that I cannot resist the temptation of recommending to you all the remarkable dissertation which George Henry Moore, Librarian of the New York Historical Society, has devoted to it.*

We come now to the Southern campaigns of 1780 and 1781. And it is not without some misgivings that I approach this part of my subject; for I am well aware that it is no easy thing in

---

* The Treason of Charles Lee, by George H. Moore, Librarian of the New York Historical Society. New York: Charles Scribner. 1860. 1 vol. 8vo.

speaking of our ancestors to guard ourselves against the insinuations of personal feeling. But the documents are within your reach to correct me if I err.

In none of the thirteen Colonies had the British arms been so uniformly successful as in the Carolinas and Georgia. They had taken Savannah, and held it against a combined attack of Americans and French by land and water. They had taken Charleston, and secured the line of the Santee by strong posts at Fort Watson and Granby, and the western districts by the still stronger post of Ninety-six, between the headwaters of the Savannah and Saluda. The battle of Camden had opened a passage into North Carolina through the broad lowlands which lay unguarded between the Catawba and the Great Pedee; and England's best soldiers, gathering around her best general, Cornwallis, were preparing to throw themselves with irresistible fury upon the feeble and disheartened remnants of the conquered army.

The population, not yet numerous in times of peace, had shrunk from the presence of hostile armies, and still more from the fierce war between Whig and Tory, till whole districts had been left desolate. Of those who still ventured to remain on their plantations and cultivate them, many were devoted to the royal cause, and many more than lukewarm in the cause of their country.

The American army was encamped at Charlotte,

between the Catawba and the Great Pedee, near the southern border of North Carolina, and about sixty miles from the British camp at Winnsboro. When General Greene took command of it on the 4th of December, 1780, it consisted of nine hundred and seventy continentals, and ten hundred and thirteen militia. A recent distribution of clothing had given each of the regulars a coat, a shirt, a pair of woollen overalls, a cap or a hat, and a pair of shoes. The blankets had been apportioned by companies, upon an average of one blanket for three men. Few of the new recruits had clothes enough to enable them to make a decent appearance on parade. They had no tents, no camp equipage, no magazines, and were subsisting by daily collections, every day made more difficult by the indiscriminate ravages of friend and enemy. As Greene looked upon them, it seemed to him "that the word difficult had lost its meaning." "I have been in search of the army I am to command," he wrote to his wife on the 7th, but without much success, having found nothing but a few half-starved soldiers, remarkable for nothing but poverty and distress." "But," he adds, "I am in hopes matters will mend. I am in good health and in good spirits, and am unhappy for nothing except my separation from you and the rest of my friends."

In advancing from Salisbury to Charlotte, Gates had no intention of renewing active operations, and a council of war had already decided to lie quiet through the winter. But Greene, convinced that his first step must be to inspire officers and men with confidence in their leader, formed his own plans independently, and proceeded to put them into execution without delay. He saw that his predecessors had been hurried into injudicious movements by consulting the wishes of the people, impatient to be freed from the presence of the enemy, rather than the means at their disposal and the true nature of the war. He recalled the King of Prussia's maxim, that in defending a country it was necessary to attend to great objects and submit to partial evils. He felt the difficulty of animating to great exertions a people who lived at such a distance from each other, and who, in spite of their danger, were intent on their private affairs. But he felt, too, that the success of the war depended upon "appearances and public opinion," and that if he would establish a character for judgment, enterprise and independence, he might hope, in spite of all his difficulties, to bring it to a successful termination.*

He chose, therefore, a new camp at Cheraw Hill, on the Great Pedee, nearly forty miles farther south than Charlotte, thus placing himself within the borders of South Carolina, and on the

---

* "Dans une guerre de cette nature, il faut du sang froid, de la patience et du calcul." — Napoléon, Note sur la position actuelle de l'armée en Espagne. Napier, Pen. War, L. 442.

enemy's right flank. But at the same time he was resolved to leave nothing to chance which prudence and forethought could secure. Three great streams intersected the region where the first and fiercest struggle would come, and in the hope of finding them navigable by batteaux, he sent out officers to explore them carefully, ascertaining the depth of water, the currents, the rocks, and everything which could favor or impede the progress of a boat. He caused a large number of boats suited to these shallow and rapid waters to be built, no easy task in the dearth of tools and artificers, and carried them with the army wherever it went. He established a depot for prisoners at Salisbury, and did everything that his means permitted to establish depots of provisions at convenient points, and open a sure communication with them. South Carolina was so completely in the hands of the enemy, that no aid could be expected from what remained of her civil government; but with the governors of North Carolina and Virginia, he kept up an active correspondence, explaining his condition, and pointing out the best modes of relief. And at the same time he did all that his circumstances permitted to restore the moral tone of his army, and instil into officers and men a spirit of discipline and soldierly pride.

Short time, however, was given him for preparation. Strong reinforcements had already reached Cornwallis, and every indication gave warning of an active winter campaign. Without waiting for his adversary to begin, he boldly took the initiative by detaching Morgan with six hundred men to join Davidson and his militia, and rouse the country west of the Catawba.

Cornwallis was perplexed. Greene might be aiming at Charleston, to which the camp at Cheraw was as near as the camp at Winnsboro. To meet this danger, he left Leslie on the east bank of the Catawba. The Whig spirit in the regions west of the Broad River and round Ninety-six, might be roused by the sudden reappearance of the American army. To meet this danger he detached his favorite officer, Tarleton, with orders to crush Morgan. Then fearing a sudden blow at Leslie, he ordered him to break up his camp on the Catawba and join the main army. Already one of the advantages of his superiority had been wrested from him by his enterprising adversary; he had lost the initiative.

Tarleton's rapidity soon brought him up with Morgan, who felt himself in a condition to fight, and who well knew how much at that moment even a partial success would encourage his countrymen. His own judicious choice of ground, and a bold movement of Colonel Howard, of Maryland, at the critical moment of the battle, gave him a complete victory, and Tarleton barely escaped with a few followers to carry to Cornwallis the unexpected tidings of his disaster. Cornwallis saw that no ordinary exertions could repair it. Still Morgan must be cut off; his five hundred prisoners must be released. Taking a day to effect his junction with Leslie, and collect the relics of Tarleton's defeat, he broke up his camp on the morning of the 19th, and pushed rapidly forward in the hope of getting between Morgan and the Dan, and thus preventing the junction of the two divisions of the American army.

But Morgan was in motion before him, and though encumbered by prisoners, and obliged to collect provisions by detachments as he marched, was at Beale's Ford, on the Catawba, sixty miles from the Cowpens, on the evening of the 23d. The next morning he crossed the river, and for the first time since the battle, could safely give his men a short breathing-space. Do not forget that the distances of those days are not to be measured by the distances of ours. The battle of the Cowpens was fought on the 17th of January, and it was not till the evening of the 25th that the tidings of it reached the American camp at Cheraw. Greene instantly put his army under marching orders, made all his preparations for advance or retreat as circumstances might require, and taking with him a sergeant's guard of dragoons, pushed rapidly across the country,—near a hundred miles' ride,—to put himself at the head of the victorious detachment, while Huger brought up the main body to the place fixed for their junction. Could he unite the two divisions of his army, and call out a sufficient body of militia, he might be strong enough to fight Cornwallis himself. But the militia failed him, and then came that celebrated retreat from the banks of the Catawba to the banks of the Dan, — one hundred and fifty miles of roads scarcely passable in the best seasons, but in February alternately mire and frozen ground, his half-clad soldiers reddening it all the way as they passed with the blood from their naked feet, and the enemy well clothed, well fed, well armed, pressing on their rear confident of victory and eager for revenge. But so well were Greene's measures taken, and such was the spirit with which he inspired his troops, that the junction with the main body was effected, and the whole army placed in safety on the north bank of the Dan. Foiled in his main object, Cornwallis turned his face southward, and raising the royal standard at Hillsboro, tried to rouse the loyalists by a proclamation announcing the evacuation of the State by the army of the Congress, and his own presence at the head of the victorious army of the King. But hardly had he begun his march from the Dan towards Hillsboro, before an American detachment was again over the river hanging upon his rear, cramping his movements, cutting off stragglers, and keeping down the Tories. The main army followed on the 23d. A fearful blow from the advanced detachment crushed a body of four hundred Tories on their way to the British camp, crushing with them the awakening spirit of loyalty; and without pausing to give his men a breathing-space, Greene took a favorable position between Troublesome Creek and the Reedy Fork, — two tributaries of the Haw, — thus covering the communications with Virginia, whence reinforcements were now coming rapidly forward, and retaining at the same time the means of retreating or advancing at will. Cornwallis followed, and pitched his camp on the Almance, another tributary of the Haw. For ten days Greene manœuvred in front of the English, constantly in motion, now on the Reedy Fork, now on Troublesome Creek, changing his camp every night, and never staying long enough in one place to allow his adversary, though ever watchful and ever active, to strike a blow. During these anxious days he never took off his clothes to sleep, — never quit the saddle but to take his pen or snatch a hasty meal. With so active and exasperated an enemy at hand, night was more dangerous than day; and every night, when all his other labors were over, he went the rounds alone, visiting every post, and making sure that every sentinel was keeping vigilant guard. It was in one of these rounds that he received what he used in after life to speak of as the greatest compliment ever paid him. Among his officers there was a namesake of his own, though not a relative, Colonel Greene, of Virginia, a bold and sturdy soldier. One night, as the General was going his round, his ear was greeted by some unequivocal sounds from the Colonel's tent, which left no doubt as to how he was passing his time. Entering in haste and rousing him by a sudden shake, "Good God! Colonel," he cried, "how can you be sleeping, with the enemy so near, and this the very hour for surprises?" "Why, General," replied the Colonel, rubbing his eyes, "I knew that you were awake."

All knew that he was awake, soldiers and officers, and the enemy too. But no one knew what the next order, or in what direction the next move would be. He called no councils, entered into no discussion, but, gathering all the information scouts and spies and constant watchfulness could give him, weighed it maturely in his own mind, and when the moment for decision was come, issued his orders and made sure that they were executed.

The promised reinforcements came at last, and choosing his own ground, he drew up his army in three lines and awaited the approach of the enemy. The battle was fierce and bloody; and though the dastardly flight of the North Carolina militia who composed the first line compelled him to relinquish the honors of the field to his adversary, he brought off his forces in perfect order, and was prepared to renew the trial the next day. But Cornwallis was too much crippled to risk another battle, or even to hold his ground; a fourth of his army was killed or disabled. His best general,

O'Hara, was seriously wounded. His favorite colonel, Webster, was mortally wounded. The desperate pursuit into which Greene had lured him had cut him off from his communications, and left him without supplies in the midst of "timid friends and inveterate enemies." Nothing but retreat could save him, and retreat must be prompt and unencumbered. Leaving seventy of his wounded behind him under the protection of a flag, he began his march towards Wilmington. A glance at the map will show you where it lies, near the mouth of the Cape Fear, on a line with Camden, and thus a little south of Winnsboro, from whence he had started eight weeks before to complete the conquest of the Carolinas. His victory, as he called it, of Guilford Court House, had forced him back towards Charleston, and left his adversary in possession of the greater part of North Carolina.

It was now Greene's turn to pursue, and welcome as a few days' rest would have been to his jaded troops, he pushed forward without delay. But at Ramsay's Mills, on the Deep River, sixty miles about from the battle-ground of Guilford, the terms of the militia's service expired; and although the enemy and certain victory were almost within their grasp, no entreaties or persuasions could induce them to stay a day beyond their time.

Thus Cornwallis again outnumbered him, and what should he do? Wait for supplies and reinforcements while taking advantage of his undisputed possession of the country, to rouse it to his support, and meanwhile give a short respite to his toil-worn regulars?

It was on the 28th of March that he was compelled to give up the hope of overtaking Cornwallis, and on the 29th he wrote to Washington that he had resolved to advance directly upon the enemy's posts in South Carolina. "Nothing," he writes to Colonel Lee, in communicating his intentions, "nothing is left me but to imitate the example of Scipio, and carry the war into Africa." On the 7th of April the gallant little army was on its way, officers and men wondering whither he was carrying them. When Cornwallis heard of his march, and the danger flashed upon his mind, he hesitated for a moment whether he ought not to go to the defence of the royal garrisons. But his army had known no rest since the campaign began, and he could not venture to call upon men who fought merely for pay, well clothed and thoroughly equipped as they were, for the sacrifices that Greene could ask from half-naked men who were fighting for freedom. To Wilmington therefore he went, the first step towards Yorktown.

Camden was Greene's first aim, the enemy's strongest post; and though it cost him the battle of Hobkirk's Hill, in which he was again compelled to leave his enemy in possession of the field, the apparent defeat again proved a real victory, and the English garrison, with Lord Rawdon at their head, destroying their works, retreated to Monk's Corner, eighty miles nearer to Charleston. Fort Watson had already fallen. Fort Mott and Fort Granby fell next. The British line of defence was effectually broken, and on the 22d of May, Greene sat down before Ninety-six. Once more he was subjected to the mortification of seeing a brilliant prize snatched from his grasp, for Rawdon, hastening forward with superior numbers, compelled him again to retreat. But the only use that the English General could make of his superiority was to withdraw his garrison and abandon the western districts to their fate. Another month of incessant activity followed, and early in July Greene pitched his camp on the high hills of Santee, and his wearied army rested from its labors. Two more moves drove the enemy down upon the seaboard, and cut them off from the interior for the remainder of the war. The first, towards the end of August, terminating in the hard-fought battle of Eutaw Springs, which forced them back upon Dorchester and Bacon's Bridge, within a few miles of Charleston. The second, in November, which drove them headlong from Dorchester, leaving them hardly a foothold outside the city but the islands on the coast, and converting what had set forth in January as the army of South Carolina, into the garrison of Charleston. When the news of this last brilliant move reached the North, Washington wrote to Laurens, "The report of the brilliant and successful movement of General Greene, by which he compelled the enemy to abandon their outposts, is another proof of the singular abilities which that officer possesses."

Thus in the South as in the North, America triumphed by the strategic skill of her generals. With an army with which no European general would have dared to look his enemy in the face, Washington year after year held his ground against the best soldiers of Great Britain, and thwarted their best concerted plans. With an army even worse appointed than Washington's, Greene, in a single campaign, faced two British armies in succession, forcing them both back upon the coast, and breaking up the strong line of well-chosen posts with which they fondly fancied they had made sure their possession of the interior. Physical superiority yielded to skilful combinations, superior discipline to superior judgment; men of talent, who had studied the art of war in the field under able generals to men who had studied it by the light of their own genius in the campaigns of Cæsar and Frederic. Read the history of the greatest commanders. See the obstacles with which they contended, and how they overcame them; study the characteristics which they displayed in the camp, on the march, and on the battle-field; penetrate the spirit of their manœuvres, and analyze the principles of their combinations then go back to the military history of our Revolution; follow Washington from Cambridge to Yorktown; follow Greene from Charlotte to Charleston; and you will find that the strategy which defended the thirteen Colonies from the overwhelming power of Great Britain was in spirit and principle the same strategy which saved Italy from Hannibal, and carried Frederic in triumph through a seven years' war, with two thirds of Europe leagued against him and but one ally at his side.

There are many other events which deserve mention, even in an outline of this war; many other names which have strong claims to our grateful remembrance. There was Sullivan's Rhode Island expedition in 1778, unsuccessful in its immediate object, but remarkable for a well-fought battle, and a skilful retreat. There was Sullivan's expedition against the Six Nations in 1779, planned with judgment and executed with energy. There was the gallant defence of Redbank, and the brilliant capture of Stony Point by storm. How many pleasant associations gather round the true-hearted and genial Knox. How well deserved was the respect which men felt for Lincoln; how well earned their confidence in MacDougall. If little Rhode Island had her Olney and her Angell, and her Christopher Greene, little Maryland had her Williams and her Howard; never was cavalry led to the charge more gallantly than the cavalry of

William Washington: never did partisan warfare bring out a bolder spirit than Marion; never was Henry Lee excelled in the skilful conduct of an advanced corps, in hanging on the enemy's rear, and beating up his quarters. Who would willingly forget the sturdy wagoner, Morgan, who with his keen-eyed riflemen decided the day at the first battle of Stillwater? or that Pennsylvanian, ever foremost in desperate encounters, eagerly scenting the battle from afar; the mad Anthony of the soldier, but to the friends he loved the high-minded, the generous, the affectionate Wayne? Gladly would I speak of these, and of many more who fought by their side, and whose memories, if we had not too often permitted ourselves to be drawn by the cares or the pursuits of the present into a wicked forgetfulness of the past, would have been preserved by statues and monuments, and all the testimonials by which a grateful people rewards the devotion of its benefactors. But all that I could do in a single lecture I have endeavored to do; still remembering, even while I selected single names as the representatives of the whole war, that neither Washington nor Greene could have brought it to a successful termination if they had not found clear heads and skilful hands to comprehend and execute their designs.

LECTURE IX

THE FOREIGN ELEMENT OF THE REVOLUTION.

WE come now to a very interesting, though a very difficult part of our subject, — the foreign element in the war of the Revolution. It is very interesting to know how much help our untrained officers received from the well-trained officers of Europe who fought by their side. It is equally interesting to know how large a proportion of those who served in the ranks and bore the brunt of the war were men of foreign birth. The last is a question of statistics for which the data are extremely imperfect, or rather, almost entirely wanting. We know that there were many foreigners among the common soldiers; for we know that on more than one occasion when men were chosen for special service, special care was taken to employ none but natives. We know that there was a German legion; and German and Irish names meet us constantly in the imperfect muster-rolls that have escaped the moths and rats, or not been burnt for kindling. But we know, also, that then as now, hundreds bore German and Irish names who had never seen Ireland or Germany. Conjecture and analogy then must supply the want of positive evidence; and the analogy in the present war bears us fully out in the conjecture that by far the greater portion of the common soldiers were natives of the land for which they fought.

Of foreign officers, the proportion in the higher ranks was much larger. Out of twenty-nine major-generals, eleven were Europeans; there were sixteen Europeans among the brigadiers; and if, as we descend to colonels, captains, and lieutenants, we find the number comparatively less, we must remember that what the greater portion of them sought in the American service was increase of rank. Few would care to serve as captains or lieutenants in the half-clad, half-starved army of America, who could be captains and lieutenants in the well-clothed and well-fed armies of France or Prussia.

But it is not by numbers that we are to estimate the services of these officers. Many of them had been trained to arms from their childhood. Many had served through the Seven Years' War, at that time the greatest war of modern history as a school of military science. All of them were practically familiar with the rudiments of their profession, the life of a camp, the duties of a field day. Ten soldiers of such make as composed the bulk of European armies might have very little influence in moulding the character of a regiment of American farmers and mechanics. But a single officer, of even moderate experience, could hardly fail to make his American colleagues painfully conscious of their deficiencies, even where the daily sight of his example did not go far towards correcting them. A colonel at a loss for some important evolution must have been greatly relieved to find that his lieutenant-colonel, or his major, knew all about it. And more than one general may have felt stronger at the head of his division, after a few weeks of daily intercourse with generals who had passed their lives in camps. It surely is not assuming too much to say that, regarded merely as a contribution to the general stock of military science, the foreign element was a very important element in the army of the Revolution.

But the war of the Revolution was a civil war; a war of opinions and convictions, in which men fought, not for a few miles more or less of a territory, that whether won or lost would add nothing to their individual aggrandizement, but for rights which involved not only their own happiness, but that of their remotest descendants. Every American who drew his sword knew that a fearful penalty was attached to his failure, — a glorious reward to his success. He had relinquished positive advantages, broken strong ties, often sacrificed cherished affections and brilliant hopes. But he had done it conscientiously as the only thing which a good citizen could do; and whatever the consequences might be, he was prepared to abide them. For him then it was a grave question, how far he ought to intrust his own and his country's cause to men who could not fully share either his hopes or his danger.

To answer this question aright, we must give a glance — unfortunately it can be but a glance, — at two characteristic features in European society at the period of the American war.

Long before that period France had placed herself at the head of European civilization. The French language had taken the place of Latin as the language of diplomacy. French literature had taken the place of the Italian as the literature of refinement and taste. Everywhere fine gentlemen endeavored to imitate the air and manners of the fine gentlemen of France. And fine ladies, as they decked themselves for the eye of the world, for the front row at the theatre, or for a presentation at court, followed with scrupulous minuteness the fashions and example of Versailles. "If I were king of France," said Frederic the Great, "not a cannon should be fired in Europe without my permission." And for many years the kings of France endeavored to do what Frederic would have done, and give law to states as their tailors and milliners gave law to drawing-rooms. Richelieu had laid deep foundations on which Louis XIV. built a dazzling superstructure. The name of country was merged in the name of king. Devotion to the sovereign became the test of patriotism. And those local attachments which have always been one of the chief bulwarks of society, were converted into those personal attachments which have often been its greatest curse.

Already when this transmutation began, men's minds had grown singularly indifferent to the obligations of nativity. Long and bloody civil wars had loosened the hold which the name of birthplace always retains in healthy minds. Turenne and Condé had alternately fought against their countrymen, and with them, and even after fighting side by side had led armies against each other. Yet France has classed them both among her favorite heroes. Frenchmen had turned their swords against France long before the army of Coblentz was enrolled. Englishmen had encountered Englishmen at the point of the bayonet on more than one bloody field. German and Swiss mercenaries, like the Condottieri of an earlier day, were long the chief reliance of every monarch in every war.

Thus when the tie of country was loosest, the tie of sovereign began to be drawn more closely. Turenne and Condé, who had shed the blood of Frenchmen freely, became the most devoted of the loyal servants of Louis. And when Louis was gone it took more than eighty years to undermine the edifice which he had built. First came the regency, and the religious element crumbled. Then the long profligacy of Louis XV., during which all the forms of reverence for the royal authority were observed, while the royal person became daily more an object of abhorrence or contempt, and last Louis XVI., on whose weak though innocent head all the sins of his fathers were fearfully visited.

It was not all at once that the idea of country could regain its natural control; nor were men conscious, at first, how far their devotion to royalty had been weakened. Their minds were filled with contradictions. School and college set Greece and Rome before them as the worthiest objects of imitation, — great republics and the heroes of republics. The philosophy and literature of the day discoursing eloquently, if not always wisely, of the rights of mankind, awakened in their breasts vague longings for noble enterprises. They ate and drank, and made love and gamed as they had always done; but their language was the language of men who feel that life has higher pleasures and worthier objects than these. And while they were thus agitated and tossed to and fro, habit conflicting with thought, and the whole theory of life with the practice of it, came the American Revolution, giving sympathy a definite object, and the love of glory a noble field. Hence the enthusiasm with which Franklin was received in Paris, and the reverence which everywhere waited on his steps.

But at the same time there was another, and perhaps a larger class, who shared this impatience of repose without sharing this longing for a nobler field of exertion. In the wars of Europe there had always been a demand for military science. A good officer could always count upon employment under one banner if he could not get it under the other. And not unfrequently, the man who saw many wars, was found in the course of them fighting with equal zeal and equal honor under both. Germany had been an exhaustless storehouse of good soldiers, from which all the princes of Europe drew freely. Switzerland sent forth her hardy sons to fight for the best paymaster, whoever he might be. Swiss guards were found in the court of every potentate that could afford to keep them. War was an honorable trade for the soldier, an honorable profession for the officer; and wherever they carried their strength or their knowledge, they were sure, when war was waging, to find honorable employment. Austria's greatest victories were won under the guidance of a foreign general. Frederic was constantly on the watch for able officers, and always ready to receive and trust them. The soldier was a citizen of the world.

Now in this class, as in every other, we must expect to find all varieties and shades of character. There would be honorable men among them, loving their profession, and ambitious of military glory as the highest glory. There would be mercenary men, ready to sell their blood to the highest bidder, and risk life for the chances of gain. There would be intriguing men, and designing men, and quarrelsome men, and fretful men; and there would be many who, with little ambition, no excessive love of gain, and no spirit of intrigue, had gone into the army as they would have gone into the Church, or engaged in any other pursuit consistent with their rank which promised them a decent livelihood.

For the greater part of these men peace was a misfortune. When armies were disbanded or regiments cut down, their occupation was gone. Even with his half pay, Captain Clutterbuck was an unhappy man till he fell upon the rare device of turning local antiquary, and found occupation for the leaden-winged hours. But what could men do who had no ruined abbeys to explore, and no half-pay to live upon? The coffee-houses of Paris, the petty courts of Germany, the watering-places and towns of the provinces were always filled in time of peace with officers whom the war had thrown out of employment; restless, impatient, and like the Mercury of Lucian's dialogue, longing for some new commotion that they might get their pay.

To those men the American war was a Godsend. Even to those among them who did not care to venture so far in quest of employment, it opened a prospect of a speedy war in Europe, in which they could not fail to find ready purchasers of the blood they were ever ready to shed. But the more active and the more ready were not to be deterred by three thousand miles of ocean and the untried perils of a country hardly better known to the best informed than the interior of Africa. Increased rank and good pay were all that they asked, and Silas Deane was ready to promise both. Soon the doors of Congress were thronged with candidates for all the highest places in the army; the tables of Congress were covered with petitions for the fulfilment of the contracts which the zealous commissioner had made in their name, and the recognition of claims which would almost have left Washington without an officer able to understand even the language of his orders.

Nor was Congress their only resource. With their vague ideas of country, and their special code of morals, there was no violation of duty in holding a commission from Congress and playing the spy for France, or Prussia, or any other power that felt sufficient interest in the question to seek for direct information. Hence some came in the double capacity of soldiers and secret agents, equally sincere and equally active in each. America gained some good officers, and the courts of Europe much valuable information.

Meanwhile, the native officers who would gladly have taken advantage of the knowledge and experience of a few good men to make up for their own deficiencies in both, became alarmed at the continuous flow of aspirants for the highest ranks, and still more at the manner in which Congress received their claims. The question of promotion had excited jealousies and discussions with the first appointments. No rule, perhaps, that could have been adopted would have given perfect satisfaction; but worst of all was the frequent violation of the commonest rules. It is well known that Arnold's discontent first arose from seeing younger officers, who had not half his claims, arbitrarily promoted over his head. And Congress, although it might never have been able to make him a good man, certainly had no small share in making him a very bad one. From the beginning of the war to the end of it, there was an apparent reluctance to give satisfaction to the army by putting the claims of its officers to rank upon a sure foundation. Men never felt safe; never felt sure that they might not suddenly find themselves called upon to receive orders from some one to whom they claimed the right of giving them. And even after Congress had grown more guarded in the distribution of honors, and these apprehensions had in a measure subsided, a sensitiveness remained, amounting almost to distrust, which in any other country and with any other army, might have led to the most disastrous consequences.

Congress itself was not free from embarrassment. Nothing could have been more hurtful to us in Europe than to send back a crowd of disappointed men who had come hither with the written promise of its accredited agent. Nothing could have been more dangerous at home than to have put places of trust and confidence in the hands of men who had no permanent interest in the cause or the country for which they had agreed to draw their swords. Still, act and decide it must. Some were accepted and remained; some were refused, and went back to complain of the injustice of Congress, and paint America and Americans in the blackest colors.

Of those who remained, the greater part, although in the strict sense of the word military adventurers, did good service. One of the serious wants of our army, and which no native genius or rapid training could immediately supply, was the want of engineers. Washington's complaints of the incompetence of even the few who claimed the name began with his first letter from Cambridge to the president of Congress; and a year later he wrote to the Pennsylvania Committee of Safety that he had but one in whom he could place confidence. Here the necessity of looking to Europe for assistance was so apparent, that Congress directed the Commissioners at Paris to engage competent engineers, with the approbation of the French court, and with the assurance of proper rank and pay. It was to this judicious resolution that we owe the services of Duportail, Launoy, Radière, and Gouvion, officers of good standing in the French army, and who brought us what we needed most, science, combined with practical skill. It was under their direction that most of the important works of the war, from 1777 to its close, were constructed. Duportail was rewarded in 1781 with a commission of major-general; and when he left the country, in 1783, carried with him the strongest expressions of the esteem and regard of Washington. Radière died in 1779, regretted by all as a valuable officer. Gouvion, like Duportail, distinguished himself by brilliant service at Yorktown, and good service everywhere. Launoy is classed by Washington with the other three as having acquired general esteem and confidence. If every foreign officer had served as they did, Washington would have been spared one of his greatest trials. But there were men among them of a very different stamp.

Shortly before the arrival of Duportail and his companions came Thomas Conway, an Irishman by birth, but who, in the course of a thirty years' service, had risen to the rank of colonel in the French army. He now was anxious to become an American citizen, as he told the credulous Silas Deane, but still more anxious to become an American general, as Congress soon discovered. With an apparent frankness, which, in the beginning, produced a favorable impression even upon the cautious mind of Washington, he stated his claims, told the story of his military experience, and, winning favor with Congress, was made brigadier-general. It was the year of the Brandywine, and his conduct on that occasion appeared all the more favorably from its contrast with the conduct of Deborre, another adventurer, who had been raised to the same rank a few weeks earlier. But it was the year, too, as all remember, of that sudden tide of unmerited success in the North which emboldened Washington's personal enemies to combine their strength against him, and set up Gates as his rival. How far this conspiracy extended in Congress and out of Congress, is not positively known. That Washington was to have been set aside, seems well established; and with him the two generals whom he most trusted, Greene and Knox. That Gates was to have been put in his place, seems equally well established; but how far he was a leader in the plot, or how far the mere tool of men more artful than himself, is not equally clear. Conway, who had been made a brigadier in May, was made inspector-general, with the rank of major-general, in December, when the plot was at its height; and even after his intrigues became known, an expedition to Canada was got up by his friends in Congress, in order to give him the opportunity of distinguishing himself at Washington's expense. But it is seldom that all the members of a conspiracy can command their passions so completely as to conceal their hopes from those with whom they live on familiar terms. Confident in the success of his schemes, Conway vented, in a letter to Gates, all the venom of his enmity to Washington, mixed with extravagant adulation of the successful general; and Gates, intoxicated by the flattery, showed the letter to Wilkinson. Wilkinson (I wish he had had a good motive for it) repeated one of the most obnoxious passages at the table of Lord Stirling, and Stirling, a frank and open-hearted man, moved both by his attachment to Washington and his indignation at the duplicity of Gates and Conway, communicated it immediately to Washington himself, in a letter which does as much honor to his heart as to his head. Once on his guard, Washington met the attack with his habitual judgment and decision. Gates blustered, shuffled, and equivocated; but, backed by strong partisans, contrived to hold his ground till the test-day of Camden, when even his warmest partisans were compelled to abandon him. Conway, too, blustered, wrote impertinent letters, tried magnanimity, injured innocence, violated independence, and all the stale tricks and subterfuges of rogues detected in their roguery; but mistaking his strength, for he had no real hold even upon his fellow conspirators, he threw up his commission in a pet, then tried to get it back again and failed; was wounded in a duel which his intemperate language had brought upon him, and, while on what he supposed to be his death-bed, wrote an humble apology to the great man whom he had injured. But the wound, though severe, was not mortal. He recovered, and made his way back to France, to live — history does not tell how, and die — no one has asked where, but leaving in American history a name second only to that of Benedict Arnold, until the rival. treasons of these latter days had robbed even that name of its bad pre-eminence.

I hurry over these scenes: nor will I dwell on the name of De Neuville, or on those claims which made many other adventurers objects of jealousy to the Americans, and even drew bitter complaints from Washington. We have no means of estimating their individual services, or of ascertaining how far they made up by knowledge and skill for the trouble they gave by their pretensions. But we do know, that the pretensions of many among them were sources of well-founded discontent to native officers, and of constant uneasiness to the Commander-in-chief, to whose door all bickerings and all complaints sooner or later made their way. There are names, however, which I would gladly dwell upon. I would gladly tell of Fleury's brilliant charge up the steep ascent of Stoney Point, and De Kalb's generous death on the fatal field of Camden. I would gladly speak of the "great zeal, activity, vigilance, intelligence, and courage" — I use Washington's words — of the Chevalier Armand, Marquis de la Roucrie. Longfellow's verses have given immortal freshness to the name of Pulaski. But the reader of Campbell knows Kosciusko only as the champion of Polish liberty.

Let me add a few words to this record of the gallant Pole, before I pass to the two great names of my subject, — Lafayette and Steuben.

Disappointed love brought him to America. "What do you seek here?" asked Washington, after reading Franklin's letter of introduction. "To fight for American freedom." "What can you do?" "Try me."

After a short service in Washington's family, as aid, he was made colonel of engineers, and sent to the Northern army. Here his military training stood him in good stead. All the important works were intrusted to his care. It was he that planned the strong line of entrenchments which proved so useful at Bemis's Heights. It is to him also that we owe the fortifications of West Point, where a romantic spot on a ledge of the precipitous wall that overhangs the Hudson is still pointed out as the Garden of Kosciusko. When General Greene was sent to take command of the Southern army, Kosciusko was placed at the head of his engineers; and during the whole of that active campaign, no one, in his appropriate sphere, was more active or more useful than the gallant young Pole in his. It was not till the war was over, and American independence secured, that he again turned his face towards Europe. One part of his task was accomplished. The hour for the other was rapidly drawing nigh; and when it came, it found him prepared to do all that it required, and bear all that it imposed, as became the friend and disciple of Washington. There ended his public career. The long years that remained, a third almost of his whole life, were passed in retirement, and nothing can exceed the dignity which his calm and consistent patriotism shed around them. Napoleon sought to lure him from his retreat, and failed. Alexander listened respectfully to his intercessions for his exiled countrymen. And when he died, the women of Poland went into mourning, and his ashes were carried reverently back from the land of exile, to sleep on their native soil in the tomb of Poland's kings.

I said that the two great names of my subject were Lafayette and Steuben, — the mercurial Frenchman, and the systematic German. Next to the two or three greatest of our own great men, no men rendered such important service as they; and it is no trifling addition to its value that it was a kind of service which none but such men could have rendered. None but a young enthusiast of high rank and large fortune could have broken through the barriers which instinct, habit, diplomacy, and even sound statesmanship, had placed between a rebel Congress and an absolute monarch. None but a soldier of long experience, deeply read in the principles of his profession, and practically familiar with their applications, would have known how to apply them to the wants of an army organized so differently and composed of such different materials from those for which tacticians had framed their precepts, and generals had written their instructions. Their characters, too, were as different as the parts which they performed: each partaking largely of those distinctive traits which belong to all Germans, on the one side, and to all Frenchmen on the other, and each equally distinguished by characteristic traits of his own.

They were both men of good talents, though neither of them could lay claim to that rarer order of mind which distinguishes the man of talent from the man of genius. They were both personally brave, cool and self-possessed in the hour of danger. They were both capable of great exertions and great endurance; both equally fond of that degree of convivial enjoyment which betokens geniality of nature rather than grossness of taste. They both possessed that species of cultivation which the habit of cultivated society gives; and read, wrote, and thought carefully whenever professional duty required careful study. But neither of them loved books for themselves, or took much pleasure in them beyond their bearing upon the practical questions in which they were more directly interested. They both had a high sense of honor, and ready sympathies, possessing and inspiring strong affections; and both, independently of the adventitious circumstances which gave them a prominent place in society, would have made themselves generally acceptable to men of refined and generous natures by the natural refinement and generosity of their own.

Here the parallel ceases. Lafayette was born to high rank and independent fortune. He had received the education of a man to whom all the paths of preferment were open; and at seventeen was already a husband and a father. His marriage with a lady of equal rank and fortune with himself had strengthened his position at court, and seemed to mark out the line of duty and ambition for him as clearly as birth and alliance could draw it. As a boy, he had already taken the first step by entering one of those regiments which raised men most rapidly, — the *mousquetaires noirs;* and when he left the French for the American army was a lieutenant. Thus he had learnt the rudiments of his profession early: was familiar with garrison duty and parade duty as far as it was incumbent upon a Marquis to know them, but had never seen actual service, and had never commanded a regiment.

Steuben was the son of a captain of engineers; — born in a garrison, and with no prospect of fortune or preferment but such as he could open for himself with his sword. His earliest associations were with armies and camps. When a mere child he had followed his father to the Crimea and Cronstadt, and played among the fortifications that the old soldier was constructing with much professional skill and absolute professional indifference as to whom they defended or who might lose his life in winning them. Then came two or three years of study in a Jesuit college, where he laid good foundations in mathematics and history, and acquired some tincture of polite literature. French, under Frederic, was as important a language for a German who wished to push his fortunes as German itself; and Steuben studied them both with equal care. But the sound of the drum broke rudely in upon these softening pursuits, and before he was fully turned of fourteen, and while Washington was learning arithmetic, and filling his copy-book with legal and mercantile forms at Mr. Williams's school, near Bridge's Creek, his future inspector-general was already serving as a volunteer in the campaign of 1744, at the siege of Prague. The upward path in the Prussian army was a hard path to climb, and many there were who left arms and legs and life itself by the way. Young Steuben entered it with the enthusiasm of a high-spirited youth, reared in the midst of warlike exercises and traditions of military glory. When the Seven Years' War broke out, he had already reached the rank of first lieutenant. Meanwhile, his leisure hours had been well employed: building up surely upon the foundations he had laid during his short college life, and making himself master of engineering and the most difficult of the scientific parts of his profession. Never before, in modern times, had its practical lessons and all its highest principles been applied as they were applied by Frederic during that bloody war; and they who, like Steuben, fought through it all, might well claim that they had studied in war's greatest school. Steuben had one advantage beyond most of his comrades, and an advantage which was at the same time the highest distinction. Frederic, who, in the distribution of his military favors never took birth or fortune or anything but merit into consideration, had chosen among his younger officers a select number to study under his own eye, teaching and examining them himself. Steuben was one of them.

With the peace of 1762 the prospect of military preferment ceased, and, withdrawing from the Prussian army, with at least one uncommon testimonial of Frederic's esteem, a pecuniary reward, he entered the service of the Prince of Hohenzollern Hechingen, as grand marshal of his court, — an office of the highest trust and dignity. The next ten years — those years during which the war on whose fortunes he was to exert such an influence was a ripening — he passed in a dignified ease, differing little from idleness: in directing the elaborate ceremonial of a court, in travelling with his new sovereign, and in social intercourse with the eminent men whom his official position made his acquaintances, and his personal qualities often made his friends. But the Prince was a Papist, and Steuben a firm Protestant, and thus, after over ten years' faithful service, he found himself compelled to resign his office, in order to escape a persecution which the priests of the court — jealous of his influence with the sovereign — had stirred up against him. At this time there was a prospect of another war, and a sudden longing for his old profession seized him. But till war should actually break out there were serious difficulties in obtaining employment in the rank he felt himself entitled to; and when the cloud passed he became again a wanderer about the pleasant places of Europe, forming new friendships and cultivating the old. His fortune, though small, was ample for his mode of life. His ambition, though not fully gratified, had been honorably rewarded; and with abundant sources of enjoyment at command, he might naturally have imagined that, at the age of forty-seven, his public career was closed forever.

But now France, already half embarked in the contest, was looking about her for the means of rendering the Americans substantial aid. Money was given secretly; arms and ammunition were supplied under an assumed name; but neither money nor arms could avail without a well-organized and disciplined army. St. Germain, the French Minister of War, an enthusiastic admirer of Frederic's military system, which he had tried ineffectually to introduce into Denmark, and was now trying to introduce into France, had no confidence in untrained soldiers, and knew that the Americans had no officer qualified to train theirs. He cast his eyes upon Steuben, whom he knew personally;

and at this moment, Steuben, wholly unconscious of his intentions, came to Paris. The negotiation was not without its difficulties. It was known that American officers were jealous of foreign officers. It was known that the Congress had refused to fulfil Deane's engagements with Ducoudray. The Commissioners themselves openly declared their inability to advance even passage-money for the voyage. The service required corresponding rank, and to secure that rank beforehand was impossible. The enthusiasm of liberty might have overborne these and all other obstacles; but Steuben had no enthusiasm for liberty. As a man of the world he knew the importance of rank. As a soldier he loved the active exercise of his profession. He had a slumbering ambition which the prospect of distinction might easily arouse. But in this untried field there was neither the certainty of employment, nor the assurance of rank, nor even the definite promise of pecuniary reward. It was an adventure, beginning in sacrifice, and full of doubt and hazard by the way.

But St. Germain's heart was in the negotiation. Beaumarchais brought his ready wit and persuasive eloquence to the task, and on the 1st of December, 1777, Steuben landed from a sixty-six days' stormy passage at Portsmouth, New Hampshire.

Lafayette had already been six months a major-general in the American army. The same court which had exerted all its influence to gain over

Steuben for the Americans, employed all its authority to prevent Lafayette from coming to their aid. Romance has no chapter more fascinating than the chapter in which sober history tells how this boy of nineteen eluded the spies and agents of a watchful ministry, and accomplished his designs in spite of obstacles that might have made the boldest hesitate. From the moment in which he had heard of the American war from the mouth of King George's brother, the Duke of Gloucester, he had felt a noble longing to take the part of a people fighting for their liberties. It was like a sudden revelation of the purpose for which rank and fortune had been given him. Life had now an object worthy of all his devotion. What were the smiles of princes to the blessings of a liberated people! What were ribbons and crosses and titles to the name of champion of human rights! What was there in the knowledge that he had helped in adding a few miles of territory or a few thousands of fellow-subjects to the possessions of an absolute monarch, that could compare with the conviction of having helped in building up a nation of freemen! How sweet would sacrifices seem in such a cause! What a serene consciousness of duty performed would mingle its soothing influences with the pains of separation from family and friends! And if he should never see them again,—if it should be his fate to die on the battle-field, as his father had died, — what a proud consolation, what an inspiring example, what a stimulant to great and noble deeds would it be for his children to know that their father had died in the cause of truth, of justice, and of humanity!

From the beginning Lafayette attached himself to Washington; not merely as the commander-in-chief, whom it was his duty to obey, but as a paternal friend, whom it was a pleasure to love. This gave a direction to his views of men and things in Congress and in camp, which preserved him from the mistakes into which so young a man, so suddenly transported into a new scene, and charged with such grave responsibilities, might easily have fallen. Washington's friends became his friends, Washington's aims his aims. No simple-hearted boy, fresh from his native village, could have demeaned himself more modestly than this young nobleman, fresh from the first circles of the most polished city of Europe. He knew that he had much to learn, and he set himself to learn it with a deep conviction of its importance, and implicit confidence in his teachers. In elementary tactics he was better grounded, perhaps, than most of his brother officers. In higher science many of them were still students as much as he. But in the government of a free people, in the art of drawing out the resources of a country in which every man had a voice and an opinion of his own, in the forming and guiding and sustaining public sentiment, all was new to him, all was as much at variance with his habits and associations as it was in harmony with his instincts and feelings. Of all these things Washington's camp was a practical school.

Nor was it less a school of systematic and untiring industry. Hard work, as well as hard fare, was the lot of most American generals; but those who sought a larger share of Washington's confidence, had a double share of both. The saddle and the writing-desk, the sword and the pen, in rapid and constant alternation, left little room for amusement, or even rest, in the active parts of a campaign; and though winter quarters brought some relaxations, there was still work enough to task the most diligent pen and the most active mind.

Lafayette fell into this new mode of life as easily as if he had been trained to it. In his manners there was a polished dignity which suited well with Washington's ideas of the proprieties of social intercourse; and, at the same time, a readiness to meet the wishes and enter into the feelings of others, which made him acceptable to men of every class. The Marquis soon became a familiar appellation in camp; and soon, too, his munificent generosity and untiring benevolence won for him, everywhere, the still dearer appellation of the soldiers' friend.

In all this he was, unconsciously, perhaps, in the beginning, but afterwards with a thorough consciousness and well-directed exertions, rendering important service to the cause to which he had devoted himself. Of the opinions and prejudices which the American Colonists brought with them from their native island, there were none which they had preserved more carefully than their derogatory opinions of Frenchmen and their prejudices against France. That one Englishman could whip three Frenchmen was as fundamental an article of Colonial as of English belief. In French politeness they saw nothing but heartless vanity. In French society nothing but sensuality and corruption. The perfidious French government was still seeking to outwit the honest, unsuspecting government of England. And even when stripped, by the peace of 1763, of her possessions on the Colonial frontier, France, although no longer an object of immediate apprehension, was none the less an object of dislike.

But American statesmen well knew that in their unequal contest with the most powerful nation of Europe, France was their first, if not their only, ally. They needed French arms. They needed French money. They might need French ships of war, and French soldiers. This reflection had led them to welcome, as a happy omen, the first appearance of military adventurers from France, and added not a little to the embarrassment of Congress when they became so numerous as to make it necessary to refuse their offers of service.

Yet the minds of these statesmen were not free from the hereditary prejudice, as the conduct of John Adams and John Jay clearly showed, at a moment when all prejudice ought to have ceased: nor the minds of generals, and still less of inferior officers, as plainly appeared in the expedition against Rhode Island. What, then, could be expected — or rather, what was not to be feared — when well-dressed and well-paid French soldiers should be brought to serve side by side with the half-naked soldiers of America?

To smooth these difficulties, to overcome these prejudices, to convert antipathy into confidence and jealousy into an honorable and friendly emulation, was the first good office which Lafayette rendered his adopted country. His money gave him the means of doing many little acts of seasonable kindness, and he did them with a grace which doubled their value. His rank enabled him to assume a tone with his dissatisfied countrymen which sometimes checked their arrogance and often set bounds to their pretensions. A true Frenchman in impulse, chivalrous sense of honor, and liveliness of perception, he taught Americans to bear more readily with qualities, which his example showed them, might easily be united with the perseverance, the firmness of principle and the soundness of judgment which they had been wont to set above all other qualities. The French alliance might have been gained without Lafayette; but the harmony of feeling which made it practically available, was in a large measure owing to the hold which Lafayette had taken upon the confidence and the affections of the American army and the American people.

And but for him that alliance might have come too late. It is true that he came to us in defiance of his government, escaping in disguise the *lettre de cachet* which a ministry, alarmed and shocked at his disobedience, had issued against him. But it is no less true that the sympathetic enthusiasm of Paris was raised to the highest pitch by this display of a chivalrous daring, which Parisians prize so highly; and that the English court was fully persuaded that he had done nothing but what his own court approved. Thus the French government found itself strengthened at home for an open declaration, and stimulated from abroad by the increasing jealousy of its powerful rival. Lafayette's hand is almost as visible in the treaty of alliance as the hand of Franklin himself.

In all that follows it is still everywhere apparent. When he had done all that, for the moment, he could do for us here, he went back to France to work for us there. "He would strip Versailles for his Americans," cried Maurepas, half annoyed, half irritated, by his urgent appeals for full and effectual succor. But his magnetic enthusiasm prevailed, and the succor came. When the work in France was done, he hastened back to America, then once more to France, and next to Spain, and all for the glorious cause to which he had devoted himself, — the cause, to his eyes, of human nature and human rights.

I have said nothing of his services in the field, — of his gallant bearing at the Brandywine; of his skilful retreat from Barren Hill; of Monmouth, and Tiverton Heights, and the brilliant Virginia campaign of 1781; for although in all of them he displayed sound judgment and high military talent, there was nothing in them which other generals might not have done as well as he. But his pure purpose, his noble aims, his intelligent zeal, his fervid enthusiasm, his modest bearing, his winning amenity, his judicious and persevering application to a great and noble purpose of the means and the influence which thousands, born to pursuits and expectations like his, were wasting in selfish pleasures and still more selfish ambition, have given him a place in American history which, of all those who fought or who worked for us, belongs to him alone.

Steuben found the American army in their winter huts at Valley Forge. Familiar from his infancy with the hardships and sufferings of military life, he had never seen such suffering before. Had he been a mere adventurer, he would have promptly retraced his steps, for there was nothing there to allure an adventurer of his rank and position. Had he been a cold and calculating man, he would have found still less to satisfy him in this first view of his future companions. But he was a man of warm feelings, quick sympathies, strong impulses. While in Europe he had hesitated whether it would be worth his while to give up the quiet enjoyments of a secure position for the hazards of an adventurous enterprize. But the prospect of military glory had aroused his slumbering ambition. The interest which the French ministers and the Spanish ambassador took in the American cause, convinced him that it was not a hopeless one. As he thought over the scenes of his early life, and recalled the excitements of the profession he had loved so dearly, his imagination kindled, and the glow of youth returned. For human liberty and human rights he had no enthusiasm, for Frederic's was not the school in which such enthusiasm was to be kindled. But he had the enthusiasm of his profession. Its details were full of interest for his accurate and systematic mind; its higher principles suggestive of questions that afforded him an exhaustless field of meditation. And as he meditated, even in the midst of the splendid frivolities of a court, he had often sighed for an opportunity to test them for himself from a higher point of view than any which he had yet reached. Thus love for his profession, the hope of military glory, the probability of an increase of fortune, combined with the persuasion of friends whom he trusted, and that restlessness and longing for change which, when youth has been passed in exciting scenes, is always sure to follow the first intervals of repose, were the motives which brought him to America.

But once here, pride, high sense of honor, and lively sympathies, led him to enter into the cause of freedom as if he had never known any other. The habits of the soldier had not blunted the sensibilities of the man, and his genial nature drew men towards him wherever he went. He was soon on an intimate footing with his brother officers; respected for his superior knowledge, and loved for his warm heart. Like Lafayette, he attached himself especially to Washington; not, indeed, with the tender veneration of the young Frenchman, but with a sincere respect and perfect confidence.

Deference for his opinion was easy, for it was always a judicious opinion, frankly expressed, and sustained by sound reasons. And confidence in his motives and reliance on his justice were easy for one whose whole life had been passed in that kind of intercourse with his fellow-men which brings out in peculiar relief all the qualities essential to harmonious relations between superior and inferior. Nor does it detract from the sincerity of his respect for Washington, although it may be justly considered as a proof of the soundness of his own judgment, and his vast intellectual superiority to such men as Lee, Gates, and Conway, that he saw that the surest way to the accomplishment of his own designs was by securing for them the approbation of the Commander-in-chief. To feel that Washington was the only man who could fill the first place was to share the feelings and convictions which enabled Greene, and Knox, and Hamilton to perform their parts so well in their own.

I have already spoken of the defective organization of the American army, — a defectiveness which extended from the drill of the common soldier to the administration of all the ramifications of the Quartermaster-General's department. Few American officers had accurate ideas of manœuvring their men, and there were no books from which they could acquire them: the elementary treatises of that day being almost as imperfect as the treatises upon the higher principles of the art. From such sources as he could command, each officer had drawn a system of his own; thus destroying all uniformity in a matter of which uniformity is the most essential element. Equally imperfect were the system of inspection, involving, among other losses, an annual loss of more than five thousand muskets, and the system of returns, by which hundreds of names were retained on the pay-rolls long after the bearers of them had left the service, and superior officers, from the commander of a brigade to the Commander-in-chief, kept in dangerous ignorance of the number and condition of their men.

To supply these deficiencies, to introduce uniform systems of manœuvre, inspection, and returns, to infuse a spirit of order and harmony into all the departments of the army, to inspire officers with self-reliance and an instinctive perception of whatever the moment might require, and men with confidence in their officers and prompt and intelligent obedience to their orders, was the task of Steuben, a task which can only be appreciated by those who take the pains to study, in detail, the difficulties with which he had to contend.

He began by examining his subject thoroughly, and preparing a full and accurate plan. With this before him, Washington could see what he proposed, and tell him what it would be safe to attempt. A routine soldier, like the Prussian general who thought to win the battle of Jena by ordering his men, in the heat of the fight, to advance their right shoulders, would have filled reams with frivolous details, and proposed a thousand impracticable things. But Steuben's mind was thoroughly imbued with the principles of his art, and keeping his great object constantly in view, he rejected many things as useless, postponed many to a more fitting time, and without leaving any opening for negligence or inexactness, adapted his instruction, with marvellous skill, to the wants and the condition of the army.

He first drafted a hundred and twenty men from the line, as a guard for the Commander-in-chief. This was his school. Twice every day he drilled them himself, teaching them to march, to wheel, to bear arms, and even to execute some elementary manœuvres. Hitherto, the American officers had left the care of drilling the soldiers to their sergeants as a thing below the dignity of an officer. The sight of a man of Steuben's rank and experience, with his glittering star on his breast, marching and wheeling with common soldiers, taking their muskets into his own hands and showing them how to handle them, produced a great revulsion in their ideas, and presently colonels and lieutenant-colonels entered cheerfully into the good work; some, perhaps, with the feeling that, like Gil Blas's uncle, they would thus learn full as much as they taught. In a fortnight his school moved and looked like soldiers; and before Monmouth came, the leaven from this little nucleus had penetrated the whole army.

Nothing contributed more to his success than the good sense with which he adapted his instruction to the circumstances, and sometimes even to the prejudices, of the men with whom he had to do. He had discovered that some officers who began by the manual exercise, as the books and all usage prescribed, had become weary, and given it up in disgust. He knew, too, that his work must be done quickly, or that it would not be done at all. He reversed the order, — began with manœuvres which interested and gave immediate results, and ended by the manual and platoon exercise. He had observed that in action Prussian soldiers, trained to fire by platoons, and to pride themselves upon loading and firing several times a minute, often, after the first discharge, loaded badly and fired as awkwardly as their enemy. Therefore, without neglecting platoon fire, he put it in its true place as a thing of secondary importance. Never before had an American army been trained like this army of Valley Forge. "Never," said Hamilton, when at Monmouth he saw a division in full retreat halt at Steuben's command, and form as coolly under a close and heavy fire as they would have formed on parade, — "never did I know or conceive the value of military discipline before."

The same happy results attended his reforms in other departments. Returns were made according to prescribed forms, and with close attention to minute and accurate specifications. By a glance at the foot of a column, Washington could at once see how many men he might count upon for actual service, how many were sick or disabled, how many of each State were enlisted for the war, and how many were to leave him at the end of the campaign. A regular and rigorous inspection brought, at stated times, the whole army under the supervision of officers eager to show their zeal in the performance of a difficult duty. Till then, as I have already said, there had been an annual loss of more than five thousand muskets, and the War Office, in making out its estimates for the year, had regularly made allowance for that number. In the returns, under Steuben's inspectorship, only three muskets were missing in one year, and those three were accounted for.

But it was not in dollars and cents that Steuben's services should be estimated, although the sums which this man, who saved nothing for himself, annually saved to his adopted country, might be counted by thousands. Like Lafayette, he brought us what none but he could have brought; and in looking at the condition in which he found us, it is difficult to conceive how we could have held out through two more campaigns without the aid which we derived from his scientific knowledge and practical skill.

And what was his reward? An eight years' struggle with poverty and its bitter humiliations; to be publicly insulted as living upon national bounty, when a tardy justice had compelled Congress to acknowledge his claims and buy them off with an annuity of $2500 a year; a grave so little respected, that a public road was run over it, laying its sacred contents bare to the rains of heaven, and the eye, and even the hand, of vulgar curiosity, till individual reverence, performing the part of national gratitude, removed the desecrated bones to a surer resting-place; and a name in American history overshadowed and almost forgotten, till a countryman of his own,* making himself, as

* Frederick Kapp, now a member of the New York bar, and whose important contributions to American history have been already alluded to in the Preface.

Steuben had done, an American in heart and feeling, without sacrificing the instincts of his nativity, gathered together, with German industry and German zeal, the scattered records of his services, and portrayed, in faithful and enduring colors, his achievements in war, his virtues in peace, his rare endowments of mind, and the still nobler qualities of his heart.

LECTURE X.

THE MARTYRS OF THE REVOLUTION.

IN speaking of the martyrs of the Revolution, I do not undertake, as you will readily conceive, to speak of all who, in that day of trial, suffered for the truth's sake. A mere catalogue would convey no idea of the peculiar merits of the sufferer or the relative value of the sacrifice. Nor would it be easy to form such a catalogue out of the imperfect materials that accident, full as often as an intelligent appreciation of their importance, has preserved. Thousands die in battle whom history never mentions; and in all great wars thousands are exposed to sufferings worse than death without even a passing allusion in the general record of misery. Here, as elsewhere, all that history can do is to select characteristic names, and by a faithful picture of individuals endeavor to give a general idea of the classes to which they belong. Out of the three hundred and sixteen who served their country in Congress from the first assumption of the powers of government in 1775 to the inauguration of the Federal Constitution in 1789, scarce thirty are known in the general history of the United States, scarce six in the general history of the world. We had twenty-nine major-generals. How many of them find a place even in the school histories which we put into the hands of our children in order to familiarize them betimes with the characters and the services of their fathers? It seems sad that so many of our benefactors should be forgotten; for it seems like wilfully rejecting the aid which society might derive from that instinctive desire to be remembered by posterity, which nature has implanted in the human heart as one of its strongest incentives to virtue. Here it is that history most needs the aid of her sister arts, — of sculpture, and painting, and poetry; whose appeals to the imagination, not confined as hers are by the rigorous laws of evidence, give a life to our conceptions of the past, which, wisely cherished and judiciously directed, seldom fails to exert an important influence upon the future. A noble act embalmed in verse, the form and features of a great man preserved in marble, the characteristic circumstances of a great event illustrated by a skilful pencil, are among the most powerful instruments which God has intrusted to our hands for the direction of individual aspirations, and the moulding of national character.

If this truth had been felt in the United States as it was felt in the republics of antiquity, the public squares of Boston would not still have been without a statue of James Otis. A century ago no face was more familiar in your streets than his; no voice so powerful in your courts of justice, in your halls of legislation, and in the gathering places of the people. When Englishmen spoke of the dangerous spirit that was daily growing more dangerous in the Colonies, the first names that came to their lips were the names of Otis and Franklin. When the leaders of sister Colonies wished to strengthen their own hands by the authority of Massachusetts, they appealed to the opinion of Otis as the most faithful expression of the opinion of his people.

Few men have possessed in a more eminent degree the qualities required for the successful guidance of the earlier periods of a struggle like that of our Revolution. He was a sound lawyer; deeply and extensively read; and all the first questions of our controversy were questions of constitutional law. He had read and thought much upon the science of government, and brought a thorough acquaintance with fundamental principles to the discussion of practical questions. He was a close reasoner, a vigorous debater, and in the appeals and apostrophes of oratory, full of an impetuous eloquence that bore down opposition. The enthusiasm that he excited was not a transient feeling, dying away with the sound of his voice, but a profound agitation of the whole nature, penetrating the heart, subduing the reason, and leaving everywhere deep traces of its passage when the headlong torrent had rolled away. He had prepared himself for his professional career by adding to the severe discipline of legal study the elegant discipline of polite literature; studying his Greek and Latin classics as he studied his English classics, and making himself as familiar with Homer and Virgil as with Milton and Shakespeare. If Milton suspended the flow of Paradise Lost in order to dictate his "Accidence made Grammar," may we not regard it as a proof of the vigor of Otis's mind that in the midst of the absorbing duties of his profession he found leisure to compile treatises on Greek and Latin prosody? High-minded, impetuous, irascible; with his political opponents haughty and overbearing, he was generous, sincere, placable, incapable of artifice or deceit; not a pure intellect, moving only in the light of reason and warming only in the pursuit of abstract truths, but a fervid mind, glowing with the sympathetic warmth of a kindred heart.

His labors belong to the first phase of the contest, and filling eight years of his active life, give him, in America, the place of defender of the constitutional rights of the Colonies against the encroachments of the Ministry and Parliament. He was the first to assert that taxation without representation was tyranny;* but his defence was strictly constitu-

---

* The expression had been used long before; Otis was the first to revive and apply it.

tional and fervently loyal; and although he may have foreseen that independence, in certain contingencies, must be the logical consequence of his doctrines, he could not foresee that contingencies so easily avoided would so speedily occur. His speech in 1761, against Writs of Assistance, marks an epoch in Colonial history; for it was the beginning of a form of legal resistance equally adapted to the nature of the dispute and the character of the people who were to sustain it. From that moment he became the acknowledged leader of the opposition: looked up to by his fellow-citizens as the champion of their rights; looked down upon by the Ministry as factious, turbulent, and unmanageable. From that moment, too, he devoted himself to public life, gradually withdrawing from his profession and concentrating his energies upon the question which, in his mind, had already assumed the proportions of a contest for freedom. And here, also, began those voluntary sacrifices, that persistent self-denial, which, for a temperament like his, were the first pangs of martyrdom. He resigned the office of Advocate-General, and with it, not merely its pecuniary rewards, but a professional distinction which he valued more than money. He placed himself in open opposition to some of his dearest friends, and voluntarily renounced many of the associations which were most necessary to his social nature. He made bitter enemies at home and abroad, and drew upon himself the calumnies and insults most galling to his generous and independent feelings. He renounced all amusements, giving himself up to his public duties with an exclusive attention, which to one who loved society and needed recreation as he did, must have required a constant exertion of self-denial in one of its rarest forms. But the sacrifice which was not too great for his will proved too great for his strength. His health failed, his overtasked mind became unequal to the incessant calls for exertion. At this critical moment he was assaulted by a political enemy, overpowered by numbers, and wounded in the head, — the first, though unfortunately not the last attempt in our annals to silence the eloquent voice by the violent hand. And now his vehement passions often got the control over him in public and private. Men wondered at his bursts of indignation, and after excusing them for a while as the eccentricities of a fervid nature, began to suspect and fear, then whisper, and at last say openly that James Otis was mad. Was not the darkness that settled upon that powerful intellect, relieved only at intervals by a softening twilight, an imperfect gleam of its original brightness, a martyrdom as full of honor, as deserving of eternal and grateful remembrance as if he had laid down his life upon the battle-field or poured forth his blood on the scaffold?

When James Otis was pleading the cause of the Colonies in the Sugar Act case and the kindred case of Writs of Assistance, Josiah Quincy, a youth of seventeen, was diligently pursuing the studies of his class at Harvard. He also brought from college a taste for letters, a deep and lasting love for the great poets and great orators of antiquity, but enlarged by a wider range of modern literature, and refined by a gentler spirit. When he first entered upon the practice of his profession, the struggle had reached a crisis of peculiar danger; the Stamp Act had been repealed, but the latent threat contained in the declaratory clause was already beginning to work out its inevitable consequences. Young Quincy loved his profession, and in tranquil times would have devoted himself to it with undivided enthusiasm. But he loved his country; he saw the danger which at that moment menaced her, more, perhaps, than ever before, and, with a clear perception of the personal sacrifice and personal peril, took his stand, from the beginning, at the side of her acknowledged champions. And soon he was in the first rank, hand in hand with Warren and the two Adamses; respected for his calm intrepidity, admired for the fluent eloquence of his pen, and trusted for the soundness of his judgment. The enthusiasm of high principles pervaded his whole nature, imparting dignity to his thoughts and an earnest gravity to his language. Will the Colonies unite? Will they persevere? were the urgent questions of this moment; and his pen poured out earnest exhortations to firm, united, and energetic resistance. As the difficulties increased and the danger grew more imminent, his spirit rose higher and his convictions became more intense. But there was a still harder trial in store for him, — a trial of moral courage under circumstances of singular difficulty. The whole community was excited as Boston had never been excited before. The first blood had been shed in her streets, and they at whose command it was shed were to be put on trial for the deed. Blood for blood, life for life, was the stern cry of the people; and who should gainsay it? Who would dare to raise his voice in defence of murder, and prove his secret alliance with tyranny by open sympathy with its minions?

Then it was that Josiah Quincy, but a little turned of twenty-six, one of the youngest members of the bar, filled with a holy sense of the obligations of his professional oath, joined his eloquent voice to the maturer eloquence of John Adams, and, saving the lives of those whom the law held innocent, saved his native city from the deep and enduring stain of judicial revenge. As we look back upon this act in the light of history, we can easily conceive that, of all the consoling reflections which sustained his spirit in the hour of death, there was none more consoling, more sustaining, than the remembrance of this deed of justice and mercy. But to his immediate contemporaries, and before their passions had cooled, it seemed like a wanton degradation of superior talents, a base abandonment of the cause of freedom. Seldom has the moral courage of a young man been so tried; never has it come out of the trial more resplendent, more worthy of the admiration of every true and honorable nature.

As the contest continued it was readily seen that he had not changed his opinion of the rights of the Colonists. Upon every important question his pen was one of those to which the friends of America looked with most confidence and her enemies with most dread. He had arguments for the understanding and fervid eloquence for the passions, and, above all, unfaltering faith and untiring zeal. But neither faith nor zeal could supply the place of that physical vigor which nature — so bountiful in other things — had denied him. His friends saw with deep anxiety the decaying strength, the sunken cheek, the hectic flush, and all the well-known symptoms of the most insidious and inexorable of diseases. A journey to the South afforded apparent relief, reviving his own hopes with the hopes of his friends. Again he gave himself up to his profession and his public duties. It was in 1774. The first Colonial Congress was about to meet, and all felt that the hopes of a successful resistance depended in a great measure upon the wisdom and temper of its resolves. It was seen, also, by leading minds, that the time had arrived when it was necessary to come to a clear understanding with their friends in England. The sword, although loose in the scabbard, had not yet been drawn. If the ministry could be brought to renounce their insane projects, the Colonies would still gladly hold on to the connection which, in spite of all that had occurred, was still endeared to all by habit, tradition, association, common laws, and a common language. To convey to their English friends an accurate statement of their own feelings and aims, and to obtain an accurate statement of theirs, had become an object of the last importance, but an object which could not be accomplished by writing, or any of the usual methods of communication. In this emergency it was resolved to send one of their own number to England, — a man familiar with the whole subject, with the limits of public opinion and the extent of individual opinion, knowing what all wished, and equally well apprised of what some foresaw.

For this delicate office, requiring so rare a combination of intellectual and moral qualities, — intellectual, because the first minds and deepest learning of England were to be met; moral, because all the allurements of refined corruption were to be encountered, — Josiah Quincy was chosen. On the 25th of September he embarked at Salem, privately, — for it was not deemed advisable to give the partisans of England time to put the government on its guard; and on the 8th of November he landed at Falmouth. Men could hardly believe their own eyes when they saw him in the streets of London. He will surely be arrested, said some. He will surely be bought over, said others. Franklin, and all who thought as Franklin did, and there was one bishop and more than one lord who thought with him, received Quincy with open arms, and listened eagerly and thoughtfully to his story of English wrongs and American resentment. Ministers, too, were anxious to see him. Lord North caused him to be sought out, for the clear-sighted, high-minded man would make no overtures. If a thorough knowledge of what America intended, a full, accurate, and straightforward account of the state of American opinion could have induced the ministry to draw back their hands, every obnoxious act would have been repealed, every soldier recalled. But behind the ministry was the King, — self-willed, obstinate, irritated; and though every word that Quincy said to North was repeated to the King, resentment, not conviction, was the only feeling it awakened. It was evident that government would not recede.

Saddened, but not disheartened, he continued his labors, seeking everywhere the friends of America and striving to confirm them in their kind feelings; meeting her enemies boldly, and using argument and eloquence to convince them of their error. In the midst of these labors his disease returned upon him more severe and menacing than ever. Skilful attendance and comparative repose gave temporary relief, and his physician held out the promise of recovery if he would only break off from his work and give himself up with undivided attention to the care of his health.

Meanwhile the storm was gathering. Before it broke, the friends of the Colonies, unable to avert it, were anxious to send a final warning to their American brethren, — a warning which they dared not trust to paper. Quincy saw clearly that to carry it was going to certain death. Repose, the waters of Bath, might give him health; and did he not owe something to his family and friends, to an aged father, of whom he was the chief hope, to a devoted wife, and children scarcely emerged from infancy, of whom he was the only stay? Had he not already sacrificed much while others were calmly looking on? Was it really the call of duty, where the hazard was so great, the reasons so nearly balanced, the excuse so evident and so plausible?

All this he felt and saw, and calmly and resolutely accepted the fatal mission. It was not like mounting a breach, for there the hot blood nerves the failing limbs, and borne on by the shouts and tumult, and fiery whirlwind of battle, men do things which at other times they would shrink from with horror. But it was placing himself calmly and deliberately in death's chosen path, and watching with unshrinking eye his swift and sure advance. The ship that he sailed in was ill provided for the accommodation of a sick man; the weather was "inclement and damp"; there was no friend to cheer him with kind words or minister to his wants. A common sailor sat by his pillow and took down, in a rude hand, his last thoughts and wishes: his country still first and foremost among them; and thus, after six weeks of solitary suffering, and just within sight of the land where wife and children and friends were anxiously awaiting his coming, he died. What sacrifice more complete, what martyrdom more holy?

Congress had its martyrs, too, if it be martyrdom to die at the post of duty for conscience' sake. The small-pox made the duty of delegate a perilous one in 1775; and among its victims was one whom the cause of American freedom could ill spare at that critical period of our fortunes. Samuel Ward had been Governor of Rhode Island, and when the first Continental Congress was chosen, became, with Stephen Hopkins, her representative. Re-elected to the Congress of 1775, he was soon distinguished for his sound judgment and practical familiarity with the management of legislative assemblies. Rhode Island was hardly large enough to give a President to the Congress, but in committee of the whole, Ward was regularly called to the chair. Few men were more assiduous in the performance of their duty; few were listened to with more respect; few possessed in a higher degree the confidence of their associates. He was among the zealous advocates of union, although the chief of his life had been passed in the political contests of a small State. He was among the early friends of Independence, foreseeing it long before it could be spoken of in debate, and looking hopefully to it, as the natural and inevitable consequence of what had already been done. And when his heart was warmest in the cause and his hopes highest, he, too, died, a victim of the small-pox in its most malignant form; but still more a victim of that noble sense of duty which taught him that for the civilian, as for the soldier, the post of honor is often the post of death. He died, too, before enough had been done to insure him a permanent place in history; too soon even to allow him to give his voice and affix his name to that Declaration of Independence for which he had labored so earnestly. And Rhode Island, like too many of her sister States, forgetful of the children who served her, when to serve her was to put life and fortune in jeopardy, permitted his bones to lie for nearly a century in a borrowed grave, and when at last, forced from their resting-place by the encroachments of an expanding population, they returned to her bosom, to return to it unheralded, and silently mingle with their native soil in the obscurity of a common burying-ground.

Domestic life, too, had its martyrs, — men and women, who, laboring earnestly in obscure fields, sacrificing much, suffering much, drew upon themselves the vengeance of their country's enemies, and sealed their devotion with their blood. Of two of these, the love and veneration of their contemporaries, piously transmitted to posterity, has preserved the memory with peculiar freshness: James Caldwell, pastor of the First Presbyterian Church of Elizabethtown, New Jersey, was distinguished from the beginning of the war as an ardent Whig; and Hannah Ogden, his wife, entering warmly into all his feelings, shared with him the hardships and dangers of his position. His vehement eloquence was directed against the enemies of his country so boldly, and acted so powerfully upon his hearers, that he was soon marked out as a man to be peculiarly dreaded, and a price set upon his head. It is easy to conceive what the influence of such a man must have been: not only eloquent in the pulpit, but living in daily intercourse with the soldiers and ministering intelligently to their wants. It is easy to conceive, too, what a life of peril and excitement the life of this noble couple must have been in a State which was so often the seat of war, and with the enemy always so near their door. More than once he was compelled to take his pistols with him into the pulpit, and lay them down by the side of his Bible. It was no false alarm: though the fatal blow first fell where least expected. In the summer of 1780 there was constant marching to and fro in the Jerseys, and many things to indicate an intention to make them the scene of active operations. For greater security, Mr. Caldwell removed his family to Connecticut Farms, a small village on the site of the modern village of Union. On the morning of the 6th of June, tidings came that the enemy were in motion. Their way led directly through the village, and the inhabitants, seizing whatever they could most readily take with them, hurried off to places of greater security, leaving their houses and the greater part of their property to the mercy of the invader. Mrs. Caldwell remained. Her husband was with his regiment at Springfield. Nine young children were a heavy burden in sudden flight. Surely her sex, their helpless age, would protect them. As the British advanced she went into a back room, and, seating herself upon the bed, with her infant in her arms, silently engaged in prayer. The nursery-maid, who had followed her into the room, with the other children, stood near her, looking towards the window, and listening to the sounds so full of menace and terror which now filled the street of the devoted village. Suddenly she saw a soldier jump over the fence and come up to the window; and as she was still telling her mistress, he levelled his musket, took deliberate aim, and fired. His musket was loaded with two balls. Both passed through the body of the mother, and she dropped dead in the midst of her children. The next day, when her husband came, under the protection of a flag, to look for her, he found the village a smouldering heap of ruins, and his new-made orphans weeping over the lifeless body of their parent. Before two years had filled their course, he too was laid, a murdered man, by her side. Their bodies lie in the burying-ground of the Broad Street Church of Elizabethtown, — a modern church, but built upon the site of the one under whose roof they had so often worshipped their God together. A marble obelisk on a granite base marks the spot; decked with a simple inscription, placed there by the descendants of those who, knowing and honoring them in their lives, bequeathed their memories as a precious legacy to the grateful reverence of posterity.

The Jerseys were the scene of many tragedies, even deeper than this. The passage of the British army in the autumn of 1776 was attended by circumstances of demoniac cruelty. All that wanton barbarity and unbridled passions could do was done; and when the whirlwind had passed, the survivor in many a domestic circle, happy and peaceful till then, looked with longing eyes upon those who had fallen in the first outbreak of violence, and envied them the calm sleep of their graves.

Thus far I have spoken only of our civil martyrs, — of those who, facing danger in a very different form from that wherein it presents itself on the battle-field, faced it with a firm and sober fortitude which on the battle-field would have won them the name of heroes. And heroes they were, of the best and rarest kind, — the heroes of conscience, of high principle, of earnest conviction, — men who serve the cause of virtue by filling the minds of those who contemplate their characters with a noble desire to live as they lived for the sake of mankind, even at the peril of dying as they died, with nothing but their faith in the ultimate triumph of truth to assure them that they had not lived in vain. If legislation were always wise, it would charge itself with the preservation of these men's memories as with one of its highest duties. It would fill public places with their busts and statues; it would seek occasion for bringing their names forward, and strengthening itself for good by showing what rewards true greatness brings. It would employ all its means, and take advantage of every fitting occasion, to dwell upon their virtues, that, by familiarizing the minds of the people with them as children, it might teach them to imitate them and emulate them as men.

In the next class, the first name that presents itself to every mind is that of Joseph Warren. It is too well known to require illustration or to justify me in dwelling upon it. It awakens the memory of a grief so deep and so universal that we feel as if we could almost weep for him as our fathers wept for him eighty-six years ago; and it comes to us with such a familiar sound, with such lively associations of pure motives, high aims, warm affections, and refined tastes, that while we think of him as of one who died for his country, we feel towards him as towards a friend who still shares with us our moments of highest aspiration and noblest resolve. It is impossible to say what Warren might have done for us had his life been spared. But it is easy to see that few lives have been so fruitful of good as his heroic death. It was the baptism of blood, — the consecration of a holy cause. Wherever the story was told it awakened mingled sensations of reverence and love and indignation. Bunker Hill became a distinct and definite object in men's minds, — not only for the fair town that lay smouldering at its foot, not only for the dead that were strewn like the new-mown hay upon its slopes, but more than all these for him, — for him that had fallen there in the pride and hope and vigor of manhood, with the name of country on his lips.

The name of Nathan Hale is less known. He was too young to take an active part in the discussions which had given Warren celebrity before the sword was actually drawn, and held too subordinate a position when he entered the army to attract the attention which he deserved. Like Quincy, he was fresh from college, loved his books, and looked upon literature as the source from which his purest pleasures were to flow. To a naturally refined and delicate mind he had added the refinement of diligent cultivation. Nature had given him lively sensibilities and a warm heart, and he had done all that he could do, by the aid of poetry and philosophy, to make them subservient to the duties of life as well as to its pleasures. His ambition for distinction was controlled by a profound sense of duty, which led him to feel that no distinction could satisfy the aspirations of his mind which did not satisfy the dictates of his conscience. "I wish to be useful," were his words to a friend who was endeavoring to dissuade him from undertaking what the world called a dishonorable thing, although Washington had said that it was indispensable to the safety of the army, — "I wish to be useful, and every kind of service necessary to the public good becomes honorable by being necessary."

With such sentiments we should naturally look for him where we actually find him, — at the camp before Boston, studying his new profession with the same zeal with which he had studied his classics, and trying to prepare his men, as he was preparing himself, for the full and satisfactory performance of their parts. Discipline was one of the first wants of the army, and he tried to make his company distinguished by the excellence of their discipline. A simple and uniform method of clothing the army was greatly needed; and turning his thoughts to the subject, he invented a uniform for his own men, simple, convenient, and comfortable. Everywhere within his sphere his duty was performed in that thorough and satisfactory manner which inspires confidence and commands respect. But no opportunity for distinguished service offered itself: he was with the regiment that Washington took over to Brooklyn during the battle of Long Island, but not in the battle itself. And when he looked back upon the year that he had passed in the army, he felt that he had as yet done nothing for his country. When, therefore, Colonel Knowlton, calling the officers of his regiment together, told them that General Washington wanted an intelligent and trusty man to enter the enemy's lines, and ascertain their position, numbers, and designs, he saw that the time which he had looked forward to was come, for that there was a work to do which even brave men might shrink from without incurring the suspicion of cowardice. The moment that the meeting of officers broke up he went directly to the tent of his friend and classmate, Captain Hull, and told him what was wanted and what he intended to do. "You are not fit for it," said Hull; "you are too frank and open for disguise. This is the work of a spy, — a man whom men use because they need him, but whom they put to death with ignominy if they detect him." It was then that Hale uttered that remarkable profession of faith which I have already quoted : — " Every kind of service necessary to the public good becomes honorable by being necessary. If the exigencies of my country demand a peculiar service, its claims to perform that service are imperious." And then, after listening to his friend's remonstrances and entreaties, he paused, took his hand affectionately, and, saying, "I will reflect, and do nothing which I do not feel to be my duty," went his way. Hull soon missed him from camp, and his heart told him too surely whither he was gone, and what the inevitable fate of one so open and artless would be.

A few days later an English officer came to the American camp with a flag and told Hamilton that Captain Hale had been arrested the day before and hanged that morning as a spy. Hull sought the officer at once and learnt from his lips the short and melancholy story of his friend.

Hale had performed his task, examined the British works, made sketches, collected information, and, with his papers concealed upon his person, was upon the point of stepping into a boat to make his way back to the army, when he was seized and carried before General Howe. Further concealment was impossible; and when we remember his character we can easily conceive that it was with a feeling of relief from odious constraint that he boldly raised his head and avowed his rank and purpose. In so clear a case no trial was deemed necessary. He was condemned to die. For convenience' sake, not mercy's, a single night was given him, for it was now evening, and Howe's quarters at a distance from the city. He passed that night in the green-house of the Beekman mansion, which ten years ago was still standing with all its associations of colonial New York. He asked to see a clergyman, but was denied, — for a Bible, but it was refused him. Next morning he was led out to death. Did he falter? did he shrink? Would he have wished that fatal step untaken? Cunningham, the Provost Marshal, would have gladly had us think so. But near Rutgers's orchard — one of whose apple-trees was to supply a gallows — an English officer had pitched his marquee, and when he saw the preparations, he asked Cunningham to allow his victim to come and sit in it till all was ready. "He was calm," said this unimpeachable witness, "and bore himself with gentle dignity in the consciousness of rectitude and high intentions. He asked for writing materials, which I furnished him, and wrote two letters, one to his mother and one to a brother officer." Shortly after, he was summoned to the gallows. All that he could add to the bitterness of death, Cunningham added; and when he heard the last words of his victim — "I only regret that I have but one life to lose for my country" — he resolved in his heart that the rebels should never know that they had a man in their army who could die with so much firmness, and destroying his letters, destroyed, as he fondly supposed, the last and only record of his dying sentiments. But Providence had not willed it so; and in this hour of desolation raised him up a friendly witness even from among his enemies; for it so chanced that the officer who had supplied him with pen and paper, was sent with a flag into the American camp on the afternoon of that very day, and from his lips, not from uncertain rumors or doubtful reports, Hull received the unquestionable testimony.

A parallel has often been drawn between Hale and André. But it is doing injustice to the self-denying American, who for conscience' sake undertook a task which, even if fully successful, could bring no reward but the sense of duty performed, with the aspiring Englishman, who for ambition's sake undertook a task which promised increase of rank and the chance of military distinction. Hale put on a disguise for a few hours under the impulse of a strong and generous motive. André carried on a treacherous correspondence for months, availing himself artfully of every means to render it effective. Had Hale succeeded in reaching the American camp, he would have made his report to his immediate commander and returned silently to the performance of his subordinate functions. Had André succeeded in reaching New York, his achievements would have been hailed by the Commander-in-chief as a brilliant display of energy, and his name transmitted to the ministry for acknowledgment and reward. They were both young, both accomplished, both engaging in their manners and winning in their address. But the English officer's act was connected with a design which, if successful, might have protracted the war for years, even if it had not turned the scale against us; thus his name became permanently associated with a great enterprise and a great treason. The enormity of Arnold's villany so overshadowed every subordinate circumstance that men never paused to weigh the measure of condemnation which a strict morality might mete out to his accomplice. They saw only the gigantic traitor, employing for the destruction of his confiding country the means which she had intrusted to his hands for her protection. They saw only that, while his presence of mind had put him beyond the reach of punishment, he had left a victim behind him, a young man full of talents and accomplishments; and as they looked upon him their hearts were saddened at the thought that such a one must lay down his young life while the master criminal lived in security. But they did not see that André's success involved the sacrifice of many innocent men, who, in that midnight assault, wherein every obstacle was removed beforehand, would have been led like victims to the slaughter. They did not see that in calmly discussing its details during the long hours of that September night, under the pensive light of the stars, and within sound of the soft ripple of the Hudson, he had been calmly laying a snare for the lives of gallant men; calmly premeditating, not an attack with equal chances upon men who might hope to defend themselves, but the slaughter of unsuspecting victims, under circumstances which, giving them no chances of defence, would, if things were always called by their true names, be branded as deliberate murder.

To Hale's undertaking no such guilt is attached. The only life that he put in jeopardy was his own. It was an individual act, by which his country might gain much, without hazard, — a self-imposed sacrifice, wherein he hazarded all, without the chance or the expectation of reward, as rewards are measured by human ambition. Should he succeed, — should he escape the other perils of war, and live to see a fireside of his own and children of his own around it, he might tell them, perhaps, how, when the patriot army was sore beset, and Washington himself at a loss on which side to look for the coming of his enemy, he had gone secretly among them at the hazard of his life, discovered their plans, revealed them to his General, and relieved that noble mind of one of its cares. But to his brother officers he could say nothing. Congress, Washington himself, might never know what he had done; and unless some chance, independent of any influence this act could have, should raise him higher, he might end his military service in the same subordinate station in which he had begun it. If acts are to be judged by the sacrifices they impose, and actors by their motives, there is but little room for a parallel between André and Hale. But the servant of the king sleeps amid poets, and orators, and statesmen, and heroes, in the hallowed precincts of Westminster Abbey; while an insignificant fort in the harbor of New Haven is the only spot which preserves the name of the republican martyr.

No occurrence of the war excited deeper or more general indignation than the official murder of Isaac Hayne of South Carolina; for it was regarded not merely as a wanton sacrifice of a worthy man, but as a brutal attempt on the part of our adversaries to retain by the threat of the halter an authority which they had not been able to preserve by the sword. The capitulation of Charleston in 1780 had thrown a large body of Carolina militia into the hands of the enemy, but a special provision in the articles of capitulation had secured them the position of prisoners on parole. The British arms continued successful; the State was overrun; and, to confirm his triumph, the English commander called upon all the militiamen on parole, not protected by the fourth clause of the capitulation, to make an immediate choice between a return to their allegiance and close confinement. Had it been the intention of the conqueror to adhere to his pledge, Hayne would have been fully protected by the article so expressly specified. But, in open violation both of its spirit and its letter, he was summoned to acknowledge himself a British subject or go to prison. The moment when this alternative was laid before him was one in which the stoutest heart might have faltered, for the small-pox was in his family, and to leave his wife and children was like consigning them with his own hands to the grave. He hastened to Charleston, and, expressly stipulating that he should not be called upon to take up arms against his country, made the fatal acknowledgment. The wife for whose protection he had taken this unwelcome step, died; he had already lost one child; a second soon followed its mother to the grave. Soon, too, he found that his stipulation, though clear, positive, and accepted by the British commander at the time, was no protection from repeated summons to join in an active defence of the English supremacy. To these summons, though often repeated, and accompanied by the threat of imprisonment, he opposed a firm refusal.

Then came Greene's advance into South Carolina, and the gradual recession of the English forces. Soon the region round Hayne's plantation was in the hands of the Americans. The English general not only was unable to enforce the allegiance he had imposed, but even to protect those who had accepted it from their irritated and victorious countrymen. Hayne's sentiments were well known. It was well known that his heart was with the Americans, and that nothing but his strong love for his family had induced him to accept the hard terms so unjustly imposed upon him at a time when, unable to do anything for his country, he might still do so much for them. Yet, without concealing his wishes, he restrained his zeal until the retreat of the enemy made it necessary to decide whether he would follow them to Charleston for a nominal protection, or obey the dictates of his conscience and join his countrymen. A calm examination of his position convinced him that an obligation of qualified allegiance, assumed because the district he lived in was in the hands of the enemy, ceased to be binding from the moment that they who imposed it were stripped of their supremacy; that having acknowledged himself a British subject for the purpose, openly avowed, of giving his personal attention to his family on the Edisto, and with an express declaration that he would not fight against his country, he was no longer a British subject when the Edisto had passed under the control of the Americans, and he was summoned, in violation of his express stipulation, to take up arms against them. He repaired to the American camp, was welcomed, placed at the head of a militia regiment, surprised, and made prisoner by militia negligence.

The English commander wanted a victim, and here was one. I will not follow the story through its sad details: the unseemly haste with which his life was hunted down, the mockery of the forms of justice, the efforts of friends to save him, the calmness with which he received the sentence of death, the fortitude with which he met it, that parting injunction to his son — a boy of thirteen — to come for his body to the foot of the gallows and give it decent burial. To tell this is the office of history, and we have not room for it here. What I wish to dwell upon is the spirit which this martyrdom awakened, and which, if the war had continued, might have swelled our list of martyrs by hundreds.

For when this occurred the American army was encamped at the high hills of Santee, resting themselves after a long and exhausting campaign. Thus the tidings reached them at a time when they had leisure and opportunity to discuss and compare their opinions. The indignation was universal; there was a common cry for vengeance. But there was but one way by which they could avenge him, and that was by retaliation. Greene's resolution was taken instantly. This must be the last judicial murder. To strike at the American loyalists would produce no effect. English officers themselves must be made to feel that the lives of Americans would no longer be taken with impunity. But at this time a large body of American prisoners who had been regularly exchanged were on their way from St. Augustine to the North, and to give full time for their safe arrival he was compelled to conceal his intention for a while even from his own army. The officers became uneasy. They knew that in asking for retaliation they were doubling their own hazards; for to be taken prisoner — and who could secure them against the chances of war? — would become a sentence of death. But they were resolved at every hazard to enforce the laws by which civilization has stript war of many of its horrors; they were resolved that the name of American and the commission of Congress should henceforth be a protection from the wantonness of systematic persecution. To give full and solemn expression to their sentiments, they drew up an address to their commander; which I will not attempt to analyze, for analysis would give you a very imperfect idea of its firm and magnanimous spirit and the calm dignity of its language. I will read it to you from the original, for the paper which I hold in my hand is the original itself. (See p. 458.)

I have already said that Greene had resolved upon retaliation the moment he heard of Hayne's murder. But the threat, supported by the battle of Eutaw and the rapid success of the American arms, proved sufficient; and this was the last instance of that barbarous policy, more unwise even than barbarous, which, during the brief duration of the English supremacy, had stained the soil of Carolina with so much innocent blood.

Thus far I have spoken of individuals, — of forms which stand out in bold relief in the transparent light of history. But what shall I say of the thousands whose sufferings, blended in one common lot, are known only as the victims of the jail and the prison-ship? Never were souls more tried than theirs; never was the crown of martyrdom won by tortures harder to bear than the tortures which they bore from week to week and month to month, till nature, sinking under the protracted agony, sought shelter in the grave. And that grave itself a few inches of sand, which the first ebbings and flowings of the tide washed away, leaving all that hunger, and foul air, and the diseases which they engender, had spared them of the image of their Maker to crumble and bleach in the wind and sun. On the shores of Wallabout Bay, alone, it is supposed that more than eleven thousand received this mockery of burial; and if we add to these the victims of the sugar-houses of New York, of the prisons and prison-ships of Charleston, and St. Augustine, what fearful proportions does the list of our martyrs assume!

It is difficult, nay almost impossible, to form an idea of these sufferings. The imagination sinks powerless before this canvas, crowded with thousands of human forms, melting in lurid light into one ghastly mass of human misery. Nor would I dwell upon them, if I did not feel that forgetfulness of the debt we owe the sufferers has had a large part in producing the sufferings of our own hour of trial. Let us take one, therefore, and fix our attention upon him, that in his sufferings we may realize more distinctly what thousands suffered with him, and in every suffering that we assign him let us be careful to add nothing which every individual of them all did not actually endure. Shall we choose him from town or country? There were hundreds and hundreds from each. Let him have come, then, from the pure air of his own fields, where he left his plough in the furrow to seize his fowling-piece or gird on the sword which his father had worn with honor in the old French war. Thrown down in the shock of battle he awakes from his trance to find himself a prisoner pent up in a close room with a crowd of prisoners. Hours pass, but no one brings them food or water. Night comes; in the stifling atmosphere, thirst, such as he had never dreamed of before, burns into his veins. He begs for a drop of water, but the sentinel at the door breaks out in a song full of mockery. He struggles to the window and tries for a breath of pure air, but the sentry thrusts him back at the point of the bayonet. Another day, another night, — food comes at last, — bread that he can hardly break, meat that even in this extremity he turns from with loathing. But O what a delicious draught in that cup of water! though it is water which, if not taken from a muddy pool, has stood in filthy vessels exposed to the sun till all its life-giving freshness was gone. Then a weary march to the river-side, — weary, because he is already faint with hunger; but, at least, it is a march in the pure air; and how sweetly does its freshness float around his brow, and check the fever that had begun to kindle its slow fires in his veins! Faint and exhausted as he is he would have gladly kept on a few miles farther, for the sake of that free-drawn breath and the sight of something besides despairing faces, the sound of something besides despairing groans. But here he stands on the river's brink, and out there at anchor, securely moored, stem and stern, lies the hulk of a huge man-of-war; the masts and bowsprit gone, but with a signal pole midships; a small tent on the stern to screen the sentry from the sun; something rising above her bulwarks, he cannot guess what, though he will soon find why it was put there; and the portholes all open, and all filled with human faces, looking out, some listlessly, some eagerly, all hopelessly. He is soon among them. A long, fixed staging, leading from the water's edge, receives him after a few strokes of the oar. The sentry at the gangway passes him roughly down; name, regiment, description of his person, are entered upon the register: the formalities are all over; he is a prisoner, and this is the Jersey.

He had good clothes on when he was taken, but they have given him rags instead; a little money, — they would have taken that, too, but when he saw them stripping his comrades he hid his money in his mouth till he had got his tatters on, and then he knew it was safe. He cannot join the groups on the main-deck, for he longs to be alone. But as he approaches the hatchway to go down below he is met by such a stifling current of foul air that he staggers back gasping for breath. Anything but this. An old prisoner observes him, and tells him that that is the air he must sleep in. By degrees, as he moves about among the groups, and what with question and reply, he begins to make acquaintances, — tells his story, hears theirs. Dinner is served out. With an appetite sharpened by almost three days of starvation, he succeeds in eating a little of the sour bread; after a few days more he will begin to taste the tainted meat. And thus thinking over the past, not daring to look forward to the future, his first day wears slowly on. And what a night is that which follows! Forced down into that pestilential air, where fever and its kindred diseases love to make their dwelling, he lays him on filthy straw and tries to sleep. But the groans of the prisoner beside him will not let him sleep; yet lie he must, for he cannot take a step without treading on the recumbent form of some fellow-sufferer, only by so much less wretched than himself inasmuch as he has become familiar with these sights and sounds and can sleep in despite of them. How gladly, yet with what a heavy heart and aching head, does he see the return of day! With it comes the rough voice of the guard from above: "Rebels, bring up your dead." And while he looks about him for the meaning of such a summons he sees a general rising and moving. Some stoop down over the bed next them and lift up its tenant, — the corpse that became a corpse while they slept, — and carry it to the hatchway to be thrown into the boat and carried off for burial. He remembers the groans that kept him awake so long, and turns to the place at his side they came from. There will be no more groaning from those lips, — livid, clammy, but O how fearfully eloquent in their appeal from tyranny to God! He shudders; a chill runs over him as he thinks that perhaps not very far off there might be a mother, a wife, children, who would have deemed it a blessed privilege to press one parting kiss upon them before they were consigned forever to the silence and darkness of the grave. But he has no time for these thoughts now, though they will come back to him at night when he again lays him down in the company of the dying. Now he must repress all his natural feelings, and help carry that body to the companion-way and see it thrown headlong into the boat.

But enough; I have exaggerated nothing; I have added nothing, although I have suppressed and omitted much. I have not dared to dip my pencil deep enough in the fearful elements of which this picture is composed to paint it in all its shocking realities. But if, with the picture such as I have it before your minds, you add that there was not one of all these sufferers who might not have purchased instant freedom by renouncing his country, you will see what kind of spirit that was which animated the martyrs of the American Revolution. And whence was that spirit drawn but from the conviction, so deep-rooted and so clearly expressed, that they were suffering for the cause of humanity: sacrificing themselves that their children and their children's children might live united and free in a land consecrated to Freedom and Union!

LECTURE XI.

LITERATURE OF THE REVOLUTION.

PART I. — PROSE.

GREAT revolutions, being attended by extraordinary intellectual activity, are generally favorable to the cause of literature. When the public mind is kept in a constant state of agitation, the mind of the individual not only partakes of the general excitement, but is often roused to a degree of exertion which it would have been incapable of in times of public tranquillity. All the great landmarks of thought are lost; principles that seemed beyond the reach of doubt are called in question; immoderate hope and immoderate fear prevail by turns, often succeeding each other with inconceivable rapidity; and the mind, tossed to and fro without respite, now grasping at one phantom and now at another, is equally eager in whatever direction it turns, and as bold in its efforts to reason as in its wildest flights of imagination; and when at last the commotion ceases, and society puts on its new form, the intellectual impulse still continues, and the new ideas which have been brought up from depths never reached before become the starting-points from which new generations set forth upon new inquiries.

But revolution, in order to give this impulse to literature, must receive its own impulse from those deeper sources in which thought and feeling are blended. It is only when men think with their hearts, if I may borrow an expression from the father of verse,* that their faculties are thoroughly roused. And to think with our hearts requires that the subject should be one from which, when once started, there is no escape. It must follow us wherever we go, meet us at every turn, intertwine itself with all the relations of life, and infuse its spirit into all our actions.

This complete possession of the human soul and absolute control of the human will does not belong to questions which have their beginning and their end in this life. Individuals may give themselves up to ambition or pleasure, classes may become absorbed in the pursuit of power or gain, but there are recesses in the human heart which neither the ambition of power nor the ambition of wealth can penetrate; and, until these recesses are reached, it is impossible to arouse the whole body of society to self-denial and continuous exertion.

Wickliffe was contemporary with Chaucer. The introduction of the Reformation was followed by

---

* Ἕως ὁ ταῦθ' ὥρμαινε κατὰ φρένα καὶ κατὰ θυμόν.
Iliad, I. 193.

the most original period of English literature. The deep convictions of the English Revolution glow with intense energy in the "Paradise Lost." Even that less original development which has often been called the Augustan age of English literature followed close upon the last great uprising of Protestant zeal in England in 1688. And never before in the whole course of its history did the French mind display such fertility and vigor as during its long contest with that arrogant spirit which, manifesting itself first in the domain of religious thought and then in the broader field of civil life, claimed equally in both the right of controlling man's action in the name of his Maker.

But the American Revolution, with all its earnestness of purpose, with all its strength of conviction, belongs, in its intellectual relations, to the domain of reason rather than to the domain of feeling. It was the expression of a belief founded, indeed, upon those instinctive suggestions in which the heart and mind act together, but a belief which appealed for confirmation to the deductions of rigorous logic and the facts of positive history. It was a legal contest, beginning with the statute-book, passing logically to Grotius and Puffendorff, and never, even in the hour of intensest excitement, losing sight of the acknowledged landmarks of thought. Hence, while it brought out in full light principles overlaid till then by old forms and customs, it started no new theories, opened no new fountains of feeling, left the floodgates of passion untouched. Its heroes were thoughtful, reasoning men, accustomed to stand on firm ground, and who felt that their new position could only be made tenable by connecting it logically with the old. They came not to create, but to eliminate; not to grasp at the future by speculative combinations, but to remove from their own path — and thereby from their children's also — the obstacles which had so long impeded the natural development of acknowledged laws. But while they thought soberly, they thought also boldly, shrinking from no remote consequence of a principle, however repugnant to common opinion; asserting in their largest comprehension the conclusions to which they had been led by close adherence to the laws of reasoning, although that unreserved assertion sometimes placed them in painful contradiction with their actual position. And thus they sometimes reached, by a severe logic, heights which are seldom reached without a vigorous effort of imagination.

When Jefferson asserted as the justification of our national existence that all men are born free and equal, he merely reduced to its simplest form of expression that fundamental truth which had been gradually making itself clearer to logical minds ever since the gathering at Runnymede.*

* The progress of the Roman "Omnes homines natura acquales sunt" from a "legal rule to a political dogma," has been sketched with a rapid but a masterly hand by Maine in his

And when Washington accepted it, he frankly accepted with it its natural corollary, although that corollary involved a radical change in the organization of labor; when Greene accepted it, he followed it to its practical consequence, and recorded it as his deliberate conviction: "On the subject of slavery, nothing can be said in its defence."

But in all this it was the reason which deduces and binds together, not the imagination which creates and stimulates, that was the guide. No fermentation of thought, no wrestling with stubborn doubts, was required to reach those truths. Nowhere in its progress did the mind find itself shrinking and shuddering on the brink of awful precipices, but ever looking forth rather from serene heights over a path which still led onward and upward.

Hence, the literature of our Revolution was chiefly a literature of investigation, reasoning, and sober thought. Men drew their inspiration from the statute-book, reached their theories by laborious induction, and seldom, when warming into eloquence, lost sight of rule and precedent. If we go to them for bold images, original forms, startling conclusions, we shall be greatly disappointed.

recent History of Ancient Law, Ch. IV. pp. 88 *et seq.* of the American edition; a work of the highest authority in itself, and which has acquired new value by the admirable introduction prefixed to it by the American editor, Professor T. W. Dwight, of Columbia College.

But they are able expounders of fundamental truths, skilful illustrators of vital principles, earnest advocates of human rights. They wrote, not to build up a literature, but to defend a holy cause; and their works, like those massive foundation walls on which modern Romans have built the palaces of a new society and the temples of a new faith, carry us back to an age of strong men building for eternity.

First among them, and still unsurpassed as a writer of pure English in a simple, graceful, and natural style, was

"Your island city's greatest son,"—

Benjamin Franklin. To write well, as I have hinted in another Lecture, was one of the earliest objects of his ambition; and starting with the conviction that "true ease in writing comes from art," he set himself to the study of this art as he set himself to the study of the art that he expected to earn his bread by, with an enthusiasm tempered by judgment. Let me give you the story in his own words.

"About this time I met with an odd volume of the 'Spectator.' I had never before seen any of them. I bought it, read it over and over, and was much delighted with it. I thought the writing excellent, and wished, if possible, to imitate it. With that view I took some of the papers, and making short hints of the sentiments in each sentence, laid them by a few days, and then, without looking at the book, tried to complete the papers again by expressing each hinted sentiment at length, and as fully as it had been expressed before, in any suitable words that should occur to me. Then I compared my 'Spectator' with the original, discovered some of my faults and corrected them. But I found I wanted a stock of words, or a readiness in recollecting and using them, which I thought I should have acquired before that time, if I had gone on making verses, since the continual search for words of the same import, but of different length to suit the measure, or of different sound for the rhyme, would have laid me under a constant necessity of searching for variety, and also have tended to fix that variety in my mind, and make me master of it. Therefore I took some of the tales in the 'Spectator,' and turned them into verse; and after a time, when I had pretty well forgotten the prose, turned them back again.

"I also sometimes jumbled my collection of hints into confusion; and, after some weeks, endeavored to reduce them into the best order before I began to form the full sentences and complete the subject. This was to teach me method in the arrangement of the thoughts. By comparing my work with the original, I discovered many faults and corrected them; but I sometimes had the pleasure to fancy that, in certain particulars of small consequence, I had been fortunate enough to improve the method or the language; and this encouraged me to think that I might in time come to be a tolerable English writer, — of which I was extremely ambitious." *

If there were time to comment upon this narrative, there are two points in it upon which I would gladly enlarge. One is, that Franklin chose for himself a model, and studied it thoroughly, — studied it as a great sculptor studies the antique; and yet, like the great sculptor, put so much of his own into his works that all that reminds you of his master in them is that fine flavor of genuine nature which they both possess in an almost equal degree. And the other, that they who, in their idle railing at Latin and Greek, cite Franklin's style as a proof of what mere English can do, forget that, if Franklin did not sit directly at the feet of Xenophon and Cicero, the master at whose feet he sat was one of the most diligent and faithful of their disciples.

One of the first things that strikes you in Franklin's writings is that he always has something to say. His sentences are not crowded with ideas like Bacon's; but, from the moment that you begin to read, you find yourself under the influence of another mind; and yet that influence is exerted so gently, his thoughts steal into your mind with such mild persuasiveness and blend so readily with

* Sparks's Franklin, Vol. I. p. 18.

your thoughts, that it is only when you come to examine yourself upon the subject, and recall the actual amount of knowledge you set out with, that you perceive how much you have added to it and what an impulse he has given you. His words are simple, — the words of common life, neither bigotedly Saxon nor studiously Latin, but the words he talked with every day, and which both from his pen and his lips found their way with equal readiness to the understandings of poor and rich, of prince and peasant. Few men have hit more happily the medium betwixt the diffusion that leads to weakness and the concision that leads to aridity. He has never too many words for forcible expression, and never too few for adequate expression. And without any obtrusive study of harmony, he arranges them with such a delicate perception of their relations as sounds, that his sentences flow with a melody that lingers soothingly in the mind long after it has ceased to reach the ear.

Like his great master, Addison, and his great contemporary, Goldsmith, he possessed in an eminent degree that rare quality of delicate humor which Englishmen, forgetful of Gasparo Gozzi, have claimed as exclusively their own. Yet, while he believed that men might often be laughed out of their foibles, he believed also that vices called for sterner rebuke; and often, as his feelings grew warm, he gave them utterance in satire, which, but for an under-current of genial sympathy which he could never wholly repress, would have blistered and burnt like the satire of Swift.

You will readily conceive that for a genius like his the controversy with England opened an ample field, calling out all the resources of wit, illustration, and argument. Living in London, as agent for four Colonies, two of them the important Colonies of Massachusetts and Pennsylvania, he was enabled to follow the progress of opinion in England, and measure from the beginning the extent of the blindness and passion which were hastening the final rupture. He would gladly have stayed it, for he thought it premature, and hence his voice was raised in warnings, grave and earnest in spirit, though often playful, sometimes ironical in form. The profoundest reasoning could not have set in a more striking light the absurdity and impolicy of the acts of Parliament for restraining American industry, than his "Edict by the King of Prussia" setting forth his claims to the sovereignty over England in virtue of the German origin of Hengist and Horsa and their companions and followers.* Still more severe in its irony, and equally profound in its wisdom, is the piece to which he gave the title, a satire in itself, of "Rules for reducing a great Empire to a small one; presented to a late Minister when he entered upon his Administration." Observe how directly he comes

* Sparks's Franklin, Vol. IV. p. 399.

to his subject, and with what a masterly touch he brings out the great underlying truth: —

"An ancient sage valued himself upon this: that though he could not fiddle, he knew how to make a great city of a little one. The science that I, a modern simpleton, am about to communicate, is the very reverse.

"I address myself to all ministers who have the management of extensive dominions, which from their very greatness have become troublesome to govern, because the multiplicity of their affairs leaves no time for fiddling.

"1. In the first place, gentlemen, you are to consider, that a great empire, like a great cake, is most easily diminished at the edges. Turn your attention, therefore, first to your *remotest* provinces; that as you get rid of them, the next may follow in order.

"2. That the possibility of this separation may always exist, take special care the provinces are *never incorporated with the mother country;* that they do not enjoy the same common rights; the same privileges in commerce; and that they are governed by severer laws, all of your enacting, without allowing them any share in the choice of the legislators. By carefully making and observing such distinctions, you will (to keep to my simile of the cake) act like a wise gingerbread-baker, who, to facilitate a division, cuts his dough half through in those places where, when baked, he would have it broken to pieces.

"3. Those remote provinces have perhaps been acquired, purchased, or conquered, at the sole expense of the settlers or their ancestors; without the aid of the mother country. If this should happen to increase her strength, by their growing numbers, ready to join in her wars, her commerce, by their growing demand for her manufactures, or her naval power, by greater employment for her ships and seamen, they may probably suppose some merit in this, and that it entitles them to some favor; you are therefore to *forget it all*, or *resent it*, as if they had done you injury. If they happen to be zealous Whigs, friends of liberty, nurtured in revolution principles, remember all that to their prejudice, and contrive to punish it; for such principles, after a revolution is thoroughly established, are of no more use; they are even odious and abominable.

"4. However peaceably your colonies have submitted to your judgment, shown their affection to your interests, and patiently borne their grievances, you are to suppose them *always inclined to revolt*, and treat them accordingly. Quarter troops among them, who by their insolence may provoke the rising of mobs, and by their bullets and bayonets suppress them. By this means, like the husband who uses his wife ill from suspicion, you may in time convert your suspicions into realities." *

I give you only extracts; you should read the whole piece for yourselves; and then turn to Swift

---

* Sparks's Franklin, Vol. IV. p. 388.

and see if he has anywhere a keener page than this. And yet do you not feel, as you read, that it was written not in bitterness but in sadness of heart?—that the benevolent old man was shuddering, as he wrote, at the miseries he foresaw, was lingering with deep yearnings over the recollection of the blessings he had enjoyed?*

Still more striking is the piece written on his death-bed, just twenty-four days before he died, and which as we read it now in the midst of a war for the extension of slavery and reopening of the slave-trade, makes us blush to think that we should

---

* As this page is passing through the press I find an important tribute to Franklin as an interpreter of nature, in Dr. Youmans's valuable introduction to the American edition of the recent English work upon the "Correlation and Conservation of Forces":—
"It was this country, widely reproached for being over-practical, which produced just that kind of working ability that was suited to transfer this profound question from the barren to the fruitful field of inquiry. It is a matter of just national pride that the two men who first demonstrated the capital propositions of pure science, that lightning is but a case of common electricity, and that heat is but a mode of motion, who first converted these propositions from conjectures of fancy to facts of science, were not only Americans by birth and education, but men eminently representative of the peculiarities of American character: Benjamin Franklin, and Benjamin Thompson, afterwards known as Count Rumford."

Of the many literary portraits that have been drawn of Franklin I cannot deny myself the pleasure of referring to that by my friend Henry T. Tuckerman in his "Biographical Essays, or Studies of Character," a work remarkable for delicate observation, accurate thought, and good writing.

still, in 1863, be so little in advance of the ground he stood upon in 1790. I have not time to read it here, but I recommend it to the thoughtful examination of all those who permit themselves to entertain doubts as to the interpretation which one of the wisest and most influential members of the Convention of 1788 put upon the first clause of the 9th Section, Article I., and the third clause of the 2d Section, Article IV., of the Constitution.

Next to Franklin's no name was more familiar to Americans from 1768 to 1775 than the name of John Dickinson, the author of the "Farmer's Letters." This eminent man was born in Maryland on the 13th of November, 1732, and while he was yet a child his parents moved to Delaware, or as it was then called, the three lower counties on the Delaware. It was there that he received the rudiments of his education, and laid the foundations of that good taste and love of general literature which became one of the chief sources of his celebrity. When old enough to choose a profession he fixed upon the law, the most attractive of all in a free state, as opening the surest path to distinction and influence, and after making a successful beginning in Philadelphia went to London and continued his studies three years in the Temple. The wisdom of this course was soon manifest, for, returning to Philadelphia with that favorable opinion which the reputation of having studied in London never failed to awaken among our England-loving ancestors, he quickly made himself a position at the bar, and obtained a good practice. Nature, too, had done her part, and given him a countenance that attracted attention and won sympathy, and an air and figure well suited to the graceful and dignified character of his eloquence. His reputation as an orator soon brought him into the Assembly, where it was readily seen that his talent for sober business was in no wise inferior to his talent for debate. The dispute with England was daily growing warmer in tone, and more comprehensive in its bearings. But for the public men of Philadelphia there was also the additional dispute with the Proprietary, which has left such deep traces in the writings of Franklin. Dickinson entered heartily into them, using both voice and pen in support of his opinions, and with a facility and vigor that soon placed him in the front rank. His first publication was a speech upon the projected change from proprietary to royal governments, which he opposed as injudicious at a time when their privileges were so evidently threatened by the policy of the ministry. This was followed in 1765 by a pamphlet, — "The late Regulations respecting the British Colonies on the Continent of North America considered"; and to this pamphlet he was probably indebted for his appointment as delegate to the Congress that was to meet that year in New York. You remember the resolutions of that Congress, how bold and how firm they are, and what an impulse and direction they gave to the spirit of resistance. It is no slight proof of Dickinson's position that with such a man as James Otis in the Assembly he should have been chosen to draft its resolves. Returning home with the additional lustre of this triumph, he resumed his labors at the bar, keeping, however, in view the great constitutional question in which all other questions were involved. Never, indeed, had such a field, so broad, so rich, demanding such depth of investigation, and such soundness of judgment, been opened to American statesmen. The Stamp Act, which had been so resolutely opposed on the continent, had been submitted to, though not without remonstrance, by the little island of Barbadoes. But in instructing their agent in London to "lay [their] complaints before his Majesty and the Parliament," the Committee of Correspondence had spoken of the resistance of their "fellow-subjects on the northern continent" as "rebellious opposition to authority," and of the spirit they were impelled by, as "popular fury." Dickinson met the charge in a pamphlet entitled, "An Address to the Committee of Correspondence in Barbadoes, occasioned by a late Letter from them to their Agent in London; by a North American"; — prefixing as a motto a passage from Shakespeare, which, like so many passages of that great poet, seemed to tell the whole story in a verse and a half: —

> "This word, Rebellion, hath froze them up
> Like fish in a pond."

"Had the charge of rebellion," begins the Preface, "been made by a private person, against the Colonies on this continent, for their opposition to the Stamp Act, I should not have thought it worth answering. But when it was made by men vested with a public character, by a committee of correspondence, representing two branches of legislature in a considerable government, and the charge was not only approved, as it is said, by those branches, but was actually published to the world in newspapers, it seemed to me to deserve notice. I waited some time, in hopes of seeing the cause espoused by an abler advocate; but being disappointed, I resolved, *favente Deo*, to snatch a little time from the hurry of business, and to place, if I could, the letter of those gentlemen to their agent in a proper light."

I have not time for extracts, but I will read you the opening paragraph, it is so true a picture of the author himself.

"Gentlemen, — I am a North American, and my intention is, in addressing you at present, to answer so much of a late letter from you to your agent in London, as casts unmerited censure or my countrymen. After this declaration, as you entertain such unfavorable sentiments of the 'popular fury' on this continent, I presume you expect to be treated with all the excess of passion natural to a rude people. You are mistaken. I am of their opinion who think it almost as infamous to disgrace a good cause by illiberal language, as to betray it by unmanly timidity. Complaints may be made with dignity; insults retorted with decency, and violated rights vindicated without violence of words."

Full as this pamphlet is of the life and spirit of political controversy, there is, at the same time, a fine literary tone about it, which shows that the excitement of public life had not estranged him from his early masters and friends. Still more apparent was this chastening influence of literary culture upon his next work, "The Farmer's Letters," published in 1767.

This work forms an epoch in the literary history of the Revolution. In no other publication had the question of taxation been discussed upon such broad grounds and with such richness and variety of illustration. The assumed character of a "Pennsylvania Farmer" permitted directness and simplicity of style, and the form of letters allowed of repetitions and returns to the same point that would have been unbecoming in a formal discourse. Unencumbered by the technicalities of professional reasoning, it was none the less faithful to the spirit of professional discipline. A man of letters might perhaps have claimed the author as one of his own fraternity, but no lawyer could have read it without recognizing the habits and influence of legal thought. Yet, to the people it came as the unstudied expression of the sentiments of a man not too far removed from them to understand their feelings, and yet so much better informed than themselves that they might, without hazard, accept him as a guide. I shall not attempt to analyze these twelve Letters, for a mere analysis would give you a very imperfect idea of their power. But I will read you a single passage, in the hope that some among you who feel curious about the means which our ancestors employed in working out their part of our great problem, may be induced to read the whole for yourselves.

"My dear Countrymen:—

"I am a *farmer*, settled, after a variety of fortunes, near the banks of the river *Delaware*, in the Province of *Pennsylvania*. I received a liberal education and have been engaged in the busy scenes of life: but am now convinced, that a man may be as happy without bustle, as with it. My farm is small; my servants are few, and good; I have a little money at interest; I wish for no more; my employment in my own affairs is easy; and with a contented, grateful mind, undisturbed by worldly hopes or fears relating to mysef, I am completing the number of days allotted to me by Divine goodness.

"Being generally master of my time, I spend a good deal of it in a library, which I think the most valuable part of my small estate; and being acquainted with two or three gentlemen of abilities and learning, who honor me with their friendship, I have acquired, I believe, a greater knowledge in history; and the laws and constitution of my country, than is generally attained by men of my class, many of them not being so fortunate as I have been in the opportunities of getting information.

"From my infancy I was taught by my honored parents to love *humanity* and *liberty*. Inquiry and experience have since confirmed my reverence for the lessons then given me, by convincing me more fully of their truth and excellence. Benevolence towards mankind excites wishes for their welfare, and such wishes endear the means of fulfilling them. *These* can be found in Liberty only, and therefore her sacred cause ought to be espoused by every man on every occasion, to the utmost of his power. As a charitable, but poor person does not withhold his *mite*, because he cannot relieve *all* the distresses of the miserable, so should not any honest man suppress his sentiments concerning freedom, however small their influence is likely to be. Perhaps he '*may touch some wheel*' that will have an effect greater than he could reasonably expect.

"These being my sentiments, I am encouraged to offer you, my countrymen, my thoughts on some late transactions, that appear to me to be of the utmost importance to you. Conscious of my own defects, I have waited some time in expectation of seeing the subject treated by persons much better qualified for the task; but being therein disappointed, and apprehensive that longer delays will be injurious, I venture at length to request the attention of the public, praying that these lines may be read with the same zeal for the happiness of *British America* with which they were written."

When this work reached London, Franklin republished it, with a preface so characteristic that I am sorry I have not time to read it to you.* In Paris it was soon translated, and coming at a time when, as we have already seen, ministers were beginning to turn their attention towards the Colonies, must have gone a great way towards convincing them that there were men among the Americans fully able to appreciate their position and defend their rights.

At home it was received not only with applause but with gratitude. "At a meeting of the freeholders and other inhabitants of this town (Boston), met at Faneuil Hall on Monday, the 24th inst.," 1768, a committee, on which we find the names of John Hancock, Samuel Adams, and Joseph Warren, reported the draft of " a letter of thanks " "to the ingenious author of certain patriotic letters, subscribed A Farmer," "saluting (him) as the *friend of Americans* and the common benefactor of mankind." " It is to you, worthy sir," they say, " that *America* is obliged for a most seasonable, sensible, loyal, and vigorous vindication of

---

* See Sparks's Franklin, Vol. IV. p. 256.

her invaded rights and liberties." Everywhere it was welcomed as the voice of a wise man. The strong felt that they had gained a strong ally; the weak, that they had found a strong arm to lean upon. It met the doubts of the wavering, exposed the sophistry of the treacherous, and, above all, enabled the great body of the people to grasp, as a conviction founded upon reason and supported by law, the principles which they had adopted from an instinctive sense of right. From that day John Dickinson became a leader of the people. "Curse him!" said one of the faint-hearted, in the perilous December of 1776, "it was those 'Farmer's Letters' of his that made all this trouble."

You would naturally expect to find him in the Congress of 1774; and among the best state papers of that Congress are the Petition to the King, the Declaration to the Armies, and the Address to the Inhabitants of Quebec, from his pen. His pen, too, was employed in preparing the last petition to the King, which, as I have already stated, was carried through Congress chiefly by his influence.

But, with all his clear-sightedness, Dickinson failed to see that the time for the Declaration of Independence was come. Of the right to break off our political connection with Great Britain he had no doubt, but he dreaded the consequences of a premature severing of ties which still had so strong a hold upon the hearts of the people. Fatal error!

and for which he atoned by losing for a while the confidence of his fellow-citizens. When the new elections came, his name was dropped. It is not true, however, as Lord Mahon has asserted, upon the authority of Mr. Jefferson, that he refused to sign the Declaration. Mr. Jefferson's memory failed him singularly in his history of that document, important as the part he bore in it was. And when he referred to the journals of Congress for confirmation, he referred unfortunately, not to the manuscript journals, but to the printed edition, in which the Congressional editors had put the signing, which did not take place till August, under the head of the resolution of the 4th of July, — a separate and independent act. By that resolution John Hancock set his name to the Declaration of Independence as President of Congress, and Charles Thompson as Secretary; and this was the shape in which it first went out to the world. In August it was engrossed on parchment, and then it was that all the members were called upon to sign it. But in the interval some new elections had taken place; and thus among the names you will find some that were not on the rolls of Congress when the act was passed, and look in vain for the names of others who took an active part in the long contest which preceded its passage and voted upon the act itself.* In August, Dickinson

---

* For a full discussion of this important question I would refer the reader to "The Declaration of Independence; or, Notes

was no longer in Congress, but — and all honor to his memory for the manly deed — he, the rich man, the man of delicate and refined habits, still hardly second among the leaders of our councils, was with the army in New Jersey, at the head of a regiment of militia.

In 1779 he was again returned to Congress, and again assisted with his pen in the preparation of those state papers which still hold their place among the noblest monuments of American intellect. The magnanimity with which he had atoned for his brief error of 1776 was rewarded by a full return of public confidence. He was successively President of Delaware and of Pennsylvania; he again found himself by the side of Washington and Franklin in the convention which gave us our noble Constitution; and he used his pen to explain and defend it, under the signature of Fabius, as he had used it twenty years before to explain and defend the rights of the Colonies under the signature of a Pennsylvania Farmer. Again, too, in 1797, he re-entered the field of political discussion to examine the delicate question of our relations with France. Eleven more years were granted him to behold the rapid growth and marvellous

---

on Lord Mahon's History of the American Declaration of Independence," by Peter Force, — *clarum et venerabile nomen*, — which I cannot write without recording my protest against the unjustifiable suspension of the "American Archives," — the greatest monument ever erected by a nation to its own history.

prosperity of the State by whose cradle he had watched so faithfully, and then in his quiet home at Wilmington, surrounded by friends who loved and honored him, he went calmly to his rest on the 14th of February, 1808.

No two men could have been more unlike than John Dickinson and John Adams; no two men more sure to come into collision almost as soon as they came into contact. But, as a writer, Adams's place is next to Dickinson for the influence which he exercised over large masses. Like Dickinson's, also, his writings are chiefly argumentative, starting from a solid groundwork of constitutional law, and fortified by collateral aids from the law of nature and of nations. But there is a vehemence in Adams which contrasts strongly with the gentle flow of Dickinson's periods, and a self-reliance bordering at times on arrogance. His strength is often the strength of an ardent nature rather than the vigor of a powerful intellect. He often grapples boldly with a subject without pausing to examine his means, and leaves upon the mind the impression of a thing earnestly begun and eagerly pursued, but not revolved with that patient and laborious investigation which is essential to the full mastery of a complex question. Upon important subjects, and when men's minds were already excited by an existing or an impending danger, he would be read eagerly; but in calmer times, his negligence, unredeemed by grace; his roughness, not always atoned for by vigor; and his hasty aggregation of materials which require a systematic and artistic arrangement to give them life and interest, will always prevent him from taking the place which, with a little more respect for others and a little less confidence in himself, he might easily have taken among the masters of political wisdom.

It is impossible to think of Adams, either as a writer or as a statesman, without soon thinking of Jefferson. Like his great opponent, Jefferson's own character is deeply impressed upon his writings. You recognize in the easier, livelier, more equable flow of his periods, a richer, more pleasure-seeking, and genial nature. You perceive in the more varied and harmonious structure of his sentences the traces of a musical sense carefully and lovingly cultivated as a source of keen enjoyment. There is a quickness in his perceptions, which is faithfully reflected in the rapid movement of his general style; and at times, as in the Declaration of Independence, a grave and solemn earnestness, rising in parts into that sober eloquence which is the natural language of conviction. Jefferson was a scholar of a wide range, loving language, science, natural history, political speculation. But, as you read him, you receive the impression of versatility rather than of depth, of vivacity rather than of power, of activity rather than of serious thought. You are entertained, interested; you get now and then new views of familiar things, new suggestions which awaken curiosity, and please by the impression of novelty; but the imagination and the heart remain cold, reason is seldom stimulated to great efforts, and you leave him rather with an increased aversion to error than a warmer love and deeper reverence for truth. But Jefferson's contributions to the literature of the Revolution were few. He was neither a controversialist nor an orator, and his brief Congressional career afforded him few opportunities for distinguishing himself by his pen. His one great work was the Declaration of Independence, now, more evidently than ever before, a work for all ages.

Of John Jay, also, it may truly be said that the style is the man. Dignity, sobriety, the distinctness of a sound reason and the warmth of a strong conviction, are the characteristics of his state papers as they were the characteristics of his mind. Sometimes, too, that warmth rises to a solemn eloquence. I have time but for one example, and I take it from the circular letter of 1779 which I have already quoted in my Lecture upon the Finances of the Revolution. The object of the letter, you will remember, was to justify the conduct of Congress with regard to emissions of paper, and enforce the necessity of fulfilling the engagements it had made in the name of the people.

" Humanity as well as justice make this demand upon you. The complaints of ruined widows and the cries of fatherless children whose whole support has been placed in your hands and melted away, have doubtless reached you; *take care that they ascend no higher.*"

I will not go to Pagan eloquence for a parallel to this, for the force of it depends upon the force of our Christian convictions, — upon our enjoined recognition of God as the God of the fatherless children and the widow. But has Bossuet a nobler passage? Or compare it rather with the opening sentence of Massillon's funeral oration on the " Great Louis," — " *Dieu seul est grand, mes frères*, — God alone is great, my brethren," — and weighing well all the circumstances, tell me which gains most by the comparison?

We are so accustomed to think of Alexander Hamilton as the confidential aid of Washington during the war and the principal author of the the Federalist after it, that we are apt to forget that he began his brilliant career by two remarkable pamphlets, one written in 1774 at the age of sixteen, and the other in 1775; and that in 1781 he wrote the Continentalist. The object of the pamphlet was to defend the action of the Continental Congress against the attacks of " A West Chester Farmer"; and he does it with a combination of argument, learning, and wit never equalled by a boy, and seldom surpassed by a man. The object of the Continentalist was to demonstrate the insufficiency of the powers of the

Confederation, and prepare the public mind for enlarging them. Although not extended beyond six numbers, it is a foreshadowing, if not a direct annunciation, of the Constitution, and of its best exponent, " The Federalist." All of these works display the marvellous precocity of Hamilton's mind and the easy vigor of his pen. It seems strange to find a boy of seventeen writing with such evident familiarity about Grotius and Puffendorff, and urging home upon his antagonist the unconscious accordance of his fundamental axioms with the godless theory of Hobbes. And it seems equally strange to find that this maturity of thought never checks the vivacity of his style, and that the style never falls below the dignity of the subject.

But the most important channel of Hamilton's influence as a writer from 1777 to 1781 was through Washington's official correspondence; in which it is as impossible to deny that he bore an important part as to deny that the similarity of tone and thought which pervade it from the beginning to the end of Washington's life, prove the importance of the part which he also took in the preparation of the documents that bear his signature.

I have already spoken of the effect produced by the writings of Otis and Quincy. I do not care to speak of Thomas Paine, although his " Common Sense" came out at a propitious moment, and contributed materially to prepare the general mind for the Declaration of Independence. But when he wrote it he had not been long enough in America to receive any definite impression from the American mind, and I cheerfully relinquish to his native island all the honor that belongs to the birthplace of such a son. Of Hopkinson, whose prose displays much of the playful vivacity which distinguishes his verse, of Samuel Adams, who wrote many of the best state papers of Massachusetts, of Livingston, and Richard Henry Lee, who wrote some of the most important state papers of Congress, and of many others who contributed by letters and pamphlets and state papers of local legislatures to the formation and guidance of public opinion, it is impossible to speak at large in a single lecture. History has not yet done full justice to their labors, nor can I see without a feeling of humiliation and painful regret, that a press which seizes so eagerly upon the journal of Semmes and the life of Stonewall Jackson, which pours out so lavishly the ephemeral productions of the American mind, and reproduces so cheerfully productions of the English mind that do us no service either practically as men and citizens or speculatively as students and lovers of the good, the beautiful, and the true, should permit these precious legacies of our fathers to lie buried and forgotten in pamphlets almost inaccessible from their rarity and newspapers almost illegible from moth-holes and faded ink. How many of the bitterest tears of the present might we have been spared by a timely study of the past!

For the newspaper press, which is too broad a field for discussion within my narrow limits, I must refer you to Frank Moore's admirable selections under the title of "Diary of the Revolution."

Of the debates in Congress we have but few and imperfect specimens; but all tradition agrees in attributing to Patrick Henry a fiery vehemence that seemed at times like inspiration; elaborate and polished concision to Richard Henry Lee, argumentative vigor to John Adams, persuasive eloquence to John Dickinson, and in various degrees many of the higher characteristics of eloquence to Jay, and Rutledge, and Mifflin, and Gouverneur Morris.

If there was less of eloquence in the pulpit, there was fervor, earnestness, and fearless patriotism. Men were not afraid of giving utterance on Sunday to the hopes that had mingled with their week-day prayers. They were not afraid to rebuke sin in the garb of state craft and policy, even at the risk of bringing politics into the pulpit. They did not fear to say that the qualities that make bad citizens make bad Christians also; that the traitor to his country is a traitor to his God. This was their faith. They proclaimed it on Sunday, they lived it in their daily lives. Bible in hand they followed their flocks to the camp, toiled with them through weary marches, preached to them with drum-heads for a pulpit, prayed with them on the battle-field, held the cooling draught to the lips of the wounded, and soothed, amid the roar of the conflict, the fainting spirits of the dying.

We are proud, and justly proud, of the Congress and the army, the statesmen and the generals of our Revolution, and close by their sides stand the patriot preachers.

LECTURE XII.

LITERATURE OF THE REVOLUTION.

PART II.— POETRY.

WE saw in our last Lecture that the prose literature of the Revolution was peculiarly a literature of reasoning and discussion. If I were to attempt to characterize the poetical literature of the Revolution I should call it a literature of syllables and rhymes. As a general rule, every noun has its adjective, every object its epithet, and through the mist of accumulated attributes you are often at a loss for the real character of the subject to which they are applied. The lines are generally correct, the number of syllables is complete, the cæsura falls in the right place, there is often thought, sometimes feeling, not unfrequently harmony and movement, but there is neither fancy nor imagination, and therefore no true poetry. Yet this period produced two epics, and elegies, odes, epistles, and occasional verses without number. Barlow is called "the child of genius"; Dwight, "the blessed"; Trumbull, "the earliest boast of fame." And for a long while no one seems to have doubted the claims of American poetry, any more than he doubted the claims of American enterprise.

Nor was English poetry much better off in her native island. Goldsmith, it is true, had put enough of it into " The Traveller " and " The Deserted Village " to redeem a whole generation of Pyes and Hayleys; and Cowper was just preparing to lead back the public taste to the paths of pure feeling and natural expression, from which it had wandered so far and so long.* But with more than half that was published and read as poetry in England, the verses of Dwight, and Barlow, and Humphreys, might have been freely compared without losing by the comparison.

It would be great injustice to the memory of an eminent man, if I were to pass by the name of Timothy Dwight without alluding to his great services as a teacher, able to point out paths which he was unable to tread, and a scholar, able to enjoy beauties which he was unable to imitate. A native of Massachusetts, where he was born in 1752, he passed the chief of his life in Connecticut, where he died as President of Yale College in 1817. Wondrous things are told of the precocity of his mind, and the marvels of his memory. He could dictate to three secretaries at a time, and preserve unbroken and distinct the flow of each separate train of thought. He tilled his farm with his own hands, keeping school, and

---

* " The Task " was published in 1784.

preaching, writing prose and poetry, theology, and an epic, and all without permitting one task to interfere with another. His pupils looked up to him with somewhat of the veneration with which Boswell looked up to Johnson, and if tradition may be trusted he was not unwilling to be thought Johnson's equal in the conduct of an argument, or the power of dictating to a social circle. It was to him and his friend Trumbull that Yale College was indebted for an enlargement of its course of study, and the introduction of a purer literary taste, and through Yale, a large portion of the young men of the first period of our history as a united people.

Dwight's hopes of poetical fame were chiefly founded upon "The Conquest of Canaan," an epic, with Joshua for a hero, and all the defects and few of the beauties of the style used by Pope in his translation of the Iliad. It was the production of his youth, which, however, when we remember that Tasso began the Jerusalem at twenty, will hardly serve as an excuse for its uniform dulness and resolute mediocrity. "Greenfield Hill," though defective in plan, is far more felicitous in execution, and parts of it may be read with pleasure even now. It is from this, although it was not written till after the close of the war, that I select a passage, both as showing Dwight's powers of versification with an acknowledged model before him, and as illustrating the view which, in common with the greater part of his contemporaries, he took of slavery.

> "But hark! what voice so gayly fills the wind?
> Of care oblivious, whose that laughing mind?
> 'T is yon poor black, who ceases now his song,
> And whistling, drives the cumbrous wain along
>
> . . . . . .
>
>   Kindly fed, and clad, and treated, he
> Slides on, through life, with more than common glee.
> For here mild manners good to all impart,
> And stamp with infamy th' unfeeling heart;
> Here Law from vengeful rage the slave defends,
> And here the Gospel peace on earth extends.
>
> "He toils, 't is true, but shares his master's toil;
> With him he feeds the herd, and trims the soil;
> Helps to sustain the house with clothes and food,
> And takes his portion of the common good.
> Lost liberty, his sole, peculiar ill,
> And fixed submission to another's will.
> Ill, ah, how great! without that cheering sun,
> The world is changed to one wide frigid zone:
> The mind, a chilled exotic, cannot grow,
> Nor leaf with vigor, nor with promise blow;
> Pale, sickly, shrunk, it strives in vain to rise,
> Scarce lives while living, and untimely dies.
> See fresh to life the Afric infant spring,
> And plume its powers, and spread its little wing!
> Firm is its frame, and vigorous is its mind,
> Too young to think, and yet to misery blind.
> But soon he sees himself to slavery born;
> Soon meets the voice of power, the eye of scorn;
> Sighs for the blessings of his peers, in vain,
> Conditioned as a brute, though formed a man.
> Around he casts his fond, instinctive eyes,

And sees no good, to fill his wishes, rise;
(No motive warms with animating beam,
Nor praise, nor property, nor kind esteem,
Blessed independence on his native ground,
Nor sweet equality with those around;)
Himself and his, another's shrinks to find,
Levelled below the lot of human kind,
Thus, shut from honor's paths, he turns to shame,
And filches the small good he cannot claim.
To sour and stupid, sinks his active mind,
Finds joys in drink, he cannot elsewhere find;
Rule disobeys; of half his labor cheats;
In some safe cot, the pilfered turkey eats;
Rides hard, by night, the steed, his art purloins;
Serene from conscience' bar himself essoins;
Sees from himself his sole redress must flow,
And makes revenge the balsam of his woe." *

Of Joel Barlow, who was born in 1755 and died in 1812, it behooves us to remember that while he pursued his studies at college during term time, he served in the ranks as a volunteer during vacation. Thus he fought at the White Plains, and was an actor in some of the scenes which he afterwards attempted to describe. Having completed his college course, he returned to the army awhile as chaplain, and from time to time, like his friends Trumbull and Dwight, composed camp songs for the soldiers. Nor should it be forgotten that his lonely death in an obscure Polish village was brought on by exposure in the service of his country. If not a great poet, he was a good,

* Part II. p. 36

loyal citizen, conscious of the high privileges which his citizenship gave him, and willing to die for them. Let us speak tenderly of the poetic shortcomings of a worthy man.

By his contemporaries he was regarded as a man of genius. Jefferson thought him the best prose writer of his time. How much was expected from him as a poet David Humphreys tells us in a letter to General Greene, announcing "The Vision of Columbus" as a work of the highest order, which some wealthy citizens of New Haven were about to give the young poet the means of completing at his ease.*

It was not, however, till eight years after this letter was written that the poem made its appearance in a modest duodecimo, with a full list of subscribers, among whom we find the names of "His Most Christian Majesty for twenty-five copies, and His Excellency George Washington, Esq., for twenty copies." General Greene's would doubtless have been there also, but he had already been lying two years in his unknown grave. The title tells as much of the plan of the poem as can well be told without rehearsing the table of contents; and its title, suggesting, as it immediately does, the idea of a history in rhyme, carries condemnation with it. I will give you a few specimens, trying to do the author full justice in my selection. The

* David Humphreys to General Greene. New Haven, April 10, 1780. Greene Papers, MS.

opening lines are not without a certain grave harmony which reminds you of greater poets.

> "Long had the sage, the first who dared to brave
> The unknown dangers of the western wave,
> Who taught mankind where future empires lay
> In these fair confines of descending day,
> With cares o'erwhelmed, in life's distressing gloom,
> Wished from a thankless world a peaceful tomb;
> While kings and nations envious of his name
> Enjoyed his labors and usurped his fame,
> And gave the chief, from promised empire hurled,
> Chains for a crown, a prison for a world.

> "Now night and silence held their lonely reign,
> The half-orbed moon declining to the main;
> Descending clouds o'er varying ether driven,
> Obscured the stars and shut the eye from heaven;
> Cold mists through opening grates the cell invade,
> And death-like terrors haunt the midnight shade;
> When from a visionary, short repose,
> That raised new cares and tempered keener woes,
> Columbus woke, and to the walls addressed
> The deep felt sorrows of his manly breast."

I pass over the earlier periods of our history. There is nothing in his treatment of them to reward the labor of an extract. But you will be curious to see how far the Muse smiles upon him when he undertakes to paint scenes which he had witnessed and men whom he had known.

> "Where dread Monmouth lifts a frowning height
> Parading armies cast a glaring light,
> Then strode the British Clinton o'er the field,
> And marshalled hosts for ready combat held.

As the dim sun, beneath the skirts of even,
Crimsons the clouds that sail the western heaven;
So, in red wavy rows, where spread the train
Of men and standards, shone the fateful plain.

"But now dread Washington arose in sight,
And the long ranks rolled forward to the fight:
He points the charge, the mounted thunders roar,
And plough the plain, and rock the distant shore.
Above the folds of smoke that veiled the war,
His guiding sword illumed the fields of air;
The volleyed flames that burst along the plain,
Break the deep clouds, and show the piles of slain;
Till flight begins; the smoke is rolled away
And the red standards open into day.
Britons and Germans hurry from the field,
Now wrapped in dust, and now to sight revealed;
Behind, great Washington his falchion drives,
Thins the pale ranks, and copious vengeance gives.
Hosts captive bow and move behind his arm
And hosts before him wing the driven storm;
When the glad shore salutes their fainting sight,
And thundering navies screen their rapid flight." *

There are better verses than these in the Vision, but none more characteristic, except, perhaps, the characters of Trumbull, Dwight, and Humphreys, at the end of the seventh book.

It is easy to see where the weakness of these verses lies. Barlow never writes with "his eye on the object," and therefore never tells us what is actually seen; never writes with his thoughts fixed upon his own emotions, and therefore never tells what is actually felt. Instead of this he gives

* Book VI. 111.

us words wrought into sonorous verses, which fill the ear, but fail to reach the mind as the representatives of real perceptions or real feeling. His heroes and scenes float before you as vague and formless as the ghosts of Ossian; and like Ossian, whom he seems to have studied more than Homer, he bewilders you by a succession of indistinct conceptions, which, having no definite shape in his own mind, leave no clear image in yours.

He has no creative imagination to invest objects and characters with a living interest, — no play of fancy to relieve the monotonous uniformity of catalogue and description; and, moreover, the grandeur of the subject bewilders and oppresses him. You look for a poem, and you find a geography, a chronicle, and a rhapsody of political speculation. The greatest of poets might have failed with such a subject. Barlow was not a great poet, and perhaps the severest censure that can be passed upon him is, that he knew so little of his own strength, and had formed so imperfect a conception of the true nature of poetry as to attempt to construct a poem out of such materials. He afterwards returned to the task again, and enlarged " The Vision of Columbus " into " The Columbiad." But it gained nothing by the expansion. If you would see Barlow at his best, read " Hasty Pudding," for there he does sing the " sweets he knows and the charms he feels."

David Humphreys, the friend whose glowing

anticipations of Barlow's success I have alluded to, was also a poet in the sense which that ill-used word is so often made to bear. He wrote with ease verses that rhymed well and flowed smoothly, and, putting a fair measure of thought into them, was read and praised by his contemporaries. Few poets, too, have had a wider range of personal experience than he, and of that kind of experience which is most easily woven into poetry. He was born in Connecticut in those Colonial days which afford such attractive scenes of rural life, — when towns and villages were little more than condensed farms, every man knowing all the inhabitants, and all uniting in harvestings, and huskings, and cider-makings,—when quiltings were the joyous gatherings of matrons and maidens, and winter firesides were thrilled by stories of Indian wars, or charmed by descriptions of home.* His school and college days were the days of discussion ripening into revolution, which gave a living interest to every lesson that he read in the history of the old republics. The war found him in a quiet retreat on the banks of the Hudson, where Nature is loveliest, and where, not many years afterwards, she revealed so much to Washington Irving that she never revealed to him. From this life of seclusion he passed to the life of camps: was Putnam's aid in 1778, and lived on so friendly a footing with the old man that he learned to look upon him as a

---

* A word which in Colonial parlance meant England.

father; was Greene's aid for a short time; was Washington's aid from 1780 to the end of the war, receiving a sword from Congress for gallant services at Yorktown, and won so largely of Washington's esteem that that man of few professions wrote him, in 1784, "I shall hold in pleasing remembrance the friendship and intimacy which have subsisted between us, and shall neglect no opportunity on my part to cultivate and improve them."* Next he went to Paris as Secretary for the Commission of Treaties, with Jefferson for his principal, and Kosciusko for shipmate; returned to become a legislator, to write "The Anarchiad" at Hartford, with Trumbull, Barlow, and Hopkins; to write a Life of Putnam at Mount Vernon, with Washington for a daily companion; then crossed the Atlantic again, and was Minister at Lisbon; and crossing it still another time, was Minister to Spain, and negotiated treaties with Tripoli and Algiers. And devoting his last as his first years to the good of his country, and mingling private with public activity, he accepted in 1812 the command of the militia of Connecticut, superintending the while, on his own land, the breed of merino sheep which he had been, if not the first, one of the first to introduce into the United States. Death, which had so often passed him by on the battle-field, came to him suddenly in 1818, at the age of sixty-five.

* The whole letter is worth reading, as an illustration of Washington the *man*. Sparks's Washington, Vol. IX. p. 6.

Yet he passed through all these scenes, and wrote long poems about some of them, without perceiving in what their poetry consisted, or leaving a single picture which posterity can go to for vigor of outline or fidelity of detail. Nature had denied him the power of looking into his own heart as the poet who would touch other hearts must look,* or of discerning in the forms of external life, which lie open to every eye, the secrets which no eye but the poet's can discern, and no mind but the poet's interpret. Like Barlow, he could not see objects as they really were, nor tell in direct and simple language what he had really seen. What lifelike portraits ought we not to have had of Washington, and Greene, and Wayne, and Knox, and Putnam, from one who had seen them and talked with them daily through the most important years of their lives and his own. Yet they come before us like the lay-figures of the artist, posed, draped, and lifeless. What scenes the summer march and winter encampment might have suggested to the true poet! but in the verses of Humphreys all the distinctive characteristics are overlaid by epithets or lost in vague generalities. It is a thing I can never think of without pain, that a man who loved his country so much and served her so well, who saw so much that we

---

* " Look, then, into thine heart, and write!
  Yes, into Life's deep stream!"
      LONGFELLOW, *Prelude to Voices of the Night*.

wish to know about, and possessed such a facility of language and versification for telling it, should not have contented himself with telling us just what he saw, and how he felt as he saw it.

Of the six long poems that he wrote, and all of which, like all of his prose, sprang directly from the scenes in which he was engaged, and bear witness to his devotion to his country, one only belongs to our present subject, — the "Address to the Armies of America." It was written in camp and while "the author was so far engaged in the duties of his profession as to have but little leisure for subjects of literature or amusement." "I was with you, my dear Colonel," writes his French translator, the Marquis de Chastellux, "when, after a glorious campaign, you composed in silence, those elegant verses, wherein you have displayed the whole extent of your genius, in only wishing to express your patriotic sentiments." "The reader," says the *Journal de Paris*, "will moreover remark with pleasure the contrast which the author has had the art to introduce, in a skilful manner, in the two very distinct parts of his poem. In the first he paints the dangers which America experienced, and the calamities of war which desolated her for so long a period. In the last he collects only delightful ideas and pictures of happiness; he unfolds to America the auspicious effects of that liberty she had obtained, and the felicity she is about to enjoy."

"The performance," says an English journal, the Critical Review, "may with some trifling exceptions, be justly styled a *good poem*, but not a very pleasing one to good Englishmen." And while good Englishmen satisfied their curiosity by public readings of it, they pacified their wounded pride by claiming the author as a countryman.

We must not forget, however, that one of the causes of this success was curiosity. Before the war the power of the American soil and climate to produce great men had been seriously called in question. It had even been gravely asserted that under their influence both men and animals soon fell below the European standard. The Revolution had shown that in military skill and statesmanship this assumption of an arrogant philosophy was false. But was it equally false in literature? Humphreys published his "Address," and hundreds of curious eyes turned eagerly to it to see.

The opening lines are grave and dignified: —

> "Ye martial bands! Columbia's fairest pride!
> To toils inured, in dangers often tried, —
> Ye gallant youths! whose breasts for glory burn,
> Each selfish aim and meaner passion spurn;
> Ye who, unmoved, in the dread hour have stood,
> And smiled, undaunted, in the field of blood, —
> Who greatly dared, at Freedom's rapt'rous call,
> With her to triumph, or with her to fall, —
> Now brighter days in prospect swift ascend;
> Ye sons of fame, the hallowed theme attend;
> The past review, the future scene explore,
> And Heaven's high King with grateful hearts adore!"

The "parent state, a parent now no more," begins hostilities, affording the poet an occasion for a simile in sonorous and swelling verses, which, at a time when men who had seen the moon and stars still admired Pope's rendering of the celebrated simile in the eighth Iliad, and mistook it for Homer, may perhaps have been admired as nature by men who had seen a thunder-storm : —

> "As when dark clouds from Andes' towering head,
> Roll down the skies and round th' horizon spread,
> With thunders fraught, the blackening tempest sails,
> And bursts tremendous o'er Peruvian vales, —
> So broke the storm on Concord's fatal plain."

Remember now what the real character of the uprising after the battle of Lexington was; remember the gathering of minute-men; remember how farmers and mechanics dropped their tools, seized their guns, and went forth singly or in small bands, or in regular companies, crowding the roads to Cambridge. See Putnam leaving his plough in the furrow, when the tidings reached him, by day, and Greene hurrying off in the dark that he might be ready to join the Kentish Guards in their march before dawn; think of the partings on the threshold, — of the mothers and sisters and wives that remained at home, — and regret with me that one who was a witness and a part of such scenes should have only told us that

> "Then the shrill trumpet echoed from afar,
> And sudden blazed the wasting flame of war;

> From state to state, swift flew the dire alarms,
> And ardent youths impetuous rushed to arms;
> 'To arms' the matrons and the virgins sung,
> To arms, their sires, their husbands, brothers, sprung.
> No dull delay, — where'er the sound was heard,
> Where the red standard in the air appeared,
> Where through vast realms the cannon swelled its roar,
> Between th' Acadian and Floridian shore, —
> Now joined the crowd from their far-distant farms,
> In rustic guise, and unadorned in arms;
> Not like their foes in tinsel trappings gay,
> And burnished arms that glittered on the day."

Bunker Hill follows: —

> "Long raged the contest on th' embattled field;
> Nor those would fly, nor these would tamely yield —
> Till Warren fell, in all the boast of arms,
> The pride of genius and unrivalled charms.
> His country's hope! — full soon the gloom was spread:
> Oppressed with numbers and their leader dead,
> Slow from the field the sullen troops retired,
> Behind, the hostile flames to heaven aspired."

Washington appears on the scene: —

> "Now darkness gathered round:
> The thunder rumbled, and the tempest frowned;
> When lo! to guide us through the storm of war,
> Beamed the bright splendor of Virginia's star.
> First of her heroes, fav'rite of the skies,
> To what dread toils thy country bade thee rise!
> 'O, raised by Heaven to save th' invaded state!'
> (So spake the sage long since thy future fate,)
> 'T was thine to change the sweetest scenes of life
> For public cares, — to guide th' embattled strife;
> Unnumbered ills of every kind to dare,
> The winter's blast, the summer's sultry air,

> The lurking dagger, and the turbid storms
> Of wasting war with death in all its forms.
> Nor aught could daunt.   Unspeakably serene,
> Thy conscious soul smiled o'er the dreadful scene."

I pass over the tributes to Brown, Scammel, and Laurens, which, according to the *Journal de Paris*, "will ever be read with sympathetic sorrow." One more passage must suffice for the dark side of the picture, and in it you will find two lines which come nearer to truth of coloring than any we have yet read: —

> "What! when you fled before superior force,
> Each succor lost, and perished each resource!
> When nature, fainting from the want of food,
> *On the white snow your steps were marked in blood!*
> *When through your tattered garbs you met the wind!*
> Despair before, and ruin frowned behind!"

Peace approaches: —

> "Anon the horrid sounds of war shall cease,
> And all the Western world be hushed in peace:
> The martial clarion shall be heard no more,
> Nor the loud cannon's desolating roar:
> No more our heroes pour the purple flood,
> No corse be seen with garments rolled in blood;
> No shivering wretch shall roam without a shed:
> No pining orphans raise their cry for bread;
> No tender mother shriek at dreams of woe,
> Start from her sleep, and see the midnight foe;
> The lovely virgin, and the hoary sire,
> No more behold the village flame aspire,
> While the base spoiler, from a father's arms
> Plucks the fair flower, and riots on its charms."

Do you not recognize in these lines a mingled imitation of Pope and Goldsmith? It is still more evident in the following passage, which is, perhaps, a nearer approach to real poetry than any he ever wrote.

> "Then, O my friends! the task of glory done,
> Th' immortal prize by your bold efforts won;
> Your country's saviours by her voice confessed,
> While unborn ages rise and call you blest,—
> Then let us go where happier climes invite,
> To midland seas, and regions of delight;
> With all that's ours, together let us rise,
> Seek brighter plains, and more indulgent skies;
> Where fair Ohio rolls his amber tide,
> And Nature blossoms in her virgin pride;
> Where all that beauty's hand can form to please
> Shall crown the toils of war with rural ease.
> The shady coverts, and the sunny hills,
> The gentle lapse of ever-murm'ring rills,
> The soft repose amid the noontide bowers,
> The evening walk among the blushing flowers,
> The fragrant groves that yield a sweet perfume,
> And vernal glories in perpetual bloom,
> Await you there; and heaven shall bless the toil,
> Your own the produce, as your own the soil."

"The Happiness of America" does not, strictly speaking, come within the limits of my subject, for it was not written till after the war. I allude to it however, because, although in nearly the same style, it is a much more poetical specimen of that style than the "Address." And that it was looked upon by Humphreys's contemporaries as a true poem, or at least as a work of great merit, may be fairly inferred from the fact that it passed through ten editions in the author's lifetime. If I should be thought to have dwelt longer upon Humphreys's defects than the subject required, remember that in the eyes of his contemporaries he was more especially the poet of the Revolution, that he was the first to attempt a picture in verse of the scenes of the war, and the first to whose pages Europeans went for indications of the poetical promise of the new nation.

It is with reluctance that I pass by that singular instance of African genius, Boston trained, Phillis Wheatley, whose verses lose nothing by a comparison with those of Dwight and Barlow. Freneau's Muse, too, began her multitudinous labors while the war was still raging, producing, at least, one piece of real value, — the lines on the battle of Eutaw; and other names might be added to the catalogue, if to make a catalogue were my aim. But it is the character of the poetry that we are studying, and the true nature of the poetical element, and these are best found in the writings of the acknowledged masters of song.

We have seen that in their serious attempts these masters failed. In humorous poetry, however, one among them was, if not fully successful, yet enough so to deserve honorable mention among the writers of his class, and to interest and amuse even the readers of an age familiar with the keen satire of Lowell and the sparkling wit of Holmes. This was John Trumbull, of Connecticut, whose long life, beginning in 1750, reached down to 1831: the friend and fellow-laborer of Dwight, and Humphreys, and Barlow, yet living to see with his own eyes the birth of a new literature, and read the early verses of Bryant and Longfellow. Trumbull's serious poems are neither very numerous nor very good. The longest of them is an "Elegy on the Times," written at Boston during the operation of the Port Bill. I select the closing stanzas both as the best and because they express with much force an opinion, which does not seem to have been confined to poets, that the loss of the Colonies would be the ruin of England: —

> "And where is Britain? In the skirt of day,
> Where stormy Neptune rolls his utmost tide,
> Where suns oblique diffuse a feeble ray,
> And lonely streams the fated coasts divide,
>
> "Seest thou yon Isle, whose desert landscape yields
> The mournful traces of the fame she bore,
> Whose matted thorns oppress th' uncultured fields,
> And piles of ruin load the dreary shore?
>
> "From those loved seats, the virtues sad withdrew
> From fell corruption's bold and venal hand;
> Reluctant Freedom waved her last adieu,
> And devastation swept the vassalled land.
>
> "On her white cliffs, the pillars once of fame,
> Her melancholy Genius sits to wail,

> Drops the fond tear, and o'er her latest shame
> Bids dark oblivion draw th' eternal veil."*

But Trumbull's true field was satire, — not the elaborate didactic satire of Pope, but the swift moving, narrative satire of Butler. Hudibras must have been his favorite study; and it must be acknowledged that he, more than once, caught the spirit of his great master. His verse has something of the same rapid and spontaneous flow, and his rhymes come with something of the same ease from remote distances. It should be remembered, however, that while Butler's style is the low burlesque, Trumbull, with great judgment, has chosen the high.†

But Butler's wit was fed from an exhaustless fountain of learning. He not only surprises you by the novelty and variety of his illustrations, but often compels you to pause and follow out the trains of thought that he suggests. Trumbull's subject, it may be said, would hardly have admitted of this, but it is equally certain that his learning fell far short of that apparent mastery over the whole field of erudition, which was a principal source of Butler's power.

The earliest of his humorous poems was "The

---

* An "Elegy on the Times," Trumbull's Works, Vol. II. (205) 217.

† See Trumbull's letter to the Marquis de Chastellux in the Appendix to the second volume of Goodrich's edition of Trumbull's Works.

Progress of Dulness," which may still be read with pleasure. But the work by which he was best known, and with which his name is universally associated, is the mock epic of "MacFingal." This work, so full of the spirit of the times, was begun in 1775, just after the battle of Lexington, and the first part was published in Philadelphia, during the session of the great Congress of Independence. Its object was purely political, to rouse the courage of the Whigs by a ludicrous yet faithful picture of the Tories. And so well was the time chosen, and so felicitous was the execution that it became a favorite with all classes, passing through thirty editions, in the author's lifetime, although, for want of a law of copyright, he derived no pecuniary advantage except from one of them. It was not till the last year of the war that the remaining cantos were added, when it assumed the form which it now bears, of a "Modern Epic" in four cantos.

I regret that my limits will not permit me to enter into a careful examination of this remarkable poem and bring it to the standard of the Lutrin, the Dispensary, and the Rape of the Lock, as well as to the standard of Hudibras. It would well repay the labor and the time; but the hour is passing and we have still more ground to go over. An outline of its plan and a few extracts as specimens of the execution are all I can give.

The plot is a very simple one, yet in its simplicity true to the life of the times. The hero, MacFingal, is a Tory of the deepest dye. Honorius is a Whig. The battle-ground is first that true New England ground, a town-meeting; and then that characteristic ground of the period, the space around the Liberty-pole. The first two books are given to the town-meeting, where MacFingal recounts the exploits of the English, the enormities of the Rebels, and draws pictures, meant to be terrifying, of their impending doom. The voice of Honorius is drowned by the clamor of the Tories, while his fluent adversary pours forth a mingled strain of narrative, prophecy, and reproach. Dinner-time comes, and the meeting adjourns. The debate is resumed in the afternoon; but meanwhile the Whigs on the outside are busily engaged in raising a liberty-pole. Their shouts rise above the voice of the orator. The audience hurry out to see what this new uproar means; MacFingal with them. At the sight of the pole he bursts into a fresh torrent of invective; calls upon the constable to read the Riot Act, and summons his adherents to aid him in tearing down the obnoxious emblem. A battle ensues. The Whigs are victorious. The unfortunate orator is seized, tried, condemned to tar and feathers, and the sentence carried into instant execution. Instructed by misfortune, MacFingal collects his friends by night in his cellar, foretells the general history of the war, and at the approach of his adversaries, who have discovered the Tory gathering and are upon the point of breaking in upon them, steals through a window known only to himself, and makes his way to Boston as best he can.

The opening will remind you of Hudibras: —

> "When Yankees, skilled in martial rule,
> First put the British troops to school;
> Instructed them in warlike trade
> And new manœuvres of parade,
> The true war-dance of Yankee reels,
> And manual exercise of heels;
> Made them give up, like saints complete,
> The arm of flesh and trust the feet,
> And work, like Christians undissembling,
> Salvation out, by fear and trembling;
> Taught Percy fashionable races
> And modern modes of Chevy Chases;
> From Boston in his best array
> Great Squire MacFingal took his way,
> And, graced with ensigns of renown,
> Steered homeward to his native town."

I pass reluctantly over the story of his origin, with the humorous allusion to Ossian; and the more humorous narrative of the conversion of his family from Jacobitism to Toryism, in which King George figures as a king

> "Whom every Scot and Jacobite
> Strait fell in love with at first sight;
> Whose gracious speech, with aid of pensions,
> Hushed down all murmurs of dissensions."

But this Highland origin manifests itself in the true form of hereditary transmission of qualities, —

> "Whence gained our Squire two gifts by right,
> Rebellion and the second sight," —

and must not, therefore, be forgotten. The latter gift is not allowed to lie idle : —

> "No ancient sibyl, famed in rhyme,
> Saw deeper in the womb of time.
>
> . . . . .
>
> He for oracles was grown
> The very tripod of the town.
> Gazettes no sooner rose a lie in,
> But strait he fell to prophesying;
> Made dreadful slaughter in his course,
> O'erthrew Provincials, foot and horse,
> Brought armies o'er by sudden pressings
> Of Hanoverians, Swiss, and Hessians,
> Feasted with blood his Scottish clan,
> And hanged all rebels to a man,
> Divided their estates and pelf,
> And took a goodly share himself.
> All this with spirit energetic
> He did by second sight prophetic."

The gift of eloquence follows, of course : —

> "Thus stored with intellectual riches,
> Skilled was our Squire in making speeches;
> Where strength of brains united centres
> With strength of lungs surpassing Stentor's."

But his eloquence is more remarkable for warmth than for logic : —

> " But as some muskets so contrive it,
>   As oft to miss the mark they drive at,
>   And, though well aimed at duck or plover,
>   Bear wide and kick their owners over,
>   So fared our Squire, whose reasoning toil
>   Would often on himself recoil,
>   And so much injured more his side,
>   The stronger arguments he applied;
>   As old war-elephants, dismayed,
>   Trod down the troops they came to aid,
>   And hurt their own side more in battle
>   Than less and ordinary cattle."

Still he was a leader, and in the statement of the fact you will observe the side hit at party majorities:—

> " Yet at town-meetings every chief
>   Pinned faith on great MacFingal's sleeve;
>   Which when he lifted, all by rote
>   Raised sympathetic hands to vote."

Such is the hero. The town,

> " his scene of action,
>   Had long been torn by feuds of faction,"

weaving " cobwebs for the public weal," which remind how

> " that famed weaver, wife t' Ulysses,
>   By night her day's work picked in pieces,
>   And though she stoutly did bestir her,
>   Its finishing was ne'er the nearer."

For the townsfolk

> " met, made speeches, full long-winded,
>   Resolved, protested, and rescinded."

It is evident that the author was not blind to the faults of his friends.

> "And now the town was summoned greeting,
> To grand parading of town-meeting."

The place of meeting is the village church, which gives him an opportunity for another stroke of satire: —

> "That house, which, loath a rule to break,
> Served heaven but one day in the week, —
> Open the rest for all supplies
> Of news, and politics, and lies."

The constable stands

> "High o'er the rout on pulpit stairs. . . . .
> The moderator's upper half
> In grandeur o'er the cushion bowed,
> Like Sol half seen behind a cloud."

What New-Englander, of even the last generation, would fail to recognize the scene?

> "Our Squire, returning late,"

finds Honorius in possession of the floor, and is compelled to listen awhile, with "sour faces," to a Whig's views of England and her policy, and how she

> "Sent fire and sword, and called it Lenity;
> Starved us, and christened it Humanity."

And,

> "spite of prayers her schemes pursuing,
> She still went on to work our ruin;

> Annulled our charters of releases,
> And tore our title deeds to pieces;
> Then signed her warrants of ejection,
> And gallows raised to stretch our necks on;
> And on these errands sent in rage
> Her bailiff and her hangman, Gage."

The portrait of Gage is not flattering: —

> "No state e'er chose a fitter person
> To carry such a silly farce on.
> As heathen gods, in ancient days,
> Received at second hand their praise,
> Stood imaged forth in stones and stocks,
> And deified in barber's blocks;
> So Gage was chose to represent
> Th' omnipotence of Parliament."

You know that serious accusations of untruthfulness were brought against the British commander. Our author traces the habit to a natural source, but adds, that with all that master's assistance he never had

> "The wit to tell a lie with art."

And MacFingal defends the royal Governor, for, says he,

> "As men's last wills may change again,
> Though drawn 'In name of God, Amen';
> Be sure they must have clearly more
> O'er promises as great a power,
> Which made in haste, with small inspection,
> So much the more will need correction;
> And when they've careless spoke or penned 'em,
> Have a right to look them o'er and mend 'em;

> Revive their vows or change the text,
> By way of codicil annexed;
> Strike out a promise that was base,
> And put a better in its place.
> So Gage, of late agreed, you know,
> To let the Boston people go;
> Yet when he saw 'gainst troops that braved him
> They were the only guards that saved him,
> Kept off that Satan of a Putnam
> From breaking in to maul and mutton him,
> He'd too much wit such leagues t' observe,
> And shut them in again to starve."

The forenoon session leaves the Tory orator in the possession of the floor, and at his suggestion the meeting adjourns for dinner. The second book opens: —

> "The sun, who never stops to dine,
> Two hours had passed the mid-way line,
> And, driving at his usual rate,
> Lashed on his downward car of state.
> And now expired the short vacation,
> And dinner o'er in epic fashion,
> While all the crew beneath the trees
> Ate apple pies and bread and cheese,
> (Nor shall we, like old Homer, care
> To versify their bill of fare,)
> Each active party, feasted well,
> Thronged in, like sheep, at sound of bell;
> With equal spirit took their places,
> And meeting oped with three *Oh Yesses;*
> When first, the daring Whigs t' oppose,
> Again the great MacFingal rose,
> Stretched magisterial arm amain,
> And thus resumed th' accusing strain."

It would be easy to fill pages with extracts from the afternoon session. I should particularly like to give you in full the character of Burgoyne and the summary of English achievements. But I must confine myself to two. And first, English benefits and American ingratitude: —

> "Ungrateful sons, a factious band,
> That rise against your parent land,
>   . . . . .
> And scorn the debt and obligation
> You justly owe the British nation,
> Which, since you cannot pay, your crew
> Affect to swear was never due.
>
> "Did not the deeds of England's Primate
> First drive your fathers to this climate,
> Whom jails and fines and every ill
> Forced to their good against their will?
> Ye owe to their obliging temper
> The peopling your new-fangled empire,
> While every British act and canon
> Stood forth your *causa sine qua non*.
> Who 'd seen, except for these restraints,
> Your witches, Quakers, Whigs, and saints,
> Or heard of Mather's famed *Magnalia*,
> If Charles and Laud had chanced to fail you?
> Did they not send your charters o'er,
> And give you lands you owned before,
> Permit you all to spill your blood,
> And drive out heathens when you could;
> On these mild terms that conquest won,
> The realm you gained should be their own?
>   . . . . . .
> Say at what period did they grudge
> To send you Governor or Judge,

With all their missionary crew
To teach you law and gospel too?
They brought all felons in the nation
To help you on in population;
Proposed their Bishops to surrender,
And made their Priests a legal tender,
Who only asked, in surplice clad,
The simple tithe of all you had:
And now, to keep all knaves in awe,
Have sent their troops t' establish law,
And with gunpowder, fire, and ball,
Reform your people one and all.
Yet when their insolence and pride
Have angered all the world beside,
When fear and want at once invade,
Can you refuse to lend them aid,
And rather risk your heads in fight,
Than gratefully throw in your mite?
Can they for debts make satisfaction,
Should they dispose their realm at auction,
And sell off Britain's goods and land all
To France and Spain by inch of candle?
Shall good King George, with want oppressed,
Insert his name in bankrupt list?

. . . . .

With poverty shall princes strive
And nobles lack whereon to live?

. . . . .

And who believes you will not run?
You're cowards, every mother's son,
And if you offer to deny,
We've witnesses to prove it by."

This, of course, is meant for Amherst, Grant, and the other revilers of American courage. The "British Lion" sits for his portrait too: —

> "Have you not roused, his force to try on,
> That grim old beast, the British Lion?
> And know you not that at a sup
> He's large enough to eat you up?
> Have you surveyed his jaws beneath,
> Drawn inventories of his teeth,
> Or have you weighed in even balance,
> His strength and magnitude of talons?
> His roar would change your boasts to fear
> As easily as sour small beer."

The partisans of England had boasted of her humanity. You remember how Gage writes to Washington that "Britons, ever pre-eminent in mercy, have outgone common examples, and overlooked the criminal in the captive."* Mac-Fingal tells us in what sense the word is used: —

> "For now in its primeval sense
> This term, *humanity*, comprehends
> All things of which, on this side hell,
> The human mind is capable;
> And thus 't is well, by writers sage,
> Applied to Briton and to Gage."

The expedition to Salem and the battle of Lexington are told with much humor and many keen strokes of satire. But it is in the future that the second-sighted orator finds amplest room for the display of his powers. Let me premise, however, before I read from this passage, that the Marshfield Resolves were a very bombastic and silly outbreak of Toryism, which found a worthy

---

* Gage to Washington. Sparks's Washington, Vol. III. p. 500, Appendix VII.

representative in a certain Abijah White; and that British officers, mistaking the winding of the "small and sullen horn" of the beetle and the whizzing of mosquitoes for more formidable sounds, wrote home, that in their evening walk on Beacon Hill they had been shot at by the Yankees with air-guns. Need I remind you that, trifles as these are, they throw a light upon the passions and feelings, the misconceptions and prejudices of the times, which nothing else could give? The silly Elijah, with his "dread array of commissions, pistols, swords, resolves," is the bullying, blustering Tory, as the Tory often appeared to our fathers. The English officers who "muskitoes take for musketeers," are the conceited, foppish cockneys, who believed that every Colonist was a savage, and that scalping, if not roasting, was as much a pastime of the Yankee as of the Indian. There were honest men among the Tories, — honest, though sadly misguided; well-informed men among the British officers, — though not well-informed enough to distinguish the right from the wrong of this contest. But if we would form a correct idea of the period we must study both classes, and for the first, MacFingal is our best authority: —

> "But now your triumphs all are o'er,
> For see from Britain's angry shore,
> With deadly hosts of valor join
> Her Howe, her Clinton, and Burgoyne,

As comets through th' affrighted skies
Pour baleful ruin as they rise;
As Ætna with infernal roar
In conflagration sweeps the shore;
Or as Abijah White, when sent
Our Marshfield friends to represent,
Himself while dread array involves,
Commissions, pistols, swords, resolves,
In awful pomp descending down
Bore terror on the factious town:
Not with less glory and affright
Parade these generals forth to fight,
No more each British colonel runs
From whizzing beetles as air-guns;
Thinks hornbugs bullets, or thro' fears
Muskitoes takes for musketeers;
Nor 'scapes, as if you 'd gained supplies,
From Beelzebub's whole host of flies.
No bug these warlike hearts appalls,
They better know the sound of balls.
I hear the din of battle bray;
The trump of horror marks its way.
I see afar the sack of cities,
The gallows strung with Whig committees;
Your moderators triced like vermin,
And gate-posts graced with heads of chairmen;
Your Congress for wave offerings hanging,
And ladders thronged with priests haranguing.
What pillories glad the 'Tories' eyes
With patriot ears for sacrifice!
What whipping-posts your chosen race
Admit successive in embrace,
While each bears off his sins, alack!
Like Bunyan's pilgrim, on his back.
Where then when Tories scarce get clear
Shall Whigs and Congresses appear?"

But I must hasten to the catastrophe. I pass over the breaking up of the meeting, the liberty-pole with its characteristic inauguration, the sideway thrust at the slave-trade, as the flag

> "Inscribed with inconsistent types
> Of *Liberty* and *thirteen stripes*,"

and how

> "Beneath the crowd without delay
> The dedication rites essay,
> And gladly pay in ancient fashion
> The ceremonies of libation;
> While briskly to each patriot lip
> Walks eager round the inspiring flip."

I pass over these and the Squire's harangue, and the fight and overthrow, to dwell for a moment on the sentence and its execution: —

> "Meanwhile beside the pole, the guard
> A Bench of Justice had prepared,
> Where, sitting round in awful sort,
> The grand committee hold their court
> While all the crew in silent awe
> Wait from their lips the lore of law.
> Few moments with deliberation
> They hold the solemn consultation;
> When soon in judgment all agree
> And clerk proclaims the dread decree, —

> "That Squire MacFingal having grown
> The vilest Tory in the town,
> And now in full examination
> Convicted by his own confession,

Finding no tokens of repentance
This court proceeds to render sentence;
That, first, the mob a slip-knot single
Tie round the neck of said MacFingal,
And in due form do tar him next,
And feather as the law directs;
Then through the town attendant ride him
In cart with constable beside him,
And, having held him up to shame,
Bring to the pole from whence he came.

"Forthwith the crowd proceed to deck
With haltered noose MacFingal's neck,
While he in peril of his soul
Stood tied half dangling to the pole;
Then, lifting high the ponderous jar,
Poured o'er his head the smoking tar.
With less profusion once was spread
Oil on the Jewish monarch's head,
That down his beard and vestments ran,
And covered all his outward man.
As when (so Claudian sings) the gods
And earth-born giants fell at odds,
The stout Enceladus in malice
Tore mountains up to throw at Pallas;
And while he held them o'er his head,
The river, from their fountains fed,
Poured down his back its copious tide,
And wore its channels in his hide:
So from the high-raised urn the torrents
Spread down his side their various currents;
His flowing wig, as next the brim,
First met and drank the sable stream;
Adown his visage stern and grave
Rolled and adhered the viscid wave;
With arms depending as he stood,
Each cuff capacious holds the flood;

> From nose and chin's remotest end
> The tarry icicles descend;
> Till all o'erspread with colors gay,
> He glittered to the western ray,
> Like sleet-bound trees in wintry skies,
> Or Lapland idol carved in ice.
> And now the feather-bag displayed
> Is waved in triumph o'er his head,
> And clouds him o'er with feathers missive,
> And down, upon the tar, adhesive.
> Not Maia's son, with wings for ears,
> Such plumage round his visage wears;
> Nor Milton's six-winged angel gathers
> Such superfluity of feathers.
> Now all complete appears our Squire,
> Like Gorgon or Chimæra dire;
> Nor more could boast, on Plato's plan,
> To rank among the race of man,
> Or prove his claim to human nature,
> As a two-legged, unfeathered creature."

The carting follows next: —

> "In front the martial music comes
> Of horns and fiddles, fifes and drums,
> With jingling sound of carriage-bells,
> And treble creak of rusted wheels.
> Behind, the crowd, in lengthened row
> With proud procession, closed the show."

The crowd disperses, and our hero and his faithful friend, the constable, remain alone. Poor MacFingal!

> "Though his body lacked physician,
> His spirit was in worse condition."

And as

"All goes wrong in Church and State,
  Seen through prospective of the grate;
  So now MacFingal's second sight
  Beheld all things in different light.
His visual nerve, well purged with tar,
Saw all the coming scenes of war.
As his prophetic soul grew stronger,
He found he could hold in no longer.
First from the pole, as fierce he shook,
His wig from pitchy durance broke,
His mouth unglued, his feathers fluttered,
His tarred skirts cracked, and thus he uttered."

The fourth canto opens with the gathering of the Tories by night in MacFingal's cellar.

"Now night came down, and rose full soon
That patroness of rogues, the moon;
Beneath whose kind protecting ray,
Wolves, brute and human, prowl for prey.
The honest world all snored in chorus,
While owls and ghosts and thieves and Tories,
Whom erst the mid-day sun had awed,
Crept from their lurking holes abroad.
  "On cautious hinges, slow and stiller,
Wide oped the great MacFingal's cellar,
Where safe from prying eyes in cluster
The Tory Pandemonium muster.
Their chiefs all sitting round descried are
On kegs of ale and seats of cider;
When first MacFingal, dimly seen,
Rose solemn from the turnip-bin.
Nor yet his form had wholly lost
Th' original brightness it could boast,
Nor less appeared than Justice Quorum,
In feathered majesty before 'em.

> Adown his tar-streaked visage, clear,
> Fell glistening fast th' indignant tear,
> And thus his voice, in mournful wise,
> Pursued the prologue of his sighs."

This book, you will remember, was written in 1782, and thus the outline of the war, which is its principal subject, is historically correct. It is not inferior to the rest of the work in spirit and humor; one passage, indeed, and that aimed less at the enemy than at the errors of his own party, is full of true invention.

> "When lo, an awful spectre rose,
> With languid paleness on his brows;
> Wan dropsies swelled his form beneath,
> And iced his bloated cheeks with death;
> His tattered robes exposed him bare
> To every blast of ruder air;
> On two weak crutches propped he stood,
> That bent at every step he trod;
> Gilt titles graced their sides so slender,
> One 'Regulation,' t' other 'Tender';
> His breasplate graved with various dates,
> 'The faith of all th' United States';
> Before him went his funeral pall,
> His grave stood, dug to wait his fall."

This disgusting figure is "the ghost of Continental money," and if you have not forgotten the lecture of the other evening, you will readily acknowledge the faithfulness of the portrait.

To do full justice to Trumbull, it would be necessary to examine many other passages, pointing out, among other things, the happy use that he makes of Homer and Virgil and Milton, and claiming for him the lines that have passed into proverbs, and been attributed to other writers. One instance will illustrate my meaning: —

> "What rogue e'er felt the halter draw
> With good opinion of the law?"

How often, and even by those who should have known better, has this been quoted as Butler's?

You will easily conceive what an impression such a work must have made at such a time, how it must have awakened the dormant mirth of many an evening circle, and called forth shouts of merriment at the winter camp-fire; awakening at the same time, slumbering faith, and strengthening wavering resolution. Of the welcome it met, its thirty editions are sufficient proof, and if you would understand the men and the passions of our Revolution, you must study it as a running commentary, a photographic illustration, of Sparks, and Force, and Hildreth, and Irving.

Of the songs and ballads of the Revolution, there is little to say. They have been carefully collected by Frank Moore, and carefully studied by the Duyckinks. They were not unsuited, perhaps, to the times, meeting, as events occurred, the popular need of a concentrated expression of popular feeling. But, though rough and unadorned, their simplicity is not the artless expression of sentiment, nor the artless picturesqueness of narrative, which belong to the old ballad. They have the stamp of a later age upon them, of the age when poetry has passed from the wandering ministrel to the author's closet, from the uncultivated classes to the cultivated classes. Now and then you meet a striking line in them, and even a fine stanza; but seldom sustained power, whether of pathos or of humor.

Of the numerous ballads on Cornwallis, "The Dance" has some lively stanzas, and one excellent one.

> "Cornwallis led a country dance,
>   The like was never seen, sir,
> Much retrograde and much advance,
>   And all with General Greene, sir.
>
> "They rambled up and rambled down,
>   Joined hands and off they run, sir,
> Our General Greene to Charlestown,
>   The earl to Wilmington, sir.
>
> "Greene, in the South, then danced a set,
>   And got a mighty name, sir,
> Cornwallis jigged with young Fayette
>   And suffered in his fame, sir."

Washington appears on the scene, and in describing him the unknown poet catches for a moment the true spirit of his art.

> "And Washington, Columbia's son,
>   Whom easy nature taught, sir,
> That grace which can't by pains be won,
>   Or Plutus' gold be bought, sir."

There is true satire in the "Etiquette," but there is no proof that it was written by an American, and therefore I make no extracts. For the same reaon I pass over the "Volunteer's Song," and the "Recess." But "Clinton's Invitation to the Refugees" is truly American, and in a strain of keen satire that Freneau seldom reached.

> "Come, gentlemen Tories, firm, loyal, and true,
> Here are axes and shovels and something to do!
> For the sake of our king,
> Come labor and sing.
> You left all you had for his honor and glory,
> And he will remember the suffering Tory.
> We have, it is true,
> Some small work to do;
> But here's for your pay, twelve coppers a day,
> And never regard what the rebels may say,
> But throw off your jerkins and labor away.
>
> "To raise up the rampart, and pile up the wall,
> To pull down old houses, and dig the canal,
> To build and destroy,
> Be this your employ,
> In the day-time to work at our fortifications,
> And steal, in the night, from the rebels your rations.
> The king wants your aid,
> Not empty parade.
> Advance to your places, ye men of long faces,
> Nor ponder too much on your former disgraces,
> This year, I presume, will quite alter your cases.
>
> "Attend at the call of the fifer and drummer,
> The French and the rebels are coming next summer,
> And the forts we must build,
> Though Tories are killed.

Take courage, my jockies, and work for your king,
For if you are taken, no doubt you will swing.
    If York we can hold
    I will have you enrolled ;
And after you 're dead, your names shall be read,
As who for their monarch both labored and bled,
And ventured their necks for their beef and their bread.

" 'T is an honor to serve the bravest of nations,
And be left to be hanged in their capitulations.
    Then scour up your mortars,
    And stand to your quarters,
'T is nonsense for Tories in battle to run.
They never need fear sword, halberd, or gun ;
    Their hearts should not fail 'em,
    No balls will assail 'em ;
Forget your disgraces, and shorten your faces,
For 't is true as the Gospel, believe it or not,
Who are born to be hanged will never be shot."

Burgoyne's defeat is celebrated in various metres. Sullivan's Island, Trenton, King's Mountain, Yorktown, are sung in verses which may have sounded well around a mess-table or a camp-fire, — may have read well in a broadside or a newspaper of the day, — but which appear tame and awkward in a printed volume. But of the humorous, nay, witty ballads, the "Battle of the Kegs" will bear a comparison with the best of its kind, and I think you will all agree with me that, though unequal in parts, there is simplicity, a happy choice of illustrative circumstances, delicacy of thought, sweetness of numbers, and a full, deep flow of natural pathos in the ballad of Nathan Hale.

BATTLE OF THE KEGS.

Gallants attend, and hear a friend,
    Trill forth harmonious ditty,
Strange things I'll tell, which late befell
    In Philadelphia city.

'T was early day, as poets say,
    Just when the sun was rising,
A soldier stood on log of wood,
    And saw a sight surprising.

As in amaze, he stood to gaze,
    The truth can't be denied, sir,
He spied a score of kegs or more
    Come floating down the tide, sir:

A sailor, too, in jerkin blue,
    This strange appearance viewing,
First damned his eyes in great surprise,
    Then said, "Some mischief's brewing.

"Those kegs, I'm told, the rebels hold,
    Packed up like pickled herring,
And they're come down t' attack the town
    In this new way of ferrying."

The soldier flew, the sailor too,
    And scared almost to death, sir,
Wore out their shoes to spread the news,
    And ran till out of breath, sir.

Now up and down, throughout the town,
    Most frantic scenes were acted;
And some ran here, and others there,
    Like men almost distracted.

Some fire cried, which some denied,
    But said the earth had quaked;
And girls and boys with hideous noise,
    Ran through the streets half naked.

And now the alarm reaches Sir William, who all this time had lain in his bed "snug as a flea," nor "dreamed of harm."

Now in a fright he starts upright,
    Awaked by such a clatter;
He rubs his eyes, and boldly cries,
    "For God's sake what's the matter?"

At his bedside he then espied
    Sir Erskine at command, sir,
Upon one foot he had one boot,
    And t' other in his hand, sir.

"Arise, arise," Sir Erskine cries,
    "The rebels, more 's the pity,
Without a boat, are all afloat,
    And ranged before the city.

"The motley crew in vessels new,
    With Satan for their guide, sir,
Packed up in bags or wooden kegs
    Come driving down the tide, sir.

"Therefore prepare for bloody war,
    These kegs must all be routed,
Or surely we despised shall be,
    And British courage doubted."

The royal band now ready stand,
    All ranged in dread array, sir,
With stomachs stout to see it out,
    And make a bloody day, sir.

The cannons roar from shore to shore,
   The small arms make a rattle,
Since wars began I'm sure no man
   Ere saw so strange a battle.

The rebel dales, the rebel vales
   With rebel trees surrounded,
The distant woods, the hills and floods,
   With rebel echoes sounded.

The fish below swam to and fro,
   Attacked from every quarter;
Why sure, thought they, the devil's to pay
   'Mongst folks above the water.

The kegs, 't is said, though strongly made
   Of rebel staves and hoops, sir,
Could not oppose their powerful foes,
   The conquering British troops, sir.

From morn till night, these men of might
   Displayed amazing courage;
And when the sun was fairly down,
   Retired to sup their porridge.

An hundred men with each a pen,
   Or more, upon my word, sir,
It is most true, would be too few,
   Their valor to record, sir.

Such feats did they perform that day,
   Against those wicked kegs, sir,
That years to come, if they get home,
   They'll make their boasts and brags, sir.

But I cannot close so serious a subject with so merry a strain. Let me ask you rather to recall what I told you, in my Lecture on the Martyrs of the Revolution, of Nathan Hale, one of the truest and noblest of those true and noble men. I trust that American poetry has yet a fitting place for him: though should even the greatest among our poets tell his story, I should be loath to have the tender and touching tribute of an unknown contemporary forgotten.

A BALLAD.

The breezes went steadily through the tall pines,
   A saying "Oh! hu-ush," a saying "Oh! hu-ush!"
As stilly stole by a bold legion of horse,
   For Hale in the bush, for Hale in the bush.

"Keep still," said the thrush as she nestled her young
   In a nest by the road, in a nest by the road;
"For the tyrants are near, and with them appear
   What bodes us no good, what bodes us no good."

The brave Captain heard it, and thought of his home
   In a cot by the brook, in a cot by the brook;
With mother and sister and memories dear,
   He so gayly forsook, he so gayly forsook.

Cooling shades of the night were coming apace,
   The tattoo had beat, the tattoo had beat;
The noble one sprang from his dark lurking-place,
   To make his retreat, to make his retreat.

He warily trod on the dry rustling leaves,
   As he passed thro' the wood, as he passed thro' the wood;
And silently gained his rude launch on the shore,
   As she played with the flood, as she played with the flood.

The guards of the camp, on that dark, dreary night,
   Had a murderous will, had a murderous will.

They took him and bore him afar from the shore,
    To a hut on the hill, to a hut on the hill.

No mother was there, nor a friend who could cheer,
    In that little stone cell, in that little stone cell;
But he trusted in love from his Father above,
    In his heart all was well, in his heart all was well.

An ominous owl, with his solemn base voice,
    Sat moaning hard by, sat moaning hard by,
" The tyrant's proud minions most gladly rejoice,
    For he must soon die, for he must soon die."

The brave fellow told them, no thing he restrained,
    The cruel gen'ral, the cruel gen'ral,
Of his errand from camp, of the end to be gained,
    And said that was all, and said that was all.

They took him and bound him and bore him away,
    Down the hill's grassy side, down the hill's grassy side;
'T was there the base hirelings in royal array
    His cause did deride, his cause did deride.

Five minutes were given, short moments, no more,
    For him to repent, for him to repent;
He prayed for his mother, he asked not another, —
    To Heaven he went, to Heaven he went.

The faith of a martyr the tragedy showed,
    As he trod the last stage, as he trod the last stage;
And Britons will shudder at gallant Hale's blood,
    As his words do presage, as his words do presage.

Thou pale king of terrors, thou life's gloomy foe,
    Go frighten the slave, go frighten the slave;
Tell tyrants, to you their allegiance they owe.
    No fears for the brave, no fears for the brave.

And now at the close of this long course permit me to give a rapid glance at the ground over which we have passed, remembering that, while history is the record of man's acts, it is still more eminently the interpreter of God's will. As the record of man's acts, we find much to humiliate and sadden us; as the interpreter of God's will, we find everything to animate us in the performance of duty, and sustain us under the trials and sacrifices which it may impose.

It is impossible at this grave moment of our country's fortunes to read the history of our War of Independence without comparing it, as we read, with that other war which is daily unfolding its vicissitudes before our eyes, — our war of fulfilment and preservation.

They are alike, for they are both wars of principle, and therefore wars of progress. There is no mistaking the cause of progress. Every responsibility carries with it a corresponding right; and true progress, if history be true, is the reciprocal evolution of responsibility from right, and of right from responsibility, and the harmonious development of both. Man's right to appropriate the earth to his own use involves the responsibility of cultivating it industriously and judiciously; and this responsibility, honestly fulfilled, gives him a right to a controlling voice in the disposal of the products of his cultivation. It was in this light that our fathers judged the legislation of the British Parliament, and in this light must their great struggle be judged.

But underlying this right was the right of personal freedom as the result of personal responsibility at the bar of God. Now this conclusion, although a logical sequence, many among them failed to reach, while those who reached it speculatively being unable to give it substantial expression by incorporating it with their new institutions, left the completion of their sacrifices and labors as a responsibility for their children, and in full faith that it would be faithfully met.

And thus our present war is the logical sequence of our War of Independence, as the War of Independence was the logical sequence of the compact signed in the cabin of the Mayflower. And thus from sequence to cause, tracing upwards the stream of time, we bind in one connected chain the Proclamation of President Lincoln with the Declaration of Independence, and the Declaration of Independence with the Charter of Runnymede. If you would judge an historical event you must study it in its sequences, you must penetrate to the right on which it rests, the responsibility which it involves, and if there be life and development in it, it is progress, and, inasmuch as it is progress, the irresistible expression of the will of God.

Thus alike in their origin, — the war of our fathers on the part of England being like our own war on the part of the South, — acts of blind resistance to the inevitable development of a great natural law, — they are also alike in many of the practical lessons which they convey. In both, while great virtues have been displayed, great errors have been committed. Our fathers erred by permitting decisive moments to pass, by neglecting the warnings of experience, and misinterpreting the lessons of history. Sometimes, too, they erred by employing palliatives, by indulging delusive hopes, by casting lingering looks behind when they should have fixed their eyes firmly on the steep and rugged path before.

And have we not erred where they erred, and even more than they? Why have we not an army of a million of men, but that we permitted the blood that rushed in indignant protest to the cheek of every true American at the sound of the first gun against Sumter to utter its protest in vain? If it was a gross error in them to raise three months' men and nine months' men, instead of men for the war, what does it become in us, with their example, written in wasted blood and protracted suffering, before our eyes? If it was madness in them to dream of reconciliation after Lexington and Bunker Hill, what shall we say of those who still continue to talk of peace without victory after Bull Run and Fredericksburg? If they failed to apply justly the lessons of history, what shall we say who, with the additional lessons of three new generations before us, have repeated all their mistakes, and not contented with repeating, have enriched them by still greater mistakes of our own?

Of these peculiar errors of ours, I will give but one example. When our fathers took up arms against England, they were in many respects like men groping in the dark. The example of the United Provinces was almost the only modern example to which they could have recourse; and I need not tell you — what your profound and eloquent Motley has shown — how unlike the two wars were in their causes, in their vicissitudes, and in the character both of the two countries and the two people. The record of this groping of our fathers is given act by act and almost day by day in the letters of Washington and his officers. There is scarce an error that we have committed which is not pointed out and illustrated in that exhaustless mine of administrative wisdom. Had our statesmen studied the correspondence of Washington with half the attention with which they have studied the ephemeral effusions of party zeal, they would never have made shipwreck, as so many of them have done, on the shoals and quicksands which he saw with so clear an eye, and marked out with so firm a hand. To neglect his warning was to undervalue his wisdom; and what an American becomes when he loses his reverence for Washington, an anecdote, for the authenticity of which I can vouch, will tell

CONCLUSION.

you better than any words of mine. I have said *he;* but the reverence which I speak of would fall very short of its office if the sentiment were confined to man, — and the subject of my story is a woman.

In the summer of 1861 an eminent artist was showing his studio to a party of ladies and gentlemen. Of all his treasures, that which he valued most was an orderly-book which had once belonged to Washington, and many pages of which were written in that firm, bold hand which every American instantly recognizes as that of the father of his country. As he was opening it, he heard a remark from one of the company, which sounded so strangely to his ears that he could not persuade himself that he had heard aright.

"What were you saying, madam?" he asked.

"I am saying that I am tired of these exaggerated praises of that cold-blooded man."

That lady is now at Richmond, presiding over those circles in which the men who would build their republic on the corner-stone of slavery do reverence to their Washington.

How, then, did our fathers conquer? They conquered by perseverance, by refusing to sheathe the sword until the purpose for which they drew it had been fully accomplished. They conquered by endurance, accepting, if not always cheerfully, yet with a wise submission, the consequences of their acts. They conquered by faith — faith in their cause as the cause of humanity, and faith in their leader as God's chosen instrument.

And by perseverance, endurance, and faith, we too shall conquer, — not this year indeed, nor perhaps even in the next, — but conquer we must, if, believing, as they believed, that our cause is the cause of religion and humanity, we too make our faith manifest by firm, consistent, and resolute action; sustaining and encouraging each other, meeting with cheerful greetings, speaking warmly of our hopes, and only so much of our fears as may be needed to infuse that wise caution which makes the accomplishment of hope sure, and repeating to ourselves and to each other the inspiring words of our great poet: —

> "Sail on, O ship of state!
> Sail on, O Union, strong and great!
> Humanity with all its fears,
> With all the hopes of future years,
> Is hanging breathless on thy fate!
> We know what Master laid thy keel,
> What workmen wrought thy ribs of steel,
> Who made each mast, and sail, and rope,
> What anvils rang, what hammers beat,
> In what a forge and what a heat
> Were shaped the anchors of thy hope!
> Fear not each sudden sound and shock,
> 'T is of the wave and not the rock;
> 'T is but the flapping of the sail,
> And not a rent made by the gale!
> In spite of rock and tempest's roar,
> In spite of false lights on the shore,

Sail on, nor fear to breast the sea!
Our hearts, our hopes, are all with thee,
Our hearts, our hopes, our prayers, our tears,
Our faith triumphant o'er our fears,
Are all with thee, — are all with thee!"

CHRONOLOGICAL OUTLINE. 447

1775.	June 15.	Washington appointed Commander-in-Chief.
"	" 17.	Battle of Bunker Hill.
"	November 29.	Congress appoints a Committee of Secret Correspondence.
"	December 31.	Montgomery killed in the attack on Quebec.
1776.	January.	Two first cantos of MacFingal published. Paine's Common Sense.
"	March.	Silas Deane sent to France as Commercial Agent.
"	March 17.	British evacuate Boston.
"	May 6.	John Adams brings forward his resolution for the establishment of State governments.
"	May 10.	Resolution passed.
"	" 15.	Preamble added.
"	June 7.	"Resolutions for Independency" moved.
"	June 10.	Committee appointed to draft the Declaration.
"	" 28.	British land and sea forces under Clinton and Parker attack Fort Moultrie and are repulsed.
"	July 2.	Independence resolved.
"	" 4.	Declaration signed by Hancock and Thompson.
"	August 27.	Battle of Long Island.
"	October 28.	Battle of White Plains.
"	November 16.	Fall of Fort Washington.
"	December 8.	Washington retreats across the Delaware.
"	" 12.	Congress adjourns to Baltimore.
"	" 19.	First number of Paine's Crisis.
"	" 21.	Franklin reaches Paris.
"	" 26.	Capture of Hessians at Trenton.
1777.	January 3.	Battle of Princeton.
"	June.	Arrival of Lafayette.
"	August 16.	Battle of Bennington.
"	September 11.	Battle of the Brandywine.
"	" 19.	First Battle of Stillwater.
"	October 7.	Second Battle of Stillwater.
"	" 14.	Battle of Germantown.
"	" 17.	Surrender of Burgoyne.
"	December 1.	Steuben arrives at Portsmouth, N. H.
1778.	February 6.	Treaty with France.
"	April 8.	John Adams arrives at Paris as Commissioner, &c.
"	June 28.	Battle of Monmouth.
"	July.	Massacre of Wyoming.
"	August.	Expedition to Rhode Island.
"	" 29.	Battle of Tiverton Heights.

1778. November. Massacre at Cherry Valley
1779. March 3. Battle of Briar Creek.
" February and July. Tryon's expeditions.
" June and July. Spain takes part in the war against England.
" July 15. Capture of Stony Point.
" " 31. Sullivan begins his march against the Indians.
" September 27. John Jay appointed Minister to Spain.
" October 9. Siege of Savannah.
" " 15. Sullivan arrives at Easton, Penn.
1780. May 12. Surrender of Charleston.
" " 29. Battle of Waxhaw Creek.
" June 23. Battle of Springfield.
" July 10. Arrival of French fleet and army.
" July 9 and August 1. Convention for armed neutrality between Russia, Sweden, and Denmark.
" August 6. Battle of Hanging Rock.
" " 16. First Battle of Camden.
" September. Arnold's treason discovered.
" October 2. Execution of André.
" " 7. Battle of King's Mountain.
" " 14. Greene appointed to the command of the Southern army.
" December 19. Francis Dana sent to St. Petersburgh.
" " 20. England declares war against Holland.
1781. January 1. Mutiny of the Pennsylvania line.
" " 17. Battle of the Cowpens.
" January and February. Greene's operations in Carolina and retreat across the Dan.
" March 15. Battle of Guilford Court House.
" April 25. Battle of Hobkirk's Hill.
" September 8. Battle of Eutaw Springs.
" October 19. Surrender of Cornwallis.
1782. Treaty with Holland.
" November 30. Provisional articles of Peace signed at Paris.
1783. April 19. Cessation of hostilities.
" September 3. Definitive treaty of peace.
" October 18. Proclamation disbanding the army.
" November 25. Evacuation of New York.
" December 4. Washington's farewell.

TABLE I.
AMERICAN COLONIAL TRADE.

Trade between Great Britain and the American Colonies, from 1697 to 1776, showing the Exports from, and Imports into, the then Colonies.

[From Hazard's United States Commercial and Statistical Register.]

	New England.		New York.		Pennsylvania.		Virginia and Maryland.		Carolina.		Georgia.	
	Exports.	Imports.	Exports.	Imports.	Exports.	Imports.	Exports.	Imports.	Exports.	Imports.	Exports.	Imports.
	£	£	£	£	£	£	£	£	£	£	£	£
1697	26,282	68,468	10,093	4,579	3,347	2,997	227,756	58,796	12,374	5,289		
1698	31,254	93,517	8,763	25,279	2,720	10,704	174,053	310,135	9,265	18,462		
1699	26,660	127,279	16,818	42,792	1,477	17,064	198,115	205,078	12,372	11,401		
1700	41,486	91,918	17,567	49,410	4,608	18,529	317,302	173,481	14,058	11,003		
1701	32,656	86,322	18,547	31,910	5,220	12,003	235,738	199,683	16,972	13,908		
1702	37,026	64,625	7,965	29,991	4,145	9,342	274,782	72,391	11,870	10,460		
1703	33,539	59,608	7,471	17,562	5,160	9,899	144,928	196,713	13,107	12,428		
1704	30,823	74,896	10,540	22,294	2,430	11,619	264,112	60,458	14,067	6,621		
1705	22,793	62,504	7,393	27,902	1,309	7,206	116,768	174,322	2,698	19,788		
1706	22,210	57,050	2,849	31,588	4,210	11,037	149,152	58,015	8,652	4,001		
1707	38,798	120,631	14,283	20,855	786	14,365	207,625	237,901	23,311	10,492		
1708	49,636	115,505	10,847	26,890	2,120	6,223	213,493	79,061	10,340	11,996		
1709	29,559	120,349	12,259	34,577	617	5,861	261,668	80,268	20,431	28,521		
1710	31,112	106,338	8,203	31,475	1,277	8,594	188,429	127,639	20,793	19,613		
1711	26,415	137,421	12,193	28,856	38	19,408	273,181	91,535	12,871	20,406		
1712	24,699	128,105	12,466	18,524	1,471	8,464	297,941	134,583	29,394	20,015		
1713	49,904	120,778	14,428	46,470	178	17,037	206,263	76,304	32,449	23,967		
1714	51,541	121,288	29,810	44,643	2,663	14,927	280,470	128,873	31,290	23,712		
1715	68,555	164,650	21,316	54,629	5,461	17,182	174,756	199,274	29,158	16,631		
1716	63,595	121,156	21,971	52,173	5,193	21,842	281,343	179,599	46,287	27,272		

450   APPENDIX.

| | New England. || New York. || Pennsylvania. || Virginia and Maryland. || Carolina. || Georgia. ||
	Exports.	Imports.	Exports.	Imports.	Exports.	Imports.	Exports.	Imports.	Exports.	Imports.	Exports.	Imports.
	£	£	£	£	£	£	£	£	£	£	£	£
1717	58,898	132,001	24,534	44,140	4,499	22,505	296,884	215,962	41,275	25,058		
1718	61,591	131,885	27,331	62,966	5,588	22,716	316,576	191,925	46,385	15,841		
1719	54,452	125,317	19,596	56,355	6,564	27,068	332,069	164,630	50,373	19,630		
1720	49,206	128,769	16,836	37,397	7,928	24,531	331,482	110,717	62,736	18,290		
1721	50,463	114,524	15,681	50,754	8,037	21,548	357,812	127,376	61,658	17,703		
1722	47,955	133,722	20,118	57,478	6,882	26,397	283,091	172,754	79,650	34,374		
1723	59,339	176,486	27,992	63,013	8,332	15,992	287,997	123,833	73,103	42,246		
1724	69,585	168,507	21,191	63,020	4,057	30,324	277,344	161,894	90,504	37,839		
1725	72,021	201,768	24,976	70,650	11,891	42,209	214,730	195,884	91,942	39,182		
1726	63,816	200,882	38,307	84,866	5,960	57,634	324,767	185,981	93,453	43,934		
1727	75,052	167,277	31,617	67,452	12,823	31,979	421,588	192,965	96,035	23,254		
1728	64,689	194,590	21,141	81,634	15,230	37,478	413,089	171,092	91,175	33,067		
1729	52,512	161,102	15,833	64,760	7,434	29,799	386,174	108,931	113,329	58,366		
1730	54,701	208,196	8,740	64,356	10,582	48,592	346,823	150,931	151,739	64,785		
1731	49,048	183,467	20,756	66,116	12,786	44,260	408,502	171,278	159,771	71,145		
1732	64,095	216,600	9,411	65,540	8,524	41,698	310,799	148,289	126,207	58,298		
1733	61,983	184,570	11,626	65,417	14,776	40,565	403,198	186,177	177,845	76,466	203	828
1734	82,252	146,460	15,307	81,758	20,217	54,392	373,090	172,086	120,466	99,658	18	1,695
1735	72,899	189,125	14,155	80,405	21,919	48,804	394,995	220,381	145,348	117,837	3,010	1,921
1736	66,788	222,158	17,944	86,000	20,786	61,513	380,163	204,794	214,083	101,147		12,112
1737	63,347	223,923	16,833	125,833	15,198	56,690	492,246	211,301	187,758	58,986		2,012
1738	59,116	203,233	16,228	133,438	11,918	61,450	391,814	258,660	141,119	87,793	17	5,701
1739	46,604	220,378	18,459	106,070	8,134	54,452	444,654	217,200	236,192	94,445	233	6,496
1740	72,389	171,081	21,498	118,777	15,048	56,751	341,997	281,428	265,560	181,821	924	3,324
1741	60,052	198,147	21,142	140,430	17,158	91,010	577,109	248,582	236,830	224,270		3,524
1742	53,166	148,899	13,536	167,591	8,527	75,295	427,762	264,186	154,607	127,063	1,022	2,653
1743	63,185	172,461	15,067	134,487	9,596	79,340	557,821	328,195	235,136	111,499	2	17,018
1744	50,248	143,982	14,527	119,920	7,446	62,214	402,709	234,855	192,594	79,141		2,291
												769

AMERICAN COLONIAL TRADE.

Year												
1745	38,948	140,463	14,083	54,957	10,130	54,280	399,423	197,799	91,847	86,815		939
1746	38,612	209,177	8,841	86,712	15,779	73,699	419,371	282,545	76,897	102,809		984
1747	41,771	210,640	14,992	137,984	3,832	82,404	492,619	200,088	107,500	95,529		24
1748	29,748	197,682	12,358	143,311	12,363	75,330	494,852	252,624	167,305	160,172		1,314
1749	39,999	238,286	23,413	265,773	14,944	238,637	434,618	323,600	120,499	164,085	51	5
1750	48,455	343,659	35,632	267,130	28,191	217,713	508,939	349,419	191,607	134,037	1,942	2,125
1751	63,287	273,340	42,363	248,941	23,870	190,917	460,085	347,027	245,491	138,244	355	2,065
1752	74,815	345,523	40,648	194,030	29,978	201,666	569,453	325,151	288,362	150,777	1,526	8,163
1753	63,395	329,433	40,553	277,864	38,527	245,644	632,575	356,776	164,634	213,009	3,057	14,128
1754	66,538	341,796	26,663	127,497	30,649	244,647	573,435	323,513	307,238	149,215	3,236	1,974
1755	59,533	384,371	28,055	151,071	32,336	144,456	489,668	285,157	325,525	187,687	4,437	2,630
1756	47,359	363,404	24,073	250,425	20,091	200,169	337,759	334,897	222,915	181,780	7,155	536
1757	27,556	465,694	19,168	353,311	14,190	168,926	418,881	426,087	130,889	213,949		2,571
1758	30,204	465,694	14,260	356,555	21,383	260,953	454,362	438,471	150,511	181,002		10,212
1759	25,985	527,067	21,684	630,785	22,404	498,161	357,228	459,007	206,634	215,255	6,074	15,178
1760	37,802	599,647	21,425	480,106	22,754	707,998	504,451	605,860	162,769	218,131	12,198	24,279
1761	46,225	334,225	48,646	289,570	39,170	204,067	455,083	545,350	253,002	254,587	5,764	23,761
1762	41,733	247,385	58,882	288,046	38,091	206,199	415,709	418,599	181,695	194,170	6,522	44,908
1763	74,815	258,854	53,998	236,560	38,228	284,152	642,294	555,391	282,366	250,132	14,469	18,338
1764	68,157	459,765	53,697	515,416	36,258	436,191	559,505	515,192	341,727	305,808	31,325	29,165
1765	145,819	451,299	54,959	382,349	25,148	363,368	505,671	383,224	385,918	334,709	34,183	67,268
1766	141,733	409,642	67,020	330,829	26,851	327,314	461,693	372,546	293,587	296,732	53,074	23,334
1767	128,207	406,081	61,422	417,957	37,641	371,830	437,926	437,628	395,027	244,093	35,856	56,562
1768	148,375	419,797	87,115	182,930	59,406	432,107	406,048	475,984	508,108	289,868	42,402	58,340
1769	129,353	207,993	73,466	74,918	26,111	193,906	361,692	488,362	387,114	306,600	82,270	56,193
1770	146,011	394,451	69,882	475,991	28,109	134,881	435,094	717,782	278,907	146,273	55,532	70,493
1771	150,381	1,420,119	95,875	653,621	31,615	728,744	577,848	920,326	420,311	409,169	63,810	92,406
1772	126,265	624,830	82,707	343,970	29,133	507,909	528,404	793,910	425,923	449,610	66,083	62,932
1773	124,624	527,055	76,246	289,214	36,652	426,448	569,803	328,904	456,513	344,659	85,391	57,518
1774	112,248	562,476	80,008	437,937	69,611	625,652	612,030	526,738	432,302	378,116	67,647	118,777
1775	116,588	71,625	187,018	1,228	175,962	1,366	758,356	1,921	579,349	6,245	103,477	
1776	762	55,050	2,318		1,421	365	73,226		13,668		12,569	

TABLE II.

List of General Officers at the Commencement and Close of the Revolutionary War.

FIRST CONTINENTAL ARMY, 1775.

Commander-in-Chief.

	State.	Date of Commis.
GEORGE WASHINGTON,	Virginia,	June 15, 1775.

Major-Generals.

Artemas Ward,	Massachusetts,	June 17, 1775.
Charles Lee,	Virginia,	do. 17, 1775.
Philip Schuyler,	New York,	do. 19, 1775.
Israel Putnam,	Connecticut,	do. 19, 1775.

Brigadier-Generals.

Seth Pomeroy,	Massachusetts,	June 22, 1775.
Richard Montgomery,	New York,	do. 22, 1775.
David Wooster,	Connecticut,	do. 22, 1775.
William Heath,	Massachusetts,	do. 22, 1775.
Joseph Spencer,	Connecticut,	do. 22, 1775.
John Thomas,	Massachusetts,	do. 22, 1775.
John Sullivan,	New Hampshire,	do. 22, 1775.
Nathaniel Greene,	Rhode Island,	do. 22, 1775.

Adjutant-General.

Horatio Gates,	Virginia,	June 17, 1775.

CONTINENTAL ARMY IN 1783.

Commander-in-Chief.

	State.	Date of Commis.
GEORGE WASHINGTON,	Virginia,	June 15, 1775.

Major-Generals.

Israel Putnam,	Connecticut,	June 19, 1775.
Horatio Gates,	Virginia,	May 16, 1776.
William Heath,	Massachusetts,	Aug. 9, 1776.
Nathaniel Greene,	Rhode Island,	do. 9, 1776
William Lord Stirling,	New Jersey,	Feb. 19, 1777

LIST OF GENERAL OFFICERS. 453

Arthur St. Clair,	Pennsylvania,	Feb. 19, 1777.
Benjamin Lincoln,	Massachusetts,	do. 19, 1777.
M. de La Fayette,	France,	July 31, 1777.
Robert Howe,.	North Carolina,	Oct. 20, 1777.
Alexander McDougall,	New York,	do. 20, 1777.
Baron Steuben,	Prussia,	May 5, 1778.
William Smallwood,	Maryland,	Sept. 15, 1780.
William Moultrie,	South Carolina,	Nov. 14, 1780.
Henry Knox,	Massachusetts,	do. 15, 1780.
Le Chevalier du Portail,	France,	do. 16, 1780.

Brigadier-Generals.

James Clinton,	New York,	Aug. 9, 1776.
Lachlan McIntosh,	Georgia,	Sept. 16, 1776.
John Patterson,	Massachusetts,	Feb. 21, 1777.
Anthony Wayne,	Pennsylvania,	do. 1777.
George Weeden,	Virginia,	do. 1777.
P. Muhlenberg,	Virginia,	do.˙ 1777.
George Clinton,	New York,	Mar. 25, 1777.
Edward Hand,	Pennsylvania,	April 1, 1777.
Charles Scott,	Virginia,	do. 2, 1777.
Jedidiah Huntington,	Connecticut,	May 12, 1777.
John Stark,	New Hampshire,	Oct. 4, 1777.
Jethro Sumner,	North Carolina,	Jan. 9, 1779.
Isaac Huger,	South Carolina,	do. 9, 1779.
Mordecai Gist,	Maryland,	do. 9. 1779.
William Irvine,	Pennsylvania,	Jan. 9, 1779.
Daniel Morgan,	Virginia,	Oct. 13, 1780.
Moses Hazen,		June 29, 1781.
O. H. Williams,	Maryland,	May 9, 1782
John Greaton,	Massachusetts,	Jan. 7, 1783
Rufus Putnam,	Massachusetts,	do. 7, 1783.
Elias Dayton,	New Jersey,	do. 7, 1783.

Major-General le Chevalier du Portail, *Chief Engineer.*
Major-General Baron Steuben, *Inspector-General.*
Colonel Walter Stewart, *Inspector of the Northern Department.*
Brigadier-General Hand, *Adjutant-General.*
Colonel Timothy Pickering, *Quartermaster-General.*
John Cockran, Esq., *Director-General of Hospitals.*
Thomas Edwards, *Judge-Advocate-General.*
John Pierce, Esq., *Paymaster-General.*

TABLE III.

A Statement of the Troops, Continental and Militia, furnished by the respective States, during the Revolutionary War, from 1775 to 1783, inclusive.

[From the Collections of the New Hampshire Historical Society.]

STATES.	1775. Conti-nental.	1776. Conti-nental.	1776. Militia.	1777. Conti-dental.	1777. Militia.	1778. Conti-nental.	1778. Militia.	1779. Conti-nental.	1779. Militia.	1780. Conti-nental.	1780. Militia.	1781. Conti-nental.	1781. Militia.	1782. Conti-n¬ntal.	1783. Conti-nental.
New Hampshire,	2,824	3,019		1,172	1,111	1,283		1,004	222	1,017	760	700		744	733
Massachusetts,	16,444	13,372	4,000	7,816	2,775	7,010	1,927	6,287	1,451	4,553	3,436	3,732	1,566	4,423	4,370
Rhode Island,	1,193	798	1,102	548		630	2,426	507	756	915		464		481	372
Connecticut,	4,507	6,390	5,737	4,563		4,010		3,544		3,133	554	2,420	1,501	1,732	1,740
New York,	2,075	3,629	1,715	1,903	921	2,194		2,256		2,179	668	1,728		1,198	1,169
New Jersey,		3,193	5,893	1,408		1,586		1,276		1,105	162	823		660	675
Pennsylvania,	400	5,519	4,876	4,983	2,481	3,684		3,476		3,337		1,346		1,265	1,598
Delaware,		609	145	229		349		317		325	231	89		164	235
Maryland,		637	2,592	2,030	1,535	3,307		2,849		2,065		770		1,280	974
Virginia,		6,161		5,744	1,289	5,236		3,973		2,466		1,215	4,331	1,204	629
North Carolina,		1,134		1,281		1,287		1,214				545		1,105	697
South Carolina,		2,069		1,650		1,650		909							139
Georgia,		351		1,423		673		87							145
	27,443	46,901	26,060	34,750	10,112	32,899	4,353	27,699	2,429	21,115	5,811	13,832	7,398	14,256	13,075

TOTAL, { Continental, 231,971
         { Militia,   56,163

TABLE IV.

Showing the Force that each of the Thirteen States supplied for the Regular Army, from 1775 to 1783, inclusive.

[From Niles's Register, July 31, 1830.]

	Regulars.		Regulars.
New Hampshire,	12,497	Delaware,	2,386
Massachusetts,	67,907	Maryland,	13,912
Rhode Island,	5,908	Virginia,	26,678
Connecticut,	31,939	North Carolina,	7,263
New York,	17,781	South Carolina,	6,417
New Jersey,	10,726	Georgia,	2,679
Pennsylvania,	25,678	Total,	231,791.

TABLE V.

Expense of the Revolutionary War.

It is not possible to ascertain with certainty the expenses of the Revolutionary War. An estimate was made, in 1790, by the Register of the Treasury, of which the following is a general abstract:—

	Dolls.	90ths.
The estimated amount of the expenditures of 1775 and 1776 is, in specie,	20,064,666	66
1777,	24,986,646	85
1778,	24,289,438	26
1779,	10,794,620	65
1780,	3,000,000	00
1781,	1,942,465	30
1782,	3,632,745	85
1783,	3,226,583	45
To Nov. 1, 1784,	548,525	63
Forming an amount total of	$92,485,693	15

The foregoing estimates, being confined to actual treasury payments, are exclusive of the debts of the United States, which were incurred, at various periods, for the support of the war, and should be taken into a general view of the expense thereof, viz.:—

	Dolls.	90ths.
Army debt, upon commissioners' certificates,	11,080,576	1
For supplies furnished by the citizens of the several States, and for which certificates were issued by the commissioners,	3,723,625	20
For supplies furnished in the quartermaster, commissary, hospital, clothing, and marine departments, exclusive of the foraging,	1,159,170	5
For supplies, on accounts settled at the treasury, and for which certificates were issued by the register,	744,638	49
	$16,708,009	75

Note. — The loan-office debt formed a part of the treasury expenditures.

The foreign expenditures, civil, military, naval, and contingencies, amount, by computation, to the sum of	5,000,000	00
The expenditures of the several States, from the commencement of the war to the establishment of peace, cannot be stated with any degree of certainty, because the accounts thereof remain to be settled; but, as the United States have granted certain sums for the relief of the several States, to be funded by the general government, therefore estimate the total amount of said assumption,	21,500,000	00
Estimated expense of the war, specie,	$135,693,703	00

TABLE VI.

Emissions of Continental Money.

The advances made from the treasury were principally in a paper medium, which was called *Continental money,* and which in a short time depreciated: the specie value of it is given in the foregoing estimate. The advances made at the treasury of the United States in Continental money, in old and new emissions, are estimated as follows, viz.:—

	Old Emission. Dollars. 90ths.	New Emission. Dollars. 90ths.
In 1776,	20,064,666 66	
1777,	26,426,333 1	
1778,	66,965,269 34	
1779,	149,703,856 77	
1780,	82,908,320 47	891,236 80
1781,	11,408,095 00	1,179,249 00
	$357,476,541 45	$2,070,485 80

By comparing this amount of paper money, issued during the Revolution, with the above estimate of the total expense in specie dollars, it will be seen that the average depreciation of the whole amount issued was nearly two thirds of its original value.

TABLE VII.

Table of Depreciation of Continental Money.

	1779.	1780.	1781.
January	7, 8, 9	40–45	100
February	10	45–55	100–120
March	10, 11	60–65	120–135
April	12½, 14, 16, 22	60	135–200
May	22–24	60	200–500
June	22, 20, 18	60	On the 31st
July	18, 19, 20	60–65	of May it
August	26	65–75	ceased to
September	20–28	75	circulate.
October	30	75–80	
November	32–45	80–100	
December	45–38	100	

TABLE VIII.

State Expenditures and Balances.

States.	Sums allowed for Expenditures.	Sums charged for advances by United States, including the assumption of State Debts.	Expenditures, excluding all advances.	Balances found due from the United States.	Balances found due to the United States.
	$	$	$	$	$
N. Hamp.,	4,278,015.02	1,082,954.02	3,195,061	75,055	
Mass.	17,964,613.03	6,258,880.03	11,705,733	1,248,801	
R. Island,	3,782,974.46	1,977,608.46	1,805,366	299,611	
Conn.	9,285,737.92	3,436,244.92	5,829,493	619,121	
New York,	7,179,982.78	1,960,031.78	5,219,951		2,074,846
N. Jersey,	5,342,770.52	1,343,321.52	3,999,449	49,030	
Penn.	14,137,076.22	4,690,686.22	9,446,390		76,709
Delaware,	839,319.98	229,898.98	609,421		612,428
Maryland,	7,568,145.38	1,592,631.38	5,975,514		151,640
Virginia,	19,085,981.51	3,803,416.51	15,282,865		100,879
N.Carolina,	10,427,586.13	3,151,358.13	7,276,228		501,082
S.Carolina,	11,523,299.29	5,780,264.29	5,743,035	1,205,978	
Georgia,	2,993,800.86	1,415,328.86	1,578,472	19,988	

ADDRESS TO GENERAL GREENE.

(See page 350.)

CAMP SOUTHERN ARMY,
High Hills, Santee, 20th August, 1781.

The subscribers, commissioned officers serving in the Southern Army, beg leave to represent to the Honorable Major-General Greene, That they are informed, not only by current reports, but by official and acknowledged authority, that, contrary to express stipulations in the capitulation of Charleston, signed the 12th day of May, 1780, a number of very respectable inhabitants of that town and others were confined on board prison-ships and sent to St. Augustine, and other places distant from their homes, families, and friends. That notwithstanding the general cartel settled for exchange of prisoners in the Southern Department, and agreed to the 3d day of May last, several officers of militia and other gentlemen, subjects of the United States, have been and still are detained in captivity.

That the commanding officer of the British forces in Charleston, regardless of the principles and even of the existence of the said cartel, hath not only presumed to discriminate between the militia and other subjects of the United States, prisoners of war, partially determining who were and who were not objects of exchange, but hath even dared to execute, in the most ignominious manner, Colonel Haynes of the militia of the State of South Carolina, a gentleman amiable in his character, respectable in his connections, and of eminent abilities: and this violent act, as cruel as it was unnecessary and unjust, we are informed, is attempted to be justified by the imputed crime of treason, founded upon the unfortunate sufferer's having in circumstances peculiarly distressing, accepted what is called a Protection from the British government.

If every inhabitant of this country, who, being bound by the tender ties of family connections, and fettered by domestic embarrassments, is forced to submit to the misfortune of falling into the hands of the enemy, must therefore become subject to such inhuman authority, and if such subjects are liable to be tried by martial law for offences against the civil government of the British nation, their situation is truly deplorable. But we conceive forms of protection that are granted one day, and retracted, violated, disclaimed, or deserted the next, can enjoin no such condition or obligation upon persons who accept them. We consider the citizens of the United States of America as independent of the government of Great Britain, as those of Great Britain are of the United States or of any other sovereign power; and think it just that indulgences and severities to prisoners of war ought to be reciprocal. We, therefore, with submission, beg leave to recommend that a strict inquiry be made into the several things mentioned, and if ascertained, that you will be pleased to retaliate in the most effectual manner by a similar treatment of British subjects, which are or may be in your power.

Permit us to add, that while we seriously lament the necessity of such a severe expedient, and commiserate the sufferings to which individuals will necessarily be exposed, we are not unmindful that such a measure may in its consequences involve our own lives in additional dangers; but we had rather forego temporary distinctions and commit ourselves to the most desperate situations, than prosecute this just and necessary war upon terms so unequal and so dishonorable.

Signatures, &c.

www.ingramcontent.com/pod-product-compliance
Lightning Source LLC
Chambersburg PA
CBHW021418300426
44114CB00010B/548